Old and New Media after Katrina

OLD AND NEW MEDIA AFTER KATRINA

Edited by

Diane Negra

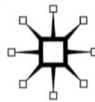

OLD AND NEW MEDIA AFTER KATRINA
Copyright © Diane Negra, 2010.

All rights reserved.

First published in 2010 by
PALGRAVE MACMILLAN®
in the United States—a division of St. Martin's Press LLC,
175 Fifth Avenue, New York, NY 10010.

Where this book is distributed in the UK, Europe and the rest of the world, this is by Palgrave Macmillan, a division of Macmillan Publishers Limited, registered in England, company number 785998, of Houndmills, Basingstoke, Hampshire RG21 6XS.

Palgrave Macmillan is the global academic imprint of the above companies and has companies and representatives throughout the world.

Palgrave® and Macmillan® are registered trademarks in the United States, the United Kingdom, Europe and other countries.

ISBN: 978-0-230-10266-8

Library of Congress Cataloging-in-Publication Data

Old and new media after Katrina / edited by Diane Negra.
　p. cm.
　Includes bibliographical references.
　ISBN 978-0-230-10266-8 (hardback)
　1. Hurricane Katrina, 2005—Press coverage. 2. Mass media—Objectivity—United States. 3. Mass media—Political aspects—United States. 4. Hurricane Katrina, 2005—Political aspects. 5. Hurricane Katrina, 2005—Social aspects. 6. United States—Social conditions—21st century. I. Negra, Diane, 1966–

HV636 2005 .G85 O43 2010
976'.044—dc22   2010007919

A catalogue record of the book is available from the British Library.

Design by Newgen Imaging Systems (P) Ltd., Chennai, India.

First edition: September 2010

10 9 8 7 6 5 4 3 2 1

Printed in the United States of America.

Contents

List of Figures   vii

Acknowledgments   ix

1 Introduction: Old and New Media after Katrina   1
Diane Negra

2 Uncovering the Bones: Forensic Approaches to Hurricane Katrina on Crime Television   23
Lindsay Steenberg

3 The Big Apple and the Big Easy: Trauma, Proximity, and Home in New (and Old) Media   41
Joy V. Fuqua

4 Expanded Medium: National Public Radio and Katrina Web Memorials   67
Maria Pramaggiore

5 Life Preservers: The Neoliberal Enterprise of Hurricane Katrina Survival in *Trouble the Water*, *House M.D.*, and *When the Levees Broke*   89
Jane Elliott

6 Discovery Channel's Nature-Reality Hybrid Shows: Representing Survival in the Wake of Katrina   113
Andrew Goodridge

7 Exile, Return, and New Economy Subjectivity in *Last Holiday*   131
Diane Negra

8 Media Artists, Local Activists, and Outsider Archivists: The Case of Helen Hill   149
Dan Streible

9 In Desperate Need (of a Makeover): The Neoliberal Project, the Design Expert, and the Post-Katrina Social Body in Distress 175
   Brenda R. Weber

10 From Mr. Pregnant to Mr. President: Prepositioning Katrina Online 203
   Jeff Scheible

Bibliography 231

Notes on Contributors 245

Index 247

Figures

1.1 Ads such as this commodify urban recovery while drawing upon long-standing stereotypes of New Orleans' local "spice."   4
2.1 *America's Most Wanted* host John Walsh on Bourbon Street with Louisiana police.   28
3.1 Visual artists such as Takashi Horisaki represent trauma through a focus on the remnants of "home." *Social Dress New Orleans—730 Days After*, Socrates Sculpture Park, Long Island City (August 2007, photograph by author).   59
4.1 A novelty keychain transforms New Orleans mayor Ray Nagin's bold complaints about the lack of government action, first broadcast on radio station WWL-AM, into an aural object. With kind permission of Steve Winn. Photo credit: Melinda Pfeiffer.   79
5.1 Documentaries such as *Trouble the Water* and *When the Levees Broke* associate the positive, agential action of survivors with the imperatives of neoliberal self-governance.   98
8.1 Helen Hill drawing in *Recipes for Disaster: A Handcrafted Film Cookbooklet.* The bomb shelter (upper right) appears in *Madame Winger Makes a Film*, as voiceover asks "fellow filmmakers" and "future filmmakers": "What Will You Do if there is a Nuclear War? Or gigantic Terrorist Attack? When your film lab is reduced to rubble, how are you going to keep making films?" Reproduced with permission.   165

9.1 Through his "Make It Right" Foundation Brad Pitt has maintained a high profile in celebrity efforts to make over post-Katrina New Orleans. 183

10.1 YouTube character Mr. Pregnant performs a post-Katrina racial burlesque. 217

Acknowledgments

I would like to warmly thank the contributors for their work in preparing the essays that make up this collection. For practical and/or intellectual contributions to this book I thank Mary Beth Haralovich, Liam Kennedy, Vicki Mayer, Kimberly Springer, Ruth Barton, and Alan Nadel as well as the participants in the 2009 Clinton Institute Summer School at University College Dublin. Grateful acknowledgment also to Monica Cullinan and the staff of the James Joyce Library at University College Dublin, the efficacious Karen Jackman, Aisling Jackman, Sarah Hartley at Taylor & Francis, Amisha Kondaskar and Junez Ali at Corbis, Lee Norton at Palgrave, and Rohini Krishnan at Newgen Imaging Systems in Chennai. Finally, I want to express my gratitude to Dolores Tierney and Eddie Besancon with whom I left New Orleans on August 27, 2005, never dreaming of how events would unfold in the city we were leaving behind.

DIANE NEGRA

Chapter 1

Introduction: Old and New Media after Katrina

Diane Negra

This book considers the media textuality of Hurricane Katrina, an event that signifies the radical eruption of incidents and images decisively outside the bounds of what is conceived as the American "way of life."[1] In its aftermath we can glimpse the ways in which citizenship, consumerism, and charity are coming together in new formulations, often in attempts to reinforce state-sponsored Christian sanctimony, the stigmatization of the poor, and the need to negotiate white middle-class guilt in such a way that national identity myths remain unthreatened. For many, Hurricane Katrina manifested not only a profoundly unequal national culture and the rupture of the social contract, it also seemed to lay bare the normalization of risk in American life. As Wai Chee Dimock has observed, Katrina stands as a public event "that casts into doubt the efficacy and security of the nation."[2]

Representations of Hurricane Katrina cannot be read outside of a neoliberal context marked by "New Economy" market fundamentalism, state-supported assaults on the environment, intense anti-immigration rhetoric in a nation that still celebrates itself as a global beacon of hope for the downtrodden, the withering role of state care for the vulnerable, and various other perversions of democracy that have flourished in recent years. Hurricane Katrina is positioned at the intersection of numerous early-twenty-first-century crisis narratives centralizing contemporary uncertainties about race, class, region, government, and public safety. For instance, the 2005 New Orleans events gave dramatic evidence of the crumbling and undermaintained American public infrastructure; in this way they stand alongside the 2003 East Coast blackout as well as smaller scale (but heavily broadcast) events such as the 2007 so-called "urban tornado" in which a hundred-year-old Manhattan steam pipe exploded, generating a large crater in midtown that killed one person and injured numerous others, and notably the I35W bridge collapse in Minneapolis a short time later.[3]

Nancy Tuana has observed that "A city is a complex material-semiotic interaction, and New Orleans rests at the heart of multiple interactions."[4] In the context of the history of U.S. imperialism, New Orleans may be seen to have functioned as an internal colonial locale where the tensions of slavery, environmental exploitation, and economic exhaustion suffused urban identity well prior to Hurricane Katrina. The city has long maintained a distinctive status within the national imaginary, its "Old South" qualities enriched and particularized by Cajun and Creole influences that have been interpreted as local "spice" or in reference to the supernatural. Many of its contemporary Hollywood film representations draw upon and further such perceptions, often featuring intense, transgressive eroticism (*Obsession* [1976], *Angel Heart* [1987], *Wild at Heart* [1990], *Interview with the Vampire* [1994]) or the romanticization of corruption. In a film such as *The Big Easy* (1987) the local population is paradoxically represented as both criminal and compliant. Outside of a grisly murder scene an unruly mob of local citizens gathers, but their political concerns quickly dissipate in the face of an opportunity for recreation. "The riot has turned into a party," a fellow cop tells police detective Remy McSwain (Dennis Quaid), who responds "I love this town." Once we understand such representations as emerging from the need to manage colonial/imperial histories we can more fully track the ambivalences at play in New Orleans' frequent depiction as resolutely, perversely local in an era of globalized connectivity.

Prior to Katrina, New Orleans maintained a singular status within an economy of carefully marketed lifestyle and tourism destinations. More than most cities, it sustained an urban brand conceptualized from the perspective of the non-resident and divorced from the daily experiences of average citizens. Once primarily seen as a place where European-American cultural affinities lived on and a "Caribbeanized" site of flamboyance, multiculturalism, and multiracialism, New Orleans was understood by many as a city whose economically anachronistic status was barely compensated for by tourism. The city's historical and contemporary associations with gambling also dovetail with new narratives of risk as a feature of the national condition.[5] Geographical vulnerability (but equally important racial, class, and financial vulnerability) constituted a key disclosure of the events of 2005. Moreover, Hurricane Katrina reverberates in a culture where so many everyday encounters are now tinged with risk, terror, anger, and competition; the increasingly authoritarian and majoritarian American emotional and financial culture as well as the possibility of alternatives to it could be starkly glimpsed in popular debates about whether New Orleans "deserves" to recover and whether its displaced population can be said to have the right of return. The inability to perceive issues of disability and ill health as constitutive elements of the vulnerability of many of those impacted by Katrina can be understood in part as a consequence of the "livestrong or die" mindset of heath triumphalism that has flourished in America in recent years, underwriting deeply classist pathways of access to medical care.

Naomi Klein has argued that "The images from New Orleans showed that this general belief—that disasters are a kind of time-out for cut-throat capitalism, when we all pull together and the state switches into higher gear—had already been abandoned, and with no public debate."[6] In the early twenty-first century the narrative of dead, dying, or injured cities is sometimes counterbalanced by the spectacle of civic rejuvenation, philanthropy, and volunteerism (nearly always on terms that accord with dominant ideological keynotes and gender, race, and class hierarchies).[7] But the effort of rebuilding itself is open to commodification as may be seen in an entry in the long-running, high profile advertising campaign for flavored Absolut vodkas. "Absolut New Orleans" features a clogged highway lane going into the city with the Superdome in the background—in such a way urban rejuvenation is fused with "local spice," and the promotion of a new Absolut product, a mango and black-pepper vodka (of all things) (figure 1.1).

In a study of consumerism and kitsch in relation to 9/11 and the Oklahoma City bombing, Marita Sturken has persuasively argued that contemporary American culture processes traumatic episodes of violence through the "tourism of history."[8] Effectively, souvenirs and trinkets, reenactment practices, museum displays, and a consumerist popular culture steer the meaning of such events in patriotically sentimentalized and ideologically neutralized directions. While Sturken's arguments are surely applicable in many ways to the commodification of disaster in New Orleans, they also need to be recast in this context, given that the unifying rhetoric of "homeland" upon which such consumer memorialization depends proved dramatically inapplicable to an event in which a majority of citizens found the government to

4 · *Diane Negra*

Figure 1.1 Ads such as this commodify urban recovery while drawing upon long-standing stereotypes of New Orleans' local "spice."

be at fault. Among the other deeply destabilizing effects of Katrina, as Carol A. Stabile has noted, was the witnessing by many citizens "for the first time in decades the effects of racism and economic despair exacerbated by the undermining of public infrastructures in the United States." For such viewer citizens "evidence of the government's abandonment of New Orleans threatened to overwhelm their sense of self and place."[9] Stabile's apt observation underscores the vital importance of spectatorship, not only in the context of what became a mediathon of television coverage in September 2005, but in the numerous ways in which Katrina's legacy appears in a range of other media forms[10] for Hurricane Katrina remains a cultural event strikingly difficult to access independent of its media representations. As Aric Mayer has usefully observed, "To put the national Hurricane Katrina experience in perspective, fewer than several hundred thousand people witnessed the storm in person. For the other 99.8 percent of Americans, the disaster was a media experience with lasting implications for the public opinion and action."[11]

This collection of essays explores the relationship between Hurricane Katrina and a range of media forms, assessing how mainstream and independent media have responded (sometimes innovatively, sometimes conservatively) to the political and social ruptures "Katrina" has come to represent. Strikingly, some media coverage in the immediate aftermath of Hurricane Katrina neglected to adhere to established protocols and conventions.[12] In certain instances this material challenged assumptions about the malfeasance of those in poverty and of an always already criminal blackness. Some of the most dramatic evidence of such coverage could be seen on heavily conservative Fox News where anomalies occasionally began to crop up in the rote call and response systems between news studios and on-site personnel. Instead of validating a view of the situation shaped in the studio and according to ideological prescription, reporters such as Fox's Shepard Smith refuted anchors' attempts to recuperate events on the ground or to validate blatantly inadequate efforts at care provision for those impacted in New Orleans. Musician Kanye West's dramatic "off-script" moment during a September 2, 2005, NBC broadcast of the benefit *A Concert for Hurricane Relief* where he protested the racial disparity between black citizens accounted as "looters" and white ones deemed "supply gatherers" and bluntly asserted that "George Bush doesn't care about black people" furthered public awareness that in the period after Katrina dissenting voices were making their way into the media mainstream. Such moments of unruly subjectivity were not frequent but they tended to harden in public memory and conveyed an ideologically contestatory mood and tone. It is the argument of this book that after an initial frenzy of media coverage, efforts to impose conservative representational discipline over an event deemed ideologically problematic have played out over a sustained period of time.[13]

Emblematic of succeeding efforts to impose social and representational order in a fast-changing environment was a broadcast of Fox reality crime series *America's Most Wanted* on September 10, 2005. Situating its longtime host John Walsh in New Orleans, the episode opened with a stark assertion of its own relevance, "our nineteenth season on the air kicks off with one of our biggest jobs...our mission to find the missing." Despite such rhetoric, close examination of the episode reveals that this "mission" is decidedly minimized in favor of the show's stock gambit of criminal apprehension. The broadcast insistently advocates on behalf of police, military, and rescue agencies, acknowledging neglect and disorder only to the minimum extent necessary and extolling that "there are stories of lawlessness and sin that erupted after the storm passed, but the bigger story is that compassion and kindness flowed like the Mississippi River" (the inappropriateness of such watery metaphors did not, apparently, register with series producers).[14] While using short segments of the show's national broadcast platform to allow separated family members to announce their locations on-air, the primary mandate of the special "Gulf Coast Recovery" episode was to stage criminal detection as social recovery. Accordingly the broadcast included a lengthy appeal to apprehend criminals who posed as contractors in post-Hurricane Andrew Florida, a profile of Mississippi police officers whose homes were flooded, introductions of police officers from other parts of the country who traveled to the Gulf region to help and the exhortation to help find two prison inmates who escaped incarceration after the storm. As Walsh puts it, "While the Mississippi police are helping their towns recover from the hurricane, you can help them by keeping an eye out for a few of their most wanted fugitives."

Aric Mayer has observed that despite the frenetic coverage accorded to it early on, post-Katrina New Orleans was a site "which seemed to defy and elude the available means of media representation,"[15] and I would argue that this unrepresentability produced a kind of unfinished agenda that lingered after the intense, immediate first phase of media coverage came to an end. It is this "unfinished business" that generates a particular representational urgency around Katrina and that a variety of media forms have subsequently addressed in the past five years. A chief goal of the essays here is to consider the ways in which Hurricane Katrina and its aftermath have/have not precipitated revision of the narrative and ideological codes of popular film and television. Do cataclysmic national events exert narrative pressure on even the most stable genres? Are certain film and television forms subject to change and contestation when representing the disaster or have standard codes and conventions proven resilient enough to evade modification in the face of the ideological/cultural exposure Hurricane Katrina has come to represent? While some contributors to this book find that a post-Katrina representational environment gives rise to programming innovations (as Andrew Goodridge argues of the survivalist nature-reality hybrid series on the Discovery Channel), others assess textual forms as varied as the romantic comedy or the NPR broadcast that seem to cling doggedly to their established formulae even as the revelations of Katrina make many of their ideological precepts untenable.[16] A strong tendency in media representations related to Hurricane Katrina is the ascription of blame and even moral deficiency to the residents of New Orleans rather than to government agencies or corporate interests as Lindsay Steenberg shows in her discussion here of the frequently punitive treatment accorded to Katrina-impacted guest characters on primetime television. Another common approach is to hype individual rejuvenation as a substitute for civic rejuvenation—a consistent device to effect this substitution is the personal or home makeover. In her essay here Brenda Weber considers the relationships in place between the Katrina legacy and the makeover as a primary televisual mode of the early 2000s.

As the foregoing examples suggest, the specific texts to be analyzed by the contributors to this book will roam widely across forms and genres. Case studies will traverse a range of texts from chick flicks such as *Last Holiday* (2006), documentaries such as *When the Levees Broke* (2006) and *Trouble the Water* (2008), and Katrina-themed episodes of prime-time television series such as *House*, *Bones*, and *Law & Order SVU*, to the landscape of cable news and the making of news personalities such as CNN's Anderson Cooper (for whom Katrina was a professional boon, perhaps the only high-profile white male public figure of whom this could be said) and disaster-themed programming on outlets such as the National Geographic and Weather Channels.

Diane Harriford and Becky Thompson point out that "Historical memory, because it is often unconsciously held, can frequently take the form of a haunting experience that follows, confronts, and interrupts people's everyday actions even though it might not manifest itself in specific, identifiable memories."[17] Although they do not come in for specific examination in this book, it is worth noting the emergence of a cluster of post-Katrina, Louisiana-set horror films including *Hatchet* (2006) and *The Reaping* (2007), which seem to process the horrors of 2005 in displaced forms and the appearance of film and television series that conceptualize New Orleans as a site for communal and personal campaigns for justice and crime-solving (notably *Déjà Vu* [2006] and the Fox drama *K-Ville*). In general, media texts that have straightforwardly sought to adapt 9/11 style discourses of heroic "law and order-ism" to a post-Katrina context have failed to muster critical approval or to stir audience interest. This has proven true for television series such as *K-Ville*, which sought (with the cooperation of the NOPD) to celebrate fictional New Orleans police officers, and for films such as *Déjà Vu*, which crudely and desperately spins a terrorist plot to impose the agenda of "homeland security" in New Orleans, opening with a spectacular sequence in which a ferry carrying hundreds of navy personnel and their families (and sailing under a banner that reads "Katrina Only Made Us Stronger") is bombed on Fat Tuesday. One of the earliest post-Katrina films with a New Orleans setting, *Déjà Vu* elides the realities of hurricane devastation by re-designating New Orleans as an investigative homeland space. By contrast, *Bad Lieutenant: Port of Call New Orleans* (2009), about a police office and former Katrina "hero" who becomes decadently corrupt, was generally positively critically assessed and pronounced a significant creative achievement for its star Nicolas Cage.

The proximity between Hurricane Katrina, the Indian Ocean Tsunami of December 2004, and the commercial success of Davis Guggenheim's acclaimed documentary *An Inconvenient Truth* in 2006 moved public awareness of environmental disaster into the cultural foreground and arguably intensified a preexisting cultural posture normalizing the permanency of disaster. Analysis of the eco-disaster film after Katrina remains outside the boundaries of this project (and a full analysis of this kind would not only engage with Hollywood fictions and works such as the IMAX film *Hurricane on the Bayou* [2006] but could even encompass precedent texts that prompt a post-Katrina rereading such as the climate change disaster film *The Day After Tomorrow* [2004]).[18] One issue under examination here is how Katrina-related media at times adhere to and at times disrupt the tradition of Hollywood films (including examples such as *Dante's Peak* [1997], *Deep Impact* [1998], *War of the Worlds* [2005], and *2012* [2009]) that take disaster as an opportunity to reconstitute the family.

Media responses to Katrina are more generically dispersed and thematically oblique than has been recognized. In this context it is crucial to understand Katrina as a media event whose meanings have been consistently fostered and furthered through the Internet.

Bearing in mind the important part played by the Internet to virtually reassemble decimated communities, friends, and peer groups after the storm, there is also considerable attention paid here to new media and the disparate textual material articulating the significance of the hurricane. Katrina-related YouTube content includes dramatic survivor videos such as those uploaded by the Guerra and Vaccarella families, memorials, survivor testimonials such as *The Truth About Hurricane Katrina*, urban video tours of decimated neighborhoods, and political calls to action. In this way, the site (launched just two months before the devastation of New Orleans) has come to serve as an "accidental cultural archive"[19] and potentially as an "enabler of encounters with cultural differences and the development of political 'listening' across belief systems and identities."[20] In his essay for this volume Jeff Scheible turns to a set of more diffuse and less direct iterations, analyzing Katrina's online presence as a means of better delineating the time and space associated with it.

Although it is not focused on in a sustained way in this book, it is important to acknowledge the scope and influence of a Katrina-influenced material culture—in this context we might consider, for instance, the early flexibility of merchandising protocols in New Orleans' French Quarter that would seem to indicate that even vast civic trauma can be rapidly commodified. T-shirts on sale in 2006 in the Quarter with such slogans as "NOPD (Not Our Problem Dude)" and "I Survived Hurricane Katrina and All I Got Was this Lousy T-Shirt (And a Plasma TV, and A DVD Player, etc. etc.)" indicate something of the way that subjects such as police abandonment and looting can be transformed (though not without ambivalence) into commercial humor. More recently fleur-de-lis t-shirts and those reading "Be a New Orleanian Wherever You Are" and Ray Nagin keychains (such as the kind discussed here by Maria Pramaggiore) indicate the ongoing scope of Katrina-related material culture and merchandising. In his essay Dan Streible documents the case of murdered filmmaker Helen Hill, whose creative work was materially damaged by the flooding in 2005. Through Streible's account, we gain a closer view of the activities of film restoration, the contours of an activist life, and the ways in which New Orleans has so often operated as cultural host for off-the-grid creative activities. A significant strand interweaving among the essays in this book involves analysis of the role of media not only in organizing public memory of Katrina but in shaping/directing affective responses to it. For example, in her essay Maria Pramaggiore examines the ways that the reflexive "anniversarizing" of Katrina on media outlets such as National Public Radio has helped to shape emotional responses to the disaster, privileging sentimentality and recollection over introspection or analysis.

A consistent element in the essays that comprise this collection is the recognition that while Katrina represented an anomalous event in some respects, it has generally been made to conform very heavily to preexisting and ongoing narrative and ideological patterns. Its media presentation, for instance, adheres to an increasingly consistent U.S. regionalization of value and morality. These sorts of dynamics are evident in the contemporary disaster film, which from *Independence Day* (1996) to *Cloverfield* (2008) has proven itself deeply invested in staging the loss of certain cities in the process of defending/reclaiming the nation. Such cities are often dubbed collateral damage of a kind in a United States that must contend against new and unprecedented threats. The broader habit of differentiating which national zones are economically/ideologically vital and which are quiescent begs the question of what kinds of "ruin" we are recognizing in the destruction of New Orleans.[21] It further invites analysis of whether/how the ruining of cities is emerging as a premiere twenty-first-century American scenario of fear and fantasy.[22]

In the twentieth century the United States accumulated little historical experience of rebuilding after large-scale destruction. It did however gain considerable experience of repressing the unmaking of such American cities as Detroit, Newark, Providence, and Baltimore, all of which saw local economies and industries dwindle away. Given the cultural proclivity in the United States to trade in competitive strength/weakness dialectics, it is not surprising that a strong impulse is to expel faltering cities as damaged parts of the national body. A "boom town" logic helps to compensate for these losses as Americans are urged to migrate to new urban centers where prospects seem bright. In the last twenty years, dramas of competitive regionalism have tended to celebrate particular cities or regions as magnet sites—Seattle, Austin, and Las Vegas among others have consistently come in for this sort of mythologizing treatment. As James Lyons has observed of Seattle in the 1990s,

> As the locale for a profusion of new technology companies, the most promising being the software behemoth Microsoft, Seattle appeared to be a model for the New American Economy, a hub for the sort of innovation, entrepreneurial spirit and élan that would lead the nation

forward into the intensified competition for jobs, markets and profits in the global marketplace.[23]

With formulations such as these in place, the economic deterioration of some cities and regions is eclipsed by the celebration of chic new urban lifestyle centers. In an era of habitual state underfunding and competitive regionalism Katrina as a cultural event exposes an intensely hierarchical, disaggregated notion of national identity.

In the drama of expendability that has frequently been staged around New Orleans since 2005, we can see the consolidation and amplification of elements that were already in place prior to Katrina. A once prosperous and thriving city, New Orleans had entered a period of long decline and was widely understood to be economically obsolescent even as other "sunbelt" cities such as Atlanta, Charlotte, and Las Vegas thrived and expanded. Commercial activity outside the city's Central Business District was sluggish and New Orleans experienced little of the gentrification Neil Smith has identified as crucial to the branding of twenty-first-century urban milieux.[24] Even as the U.S. economy surged in the late 1990s and early 2000s New Orleans was figured in many respects as an anomalous space, a socially and financially decrepit city that had been "left behind" in the rush toward hypercapitalist development and financial speculation. In such accounts New Orleans is understood as the site of a culture that is unable/unwilling to change (or to change in the right ways). This rhetoric of "left behindness" is apparent, for instance, in Richard Florida's 2002 account of the regionalization of class and creativity in which he designates New Orleans as one of several regions "being bypassed in the shift to the Creative Economy." Cities such as Buffalo, Grand Rapids, Greensboro, and New Orleans, Florida maintains, "are being left almost totally behind in this process."[25]

Left behindness as it was broadly constituted in American economic and social discourses of the early millennium is, of course, fully implicated with neoliberal self-reliance. Such rhetorical/ideological systems maintain absolute adherence to a national narrative of ongoing progress in which citizens are imagined as simply choosing to take part or not. National disapproval of New Orleans post-Katrina has consistently caricatured its "do-nothing" citizens, relying upon neoliberal discourses of self-sufficiency and studious avoidance of structural features that produce social vulnerability.[26] Andrew Rojecki has aptly noted the "absence of a vigorous discussion in the mass media on the possibility and desirability of rebuilding

New Orleans and protecting it from future flooding."[27] In Rojecki's comparative study of print and media responses to the Great Flood of 1927 and to Katrina he finds that one of the most striking features of the news coverage of Hurricane Katrina was a distinct lack of a sense of national common cause with those impacted. In addition to a "them not us" formulation, the contemporary event moreover was often discursively linked to fatalism, religion, and scientific superficiality. The cultural event of Katrina in many ways confounded positive spin, laying bare a national culture in thrall to socially destructive forms of capitalism that privatized gains and socialized losses.

Several years on, public opinion seems if anything to have hardened against New Orleans; its politicians and its population are frequently characterized using the now-familiar rhetoric of the political right, which rewrites social/economic vulnerability as a failure of citizenship. Indeed, one of the most striking features of Katrina-related public discourse is the consistent expression of condemnation, umbrage, and distaste toward storm victims. Posted comments on follow-up news coverage (which often express deep hostility toward the residents of New Orleans) seemingly give credence to Barbara Ehrenreich's notion of an "empathy deficit" in contemporary U.S. culture.[28] For Ehrenreich, a cultural climate stressing the social obligation to display positive thinking belies a deep and widespread sense of helplessness in American life.[29]

The emphatically negative assessments so conspicuous in post-Katrina rhetoric also trade in part on the remnants of a very old idea that would seem to be intrinsic to American logics of capital—the concept of "creative destruction," in which as Kevin Rozario has pointed out disasters are framed as "events that transform space in ways that promote economic expansion and present (some) investors and businesses with opportunities for the accumulation of capital."[30] As Rozario contends, the combination of Puritan dogma, nation-building ideologies, and unfettered capitalism helped to produce an American tendency (evident as early as 1727 in responses to a New England earthquake) to interpret disaster in opportunistic ways. Yet by the early twenty-first century this interpretive rubric had substantially broken down—when Hurricane Katrina struck New Orleans the gaping hole in the landscape of lower Manhattan that had come to be known as "Ground Zero" was still starkly apparent. Moreover, New Orleans was a place in which automatic assumptions about post-disaster regeneration and urban renewal would be troubled by the reality that the "the old" and "the quaint" carried distinctive urban commercial value (admittedly, this was far more true of some districts than of others). Writing prior to 9/11 and Hurricane Katrina, Rozario would observe that at the dawn of the twenty-first century "old optimisms about the benefits of disaster are finally wearing thin."[31] Even so, faint traces of a centuries-old American expectation that calamities could be beneficial may play a part in the censure of New Orleans citizens after the levees broke. This sort of thinking is also apparent in a film such as *Last Holiday* (2006), which, as I discuss in this volume, anchors a fantasy of entrepreneurial success in an economically purified post-Katrina New Orleans.

A further way in which we may understand the reactions of condemnation toward New Orleans and its citizens is to note the tremendous rise in recent years of contemporary Christian apocalypse fiction. It is not unlikely that some Americans may process their response to disaster taking substantial cues from this material, which paints a world of stark contrasts between the "deserving" and the "undeserving." The best-selling (and culturally and ideologically prominent) *Left Behind* novels of Tim LaHaye and Jerry B. Jenkins, for instance, turn on eschatological readings of the Bible, heavily emphasizing a moralistic selection process determining who will be saved and who will be damned in "The Rapture," the moment of instantaneous divine last judgment. Andrew Strombeck has persuasively argued that "as much as the books reflect a narrow, Christian Right agenda, they also reinforce a more hegemonic ideology,"[32] one that is specifically supportive of neoliberal privatization. Torin Monahan has more precisely noted that "Rapture fiction performs a drama of extremism, consumerism, isolationism and social polarization, thereby tolerating—and arguably helping to normalize—the structural conditions and social practices that are at the root of many social problems."[33] Hurricane Katrina is significant for its uncanny enactment of the "left behind" trope, a trope that emerges largely out of these series of Christian novels and films but which can be more usefully re-purposed to conceptualize the social and material consequences of radical inequality in early twenty-first-century America. Further traces of the association between Hurricane Katrina, social abandonment, and contemporary necropolitics can be glimpsed in *Left 4 Dead 2*, the cooperative first-person shooter game launched for Microsoft Windows and Xbox in November 2009, in which the zombie-killing fight for survival after an apocalyptic pandemic culminates in New Orleans. What I am arguing here is that Katrina lays bare a set of necropolitical relations at work in the twenty-first-century

United States (that is to say relations between the power of the state and the power over life and death). Katrina texts work to suppress or activate those relations (sometimes in unexpected ways).

Many of the essays in this collection will examine the ways that fiction and nonfiction media forms conceptualize/challenge a view of those impacted by the storm as deviant or deficient citizens, members of a left behind remnant public. Toward this end, virtually all of the contributors engage with neoliberalism as a key explanatory framework for the representational practices associated with Katrina. This does not mean that they all reach the same conclusions and while some see the media genres or forms they assess fitting within that framework, in other cases they are deemed to exceed or resist it. It is in this context, for instance, that Jane Elliott examines paradoxical representations of self-preservation in two documentary films and an episode of television medical drama *House*.

This collection will examine, then, the ways that Katrina was experienced by so many in mediated form as well as the afterlife of the storm and its locales in media imagery. It undertakes such analysis at a time when press accounts are hyping Louisiana's accumulating track record as a site of media production, with a record number of films and television series being filmed statewide (in part due to a set of tax incentives first established in 2002) and Louisiana seemingly a particular point of attraction for television "auteurs" such as David Simon (currently in production on *Treme*) and Alan Ball. The expansion of media production has been extolled as a "silver lining" to the catastrophe of the storm and as a form of potential economic salvation in the region.[34] Yet even as a growing number of productions bid for local verisimilitude, many carefully (even elaborately) negotiate the traumatic residue of the storm. HBO's Louisiana-set (though only partly Louisiana-filmed) *True Blood* makes a brief reference to Katrina in its pilot but its setting in small-town Bon Temps is (officially) untouched by the storm.[35]

In its cursory engagement with Katrina and "Bon Temps" locale, *True Blood* generates the fantasy that the hurricane represents a one-time interruption of the status quo with minimal impact on white hegemony and traditionalist communities. Through its "Bon Temps" setting moreover the series references the promise of ongoing leisure and an uninterrupted way of life in the slogan long associated with New Orleans: "Laissez les bon temps rouler." Its first season episodic development playing out in a world free of impact from Katrina, *True Blood* prefers to trade in well-established conventions associating the

Deep South with gothic-tinged horror.³⁶ Yet its intensely romantic localism diverts attention away from a contemporary intensification of regional inequalities (demonstrable in widening regional gaps in mortality rates, etc.) and is linked to a pattern of historical detours that seems to be accumulating in post-Katrina media.

Disney's animated feature *The Princess and the Frog* (2009) (which I discuss at greater length later in this volume), for instance, finds it convenient to construct New Orleans as Jazz Age phantasmagoria, its "Old New Orleans" setting bespeaks a tendency to evade a problematic contemporary urban locale by foregrounding romantic history (in the form of an African American princess, jazz-playing alligator, and voodoo priestess fairy godmother). The film's impulse to stage a compensatory dreamland that substitutes "Old South" clichés for present-day realities culminates in the trailer's audacious last dialogue line "Dreams do Come True in New Orleans."³⁷

This is not to suggest that all recent New Orleans-set media texts are so historically and ideologically evasive. In the Academy Award nominated *The Curious Case of Benjamin Button* (2008) an F. Scott Fitzgerald short story is distinctively adapted to acknowledge the Katrina context.³⁸ As the elderly protagonist Daisy lays dying in a New Orleans hospital while the hurricane approaches, the story of her life with Benjamin (a man whose aging process runs in reverse) is revealed to us in flashback. The film emphatically insists on the richness and fullness of the lives lived by its New Orleans protagonist couple and in this way compensates for the anonymous and abject deaths of some elderly residents (who included hospital patients) during the storm. Equally attuned to the Katrina context are two of the film's strongest thematic keynotes: the acceptance of counter-hegemonic experiences of temporality and "progress" and the affinity with and mastery of water. *Benjamin Button* rejects notions of the grandeur of war and industrial capitalism, celebrating instead the social health of small-scale enterprises and local communities. Benjamin's unusual relationship to time is connected to New Orleans itself in the image of a clock installed in the city's train station. The clock-maker, bereft after the death of his son in World War I, designs the clock to run backward, and the closing image of the film is of the now-warehoused clock still ticking away in reverse as flood waters rush in. Equally striking is the fact that a range of the film's characters (including Benjamin, his father, and a woman with whom Benjamin has an affair and who becomes the oldest woman to swim the English Channel) all manifest a sense of self-discovery, serenity, and pleasure in relation to water. *Benjamin Button* is a film that seems to recognize the fallibility of commitment to fixed ideas about linear historical progress. It celebrates pre-Katrina New Orleans as a site where human strength and emotional tranquility are connected to coastal culture and as a city culturally receptive to the "curious," construed in the film as counter-hegemonic experiences of temporality, linearity, and history. In this sense, and despite its adherence to a problematic limited racial economy in which such experiences of civic richness are available only to white characters that limits its ideological authority and narrative effectiveness, the film stands out among post-Katrina media texts for its humane vision.

Old and New Media after Katrina considers media discourse about citizenship in the wake of the storm, particularly the ongoing effort of mainstream U.S. media to sort citizens into victims, criminals, and heroes. Where 9/11 speedily and durably installed a set of themes and archetypes of cultural heroism that helped to inscribe a narrative of worthy self-sacrifice and barbaric terrorism, the events associated with Katrina, although they did indeed generate a range of heroic actions, did not lead to the lionization of particular individuals or groups. Explanations for this are surely rooted in if not limited to the fact that in the latter instance those most conspicuously impacted were the black urban poor rather than white professionals. As a number of critics have observed, 9/11 coverage tended to prefer suburban breadwinners and an intensely re-valorized class of white male firefighters and police officers, in many cases conferring upon them the status of martyrs.[39] It is perhaps also noteworthy that most 9/11 victims were killed while at work or going to it while Katrina victims died in the homes they were perceived to have fully "chosen" to stay in. In this way 9/11 victims were emphatically linked to the idealized daily rhythms of American capitalism and seats of financial and governmental power while Katrina victims were presented in compliance with a set of preexisting stereotypes about the idle urban poor in a city where "black gangsterism" was understood to thrive. In many respects, then, Katrina can be seen as an event that punctured 9/11 mythologies and unraveled many of its associated certitudes.

Old and New Media after Katrina is finally a book about loss (at personal, civic, and national levels). Among other things, it takes part in a cultural/academic trend toward the study of disaster (and often its heavily mediated character). Such study is increasingly recognized as central to the thoughtful experience of citizenship in the early twenty-first century. (For instance, in autumn 2007, all incoming freshmen at the University of California-Berkeley were assigned a set of summer readings around the theme of disaster.) While a growing body of scholarship addressing Hurricane Katrina and its social outcomes has emerged from disciplines such as sociology, urban studies, and cultural studies in recent years, most academic studies at this point note the mass mediated character of this cultural event without really analyzing it. As illustrated by the summer 2008 mediathon hyping anxious anticipation for Hurricane Gustav (in which several New Orleans area levees were overtopped but none breached) the need for symbolic eradication of Katrina traumas persists and the legacy of the 2005 events is still very much with us, politically, economically, socially, and ideologically. This collection seeks to provide a timely and intellectually fruitful assessment of the complex ways in which media forms and national events are currently entangled and to address a range of readers interested in, provoked by, and concerned about the culture of media spectacle, the bifurcation of wealth and social health in America, and the parlous status of early twenty-first-century American democracy.

Notes

1. I am aware of the inadequacy of the term "Hurricane Katrina" but have elected to retain it for clarity. Some critics prefer terms such as "Katrina circumstance" or "Katrina Event." Nicole R. Fleetwood, for example (and Lindsay Steenberg in this volume following her usage), employs the latter term to describe not only the storm and the floods, but "the material and social impact of the storm, as well as the complex set of social, technological, and economic narratives and processes reported by the news media." "Failing Narratives, Initiating Technologies: Hurricane Katrina and the Production of a Weather Media Event," p. 768.
2. "World History According to Katrina," p. 35.
3. Just as 9/11 is disproportionately representationally confined to the spectacle of Ground Zero destruction, media representations of Katrina are largely focused on the impact in New Orleans. The general elision of the storm's effects on coastal Mississippi harmonize with the subsequent unrepresentedness of Hurricane Rita, which succeeded Katrina by just a few weeks and took a heavy toll on the Western Louisiana coast. This book self-consciously participates in this dynamic partly in an effort to match the general tendencies of media coverage of Hurricane Katrina.

4. "Viscous Porosity: Witnessing Katrina," p. 195.
5. See Randy Martin's *An Empire of Indifference: American War and the Financial Logic of Risk Management* where he distinguishes between a privileged class marked by its ability to take risks with capital and an underclass deemed to be perpetually "at risk."
6. *The Shock Doctrine: The Rise of Disaster Capitalism*, p. 408.
7. One instance of such activity at its most crass can be found in a first season episode of the MTV reality sitcom *Keeping Up with the Kardashians*. Visiting New Orleans, "celebutante" Kim Kardashian and her siblings fall into conversation with a local woman at Café du Monde and contrive to buy the woman and her family (whose storm-damaged home is being renovated) a range of home furnishings to replace those they lost.
8. See *Tourists of History: Memory, Kitsch and Consumerism from Oklahoma City to Ground Zero*.
9. "No Shelter from the Storm," p. 684.
10. The status of Katrina as a media event was further underscored in a high-profile exchange between ABC News' Ted Koppel and FEMA director Michael Brown on September 1, 2005, when Koppel incredulously disputed Brown's claims about FEMA's awareness of conditions on the ground in New Orleans asking "Don't you guys watch television? Don't you guys listen to the radio?"
11. "Aesthetics of Catastrophe," p. 179.
12. It is worth bearing in mind that until the levees broke, Hurricane Katrina was being assiduously covered in the national media according to the sensationalist protocols of contemporary weather coverage. In "TV in the Season of Compassion Fatigue," I write about watching The Weather Channel coverage of New Orleans with other evacuees as Katrina came ashore. Even a group with profound personal and material investments in the city maintained a striking initial adherence to viewing protocols that inscribe titillation and thrill in the coverage of destructive weather events. Among the functions of such coverage is the normalization of features of daily life in the United States that might otherwise be subject to scrutiny including lengthy car commutes (often in the absence of mass transportation options), exceptionally high rates of home ownership, diminished property insurance coverage, and a repertoire of consuming behaviors that are called forth as privileged acts of citizenship in intense or unusual weather conditions. Andrew Ross reads weather coverage in light of many of these concerns in "The Drought this Time" in *Strange Weather: Culture, Science and Technology in the Age of Limits*. His interest is in "the way in which the weather is used to naturalize the social" (237) and "a social history in which 'the weather' has been shaped and appropriated by various state and commercial interests" (228).

13. Though I hasten to add that forms of visual culture outside the mainstream often work differently as Joy Fuqua shows in her study here of two visual artists whose installations specifically redress the positioning of storm victims as extra-national "refugees," looking to forge specific ideological and affective links between the post-Katrina Gulf Coast and post-9/11 New York.
14. A similar obliviousness is illustrated when Walsh tells a U.S. marshal during the broadcast that "You guys are doing a heck of a job," and then repeats this phrasing at the close of the episode. The phrase "heck of a job" had of course entered popular consciousness as shorthand for the callousness, cronyism, and ineptitude of the Bush administration when President Bush praised FEMA director Michael Brown on September 2, 2005, by using that very phrase. Lindsay Steenberg discusses this phrasing and episode of *America's Most Wanted* further in her essay in this volume.
15. "Aesthetics of Catastrophe."
16. In exploring *Survivorman* and a rash of other cable programs that have come to television in the years after Katrina and are dedicated to depicting men testing their mettle against nature, Goodridge notes that the impulse to stage individualist survivor scenarios exceeds televisual representation alone, as is amply demonstrated in print bestsellers such as Neil Strauss' *Emergency: This Book Will Save Your Life* (2009).
17. Diane Harriford and Becky Thompson, *When the Center Is on Fire: Passionate Social Theory for Our Times*, p. 55.
18. Illustrating the preference of the majority of Katrina-related media for (seemingly) apolitical accounts, *Hurricane on the Bayou*, as Anna Hartnell has shown, avoids depictions of human action in favor of an emphasis on the potency of "Nature." For Hartnell, such a depiction fits into a broader matrix of post-Katrina disaster tourism that is "accelerating the widening gulf between New Orleans's party town veneer and its disenfranchised majority" and frequently relies upon "a depoliticized environmentalism that is divorced from any kind of social justice narrative." "Katrina Tourism and a Tale of Two Cities: Visualizing Race and Class in New Orleans," p. 745.
19. Jean Burgess and Joshua Green, *YouTube: Online Video and Participatory Culture*, pp. 89–90.
20. Ibid., p. 77.
21. Jerry Herron has produced an astute reading of Detroit in similar terms. See "Detroit: Disaster Deferred, Disaster in Progress."
22. Such a reading would comply with Henry Giroux's assertion that "Today, a predatory mode of politics and its accompanying representations, images and discourses are constitutive of how American society has increasingly come not only to privilege death over life but also to view death as a form of entertainment." "Beyond the

Biopolitics of Disposability: Rethinking Neoliberalism in the New Gilded Age," p. 593.
23. *Selling Seattle: Representing Contemporary Urban America*, p. 3.
24. See "Gentrification Generalized: From Local Anomaly to Urban 'Regeneration' as Global Urban Strategy."
25. *The Rise of the Creative Class*, p. 248.
26. A consistent element in public discourse (such as posted Internet responses on national newspaper websites) related to events such as the spring 2008 floods in the upper Midwest has stressed that victims of such disasters (who were perceived to be universally white) did not whine or ask for government handouts. In the drama of competitive regionalism the Midwest is presented as stoic and abiding in contrast to a "low" black Southernness and New Orleans' natural state is to be flooded while in the farmlands of the Midwest such floods are anomalies that spur narrative of recovery and restoration. The contrastive regionalism in such accounts relies on a virtuous white Midwesternness counterposed with a criminal and calculating Southern blackness.
27. "Political Culture and Disaster Response: The Great Floods of 1927 and 2005," p. 957.
28. *Bright-Sided: How the Relentless Promotion of Positive Thinking Has Undermined America*, p. 56.
29. Ibid., p. 59.
30. "What Comes Down Must Go Up: Why Disasters Have Been Good for American Capitalism," p. 74.
31. Ibid., p. 95.
32. "Invest in Jesus: Neoliberalism and the Left Behind Novels," p. 161.
33. "Marketing the Beast: Left Behind and the Apocalypse Industry," p. 825.
34. See Rick Jervis, "Movie and TV Crews Help Louisiana Recover."
35. In its adaptation from a well-known series of novels, HBO's *True Blood* seems both to require a reference to Katrina for purposes of verisimilitude and to want to get that reference out of the way early. The pilot thus opens with an exchange between a young convenience store patron and a clerk who tells him, "You didn't know that New Orleans is a mecca for the vampire," to which he replies, "Seriously, I mean, New Orleans? Even after Katrina? Didn't they all drown?" For discussions of the regional and national politics in which *True Blood* is embedded, see Lisa Nakamura et al., "Vampire Politics," and Stephen Shapiro, "*True Blood* and *Mad Men*'s Passive Revolution: Utopian Reaction in the Age of Obam(a)mnesia."
36. *True Blood* relies on tensions between vitality and mortality to perpetuate a well-established pattern of popular representations of the South as subject to what Tara McPherson deems "a "cultural schizophrenia." As she notes, "the region remains at once the site of the

trauma of slavery and also the mythic location of a vast nostalgia industry." *Reconstructing Dixie: Race, Gender, and Nostalgia in the Imagined South*, p. 4.

37. In a similar vein another post-Katrina film release is *Hurricane Season* (2009) a feel-good success narrative about a state-championship-winning basketball team comprised of Katrina evacuees. The film's cast members include New Orleans native and rap star Lil Wayne. Upcoming in 2010 is *Mardi Gras*, a sex comedy about a group of male college students that seems to want to reposition New Orleans as the urban destination of choice for spring-break exploits.

38. This entails in the first instance shifting the setting from Baltimore to New Orleans.

39. In *The Terror Dream: Fear and Fantasy in Post-9/11 America* Susan Faludi reminds us of the traumatic spectacle of rescuer impotence on 9/11 and notes that "the national frenzy to apotheosize these people suggested a deep cultural unease beneath the hero worship" (pp. 63–64). In a set of popular films of the immediate post-9/11 period, New York tycoons were frequently morally rehabilitated, demonstrating a renewed commitment to civic concerns and a socially benevolent capitalism. See my essay "Structural Integrity, Historical Reversion and the Post-9/11 Chick Flick" for a fuller discussion.

CHAPTER 2

UNCOVERING THE BONES: FORENSIC APPROACHES TO HURRICANE KATRINA ON CRIME TELEVISION

Lindsay Steenberg

Crime television reflects American culture's desire to see the spectacle of trauma and its equal need for a rational narrative to contain it. The search for the motive behind a violent act informs its investigative structure and provides professional motivation for its (traumatized) investigators. Within what cultural theorist Mark Seltzer calls "wound culture," crime television offers an opportunity for televisual spectators to gather around the wound, to visualize a "sociality [which] is bound to the excitations of the torn and opened body, the torn and exposed individual."[1] Crime programs also offer the reassurance of a functioning system of scientifically informed justice, embodied by an exceptional investigator or interlocutor who can personally work through the trauma of living in a violent and risk-attuned culture.

The events surrounding Hurricane Katrina's devastation of the city of New Orleans in August 2005 made a deep impression on the collective American imagination, and crime television was quick to incorporate this national trauma into its established systems of law and order. Episodes of several established crime shows such as *Law and Order: Special Victims Unit* (NBC 1999–) and *America's Most Wanted* (Fox 1988–) imagined a post-Katrina New Orleans in which criminals used the chaos of the storm's aftermath as an opportunity to commit crime and conceal evidence.[2] These fictional series set their stories during the reconstruction rather than the initial destruction in order to frame the Katrina event within existing crime conventions.[3] These conventions emphasize closure, and the unquestionable authority of law enforcement representatives in the service of a moral justice imagined as separate from legal due process. Because of their increased foregrounding of the procedures of forensic science, crime television programs, such as those mentioned earlier, focus on reconstruction as a key method of locating buried and unambiguous truths about violence. In the case of the Katrina episodes, the hurricane aftermath becomes a generic space of excavation organized to expose pathological individuals and their deliberate crimes. This is symptomatic of a politically conservative orientation that permits emphasis on "recovery" and "rebuilding" and diminishes emphasis on the immediate duress of the storm, or any underlying sociopolitical circumstances at odds with narratives of recovery. The tropes of television forensic science (its definitive closure, unambiguous truths, and spectacles of simulation and reconstruction) facilitate and even encourage such a depoliticized and archeological treatment of the Katrina event.

A number of crime programs and many news features aired in 2005 in the immediate aftermath of the hurricane dealt (explicitly or allegorically) with conflicts raised by the Katrina event. Coverage of the event appears on reality television in such broadcasts as *NOPD: After Katrina* (November 1, 2005), a documentary style program clearly based on the successful FOX series *Cops* (1989–), which follows police officers during and directly after the storm. The crime drama *K-Ville* (Fox 2007–) concentrated its focus on the specificity of crime in post-Katrina New Orleans, following a familiar and established cop/buddy format: two partners, one white and one African American, struggle to get along despite their differences. In this case, their struggle is framed by the context of post-Katrina New Orleans. Most of the series' storylines focus on Katrina related crimes and situations; for example, one episode concerns a child who is assumed to have been killed in the storm and has been adopted despite her father's wishes. Despite its Katrina-specific storylines and post-Katrina setting, *K-Ville* uses many of the same tropes as other cop shows set in "exotic" locales, for example, the New Orleans set *Bourbon Street Beat* (ABC 1959–1960)[4] and the successful *Hawaii-Five-O* (CBS 1968–1980). Like these earlier series, *K-Ville* relies on the "local color" of its backdrop for its appeal: jazz music and bayou locales are integral to its fictions and one of the lead cops Marlin Boulet cooks Cajun food and peppers his speech with creole. This characterization of New Orleans as exotic and old/otherworldly remains a key part of its network televisual representation.

Rather than focus on *K-Ville*, my intention is to interrogate a wider pattern in contemporary mainstream crime television that entails incorporating national crises such as the Katrina event into already established patterns of forensic investigation. The FBI-centered missing persons drama *Without A Trace* produced an episode entitled "The Calm Before" focusing on lead investigator Jack Malone's journey to New Orleans to honor a dying man's wish to make up for the people he was unable to save during the storm. The FBI profiler drama *Criminal Minds* focused its post-Katrina episode ("Jones") on a female copycat of Jack the Ripper who uses the chaos of the aftermath of Katrina to murder the men who raped her. Like *K-Ville*, "Jones" relies on the exotic and permissive "Europeanness" of New Orleans as a place that can conceal and facilitate the imitation of an iconic old world serial killer such as Jack the Ripper. An episode of *Law and Order: Special Victims Unit* entitled "Storm" sticks to the program's consistent thematic concerns about sex-based crimes, following the story of sisters who were abducted during the storm and subsequently abused. As in most episodes of the program, Detective Olivia Benson demonstrates her professional tenacity by taking on the emotional and investigative burden of the case personally.

These one-off episodes have more in common than their Katrina narratives. They all fit Katrina stories within their existing procedural and thematic structures, and read New Orleans as an exotic or alien urban landscape (made even more so by the devastation of the Katrina event). Furthermore, each episode follows detectives who are able to individually complete journeys of recovery and reconstruction that come to stand in for (and reify) the problematic process of recovery and reconstruction undertaken by the U.S. government and FEMA on the Gulf Coast. This essay looks at two very successful crime programs, both airing on Fox (the same network that produced *K-Ville*): the long-running crime appeal show, *America's Most Wanted* (*AMW*) and the forensic themed drama, *Bones* (Fox 2005–).[5] These programs are representative of a hegemonic forensic approach to violence that is framed as reconstructable, apolitical, and, ultimately, understandable.

AMW's direct address to the spectator insists that progress in New Orleans' reconstruction (of the city and its citizens) is proceeding well with the help of responsible individuals and organizations (often framed as: "viewers, like you") and, especially, through the compassionate and tenacious efforts of law enforcement agencies. Host John Walsh ends the broadcast by congratulating the police forces working in New Orleans, "They're doing one heck of a job." This congratulatory tone is typical of the show, which frames its crime reconstructions and calls for public help through its privileged position as partner and extension of law enforcement agencies.

Bones, a Fox series of more recent origin, represents the apotheosis of the popular cycle of forensic crime shows. It uses all the conventions of forensic fiction to excess—its experts are better educated and more specialized, its crimes are more bizarre, and its corpses more severely decomposed or damaged than in previous iterations of the subgenre. Its Katrina episode ("The Man in the Morgue"), as I shall discuss in more detail in the second half of this essay, frames the Katrina event through the exoticism of voodoo and through the personal injuries suffered by lead investigator Dr. Temperance Brennan. In this episode, as in the series as a whole, Brennan and her FBI partner, Seeley Booth, use forensic science to resolve cases that miniaturize and particularize broader national, historical, and social crises. Through forensic framing, a national trauma (like the Katrina event) is depoliticized and "solved" by dedicated individual professionals.

The forensic science celebrated and spectacularized on both *Bones* and *AMW*, and in popular culture more generally, is articulated as distinctly tabloid in character. Cultural theorist Kevin Glynn has defined a transmedia tabloid modality, one that prefers emotionality, resists objectivity, and incorporates the "deviant" ignored by the mainstream. He describes tabloid forms, especially tabloid crime shows such as *AMW*, as given to themes of victimization, gender confusion, and the paranormal.[6] In using the term tabloid to describe forensic science, I want to highlight its inclusion of many different types of knowledge—historical, mythical, and cultural as well as more traditionally empirical modes. Tabloidized representations of the forensic are driven by spectacle and blur the factual with recreation and simulation. They compress several historically disparate scientific schools of thought into a postmodern aesthetic that flattens epistemology into a screen spectacle and fractures the meta-narrative of Enlightenment rationalism while nostalgically longing for it. The authority claimed by such representation is legitimized through a bricolage of knowledge sources—while one may be questioned, not all can be dismissed outright. Thus, tabloid forensic science (whether embodied by "experts" such as fictional scientist Dr. Brennan on *Bones* or *AMW* host John Walsh) is an authoritative discursive mode that invites viewers to draw conclusions about the national crises it represents.

"One Heck of a Job": Moral Authority on
America's Most Wanted

AMW constructs the authority of host John Walsh through his extratextual life as a victim of crime and an advocate for victim's rights, and through his position as moral translator of tabloid forensics. In 1981 Walsh's six-year-old son, Adam, was kidnapped and murdered. According to the *AMW* website, this spurred Walsh to become a crusader for victim's rights and missing children's organizations. Walsh looked to the media, in particular, as a means of realizing his concerns. He authorized two made-for-television films based on his son's murder: *Adam* (1983) and *Adam: His Song Continues* (1986). In addition to becoming the host and figurehead of *America's Most Wanted* in 1988, Walsh has hosted a talk show, *The John Walsh Show* (ABC 2002–2004), authored several books, and has even teamed up with the makers of Baby Einstein to produce a DVD series about children's safety.[7] Walsh was also the architect of the Adam Walsh Child Protection and Safety Act, which was passed in 2006. The *AMW* website describes the Act as a "tough-as-nails law" designed to "track and apprehend convicted sex offenders who disappear after their release from prison."[8]

Elayne Rapping argues that the victim's rights movement of the 1980s, of which John Walsh's celebrity is axiomatic, marks a shift from rehabilitation toward retribution and a vengeance oriented right-wing approach to crime and criminals.[9] This is exemplified by Walsh's "tough-as-nails" approach to victim's rights and by the addition of the subtitle *America Fights Back* to *AMW* in 1995. On *AMW*, such a hard-line approach distinctly flavors Walsh's voiceover remarks. Walsh passes continual judgment on criminals—not only in terms of their criminal acts but also with respect to their capacity to be good family members and citizens. Walsh comments that one suspect "thought nothing of putting his loved ones in the path of danger" and ends segments with calls to arms such as: "let's get him off the streets tonight" and "let's track him down!"

John Walsh's *AMW* persona depends on a "tough-on-crime" reputation that the series seeks to justify through his personal history of trauma. Walsh's *AMW* role also depends on its close association with the law enforcement community. The series is produced with the active support of the FBI and John Walsh is positioned as our insider source at the agency, singularly able to translate to the public the importance of the job that law enforcement does, the methods they use to accomplish their goals, and how we (the community of viewers) can aid and participate. A standard episode sees Walsh positioned in a studio squad room with ringing telephones, computers, and maps. He frames, through direct address to the camera and voiceover, the reconstructions and interviews to come. He urges the public, addressing us exclusively as members of families and communities, to get involved in the law enforcement process—primarily through vigilant surveillance.

The episode of *AMW* filmed in New Orleans (and briefly discussed by Diane Negra in this book's introduction) addresses the chaos created by the Katrina event and is, to a certain extent, an exception to the show's standard format. Here there is no squad room. Instead, Walsh walks the streets of New Orleans escorted by the U.S. Marshals and the police; a display that resonates with the militarization of public space in post-Katrina New Orleans (figure 2.1). He talks easily with the cops, congratulating them on their work and explaining to the audience what has already been done to help the people of the city. *AMW*'s approach to the Katrina event meshes with the crime appeal program's general approach to crime through

Figure 2.1   *America's Most Wanted* host John Walsh on Bourbon Street with Louisiana police.

a composite of recreation, interviews, and flashy computer graphics. Shots of Walsh walking with the police through the evacuated tourist areas of urban New Orleans (e.g., Bourbon Street) are intercut with shots of unidentifiable wreckage (houses, vehicles, garbage) and interviews with displaced survivors. *AMW*'s framing of post-Katrina New Orleans as post-apocalyptic is in keeping with portrayals in the fictional crime programs. *Bones* and *Criminal Minds* both open their New Orleans stories with archival news footage of the storm and its aftermath, using iconic images associated with disaster: washed away cars, destroyed houses, ruined cityscapes, and so on. *AMW* and *Bones* use this post-apocalyptic imagery to champion their forensic reconstructive process as a logical and effective coping strategy. Walsh introduces the individual segments as he tours this post-apocalyptic version of the city, frequently stopping to comment and congratulate his police escort. The individual segments of the show are not all related to Katrina, profiling among others an escaped career criminal, a pedophile, and a lying husband who rapes his step-daughter and tries to kill her mother. Walsh loosely relates all the disparate segments through the opposition of good and bad families (a rhetoric common to *AMW* and reality crime shows such as *Cops*).

Although the Katrina episode features *AMW*'s usual recreations of crimes and appeals for public help, it also provides air time for Katrina victims looking for family members and offers, like quality crime dramas, commentary on the tragedy. Ultimately Walsh's commentary on Katrina is similar to his commentaries on all crimes (whether they concern missing children, murder, or abuse). He calls for communities of families to be vigilant in watching for deviance, tempering his alarmist warnings with a revenge-oriented rhetoric advocating right-wing "war on crime" solutions.

Crime dramas and reality crime programs alike depoliticize the Katrina event through a neoliberal system of checks and balances. In a discussion of the reality crime program *Judge Judy* (1996–) Laurie Ouellette suggests neoliberalism is "generally understood as a troubling world-view that promotes the 'free' market as the best way to organize every dimension of social life."[10] She asserts that reality crime programs such as *Judge Judy* "train TV viewers to function without state assistance or supervision as self-disciplining, self-sufficient, responsible, and risk-averting individuals."[11] I argue that Ouellette's claims about the functions of neoliberalism apply equally to "quality" crime dramas as to tabloid reality programs. That is, specifically through a system of checks and balances that insists that if dedicated, righteous individuals commit themselves personally to reconstructing and "solving" political/historical disasters such as the Katrina event, they can make up for any failings on the part of the state. What differentiates reality from "quality" or narrative crime dramas is tone. While reality programs such as *Cops*, *Judge Judy*, and *AMW* favor hard-line positioning of dichotomies of good and evil (us and them) in framing this system of checks and balances, crime dramas such as *Without a Trace*, *Law and Order: SVU*, and *Bones* are more mournful in their approach, articulating the checks and balances system as a process of working through national traumas (like the Katrina event).

Jack Malone, the patriarch of *Without a Trace*, shakes his head over the events in New Orleans saying, "There is no excuse for what they let happen there." The Katrina episode of *Criminal Minds* opens with a quotation from Robert F. Kennedy: "Tragedy is a tool for the living to gain wisdom, not a guide by which to live." Typically, *Criminal Minds* opens and closes with an aphorism that summarizes what the profilers have learned from the case at hand. In framing its story of post-Katrina New Orleans with the quotation by Kennedy, the program makes sinister recommendations that the nation must move on from the Katrina event having learned a lesson and become stronger—much as the profiling team has done after their encounters with serial killers in other episodes. While *Without a Trace* and *Criminal Minds*, like other crime dramas, acknowledge the political mistakes that were made in 2005, they significantly elide any notion that blame could lie with the institutions their protagonists represent (the FBI). They imply that something went wrong, but never mention exactly what, and ignore the circumstances or apparatuses that might be to blame. In both series' Katrina episodes, dedicated FBI teams are able to make right these ambiguous and unnamed oversights. *AMW*, on the other hand, treats Katrina not as an event, but as a single disruptive moment limited to experiences of the hurricane itself, framed as a natural disaster beyond human control. For *AMW*, the story of the storm's aftermath is limited to reconstruction efforts and to celebrations of the human (read American) spirit. The broadcast's Katrina related sequences follow the stories of families reunited (often through the efforts of viewers of AMW) and the efforts of off-duty police officers from around the country traveling to New Orleans to volunteer their time and labor. The Katrina related crimes covered in the show focus on the risks that New Orleans may face in the future. For example, one segment names fugitive builders who cheated many Floridians in the wake of Hurricane Andrew.

Because John Walsh has experienced violence in his past, and continues to face that violence as our representative on *AMW*, he is uniquely positioned as able to make sense of tragedy—from the small scale of a missing child or crooked contractor, to the large scale of national catastrophes. His ability to make sense of tragedy depends upon his persona's combination of moral and official authority. These two points coalesce around Walsh's tough-as-nails common sense and its ability to translate (morally and narratively) complex forensic procedures.

Tabloid forensic science is now, undoubtedly, a preoccupation of popular wound culture. Forensic science is a key part of how we visualize and mediate violence, crime, and the horrors of the human body. As discussed, successful crime dramas such as the *CSI* franchise feature forensic science as their key procedure. Forensic-themed merchandise, often aimed at children, sells quickly and forensic-themed events are staged across America, from museum exhibits (the touring "CSI Experience") to corporate team-building events, and themed summer camps.

The spectacle of death and disaster offered by forensic science is legitimized by its authoritative, scientific, and pedagogical functions. On television series such as *Bones* and *C.S.I.: Crime Scene Investigation* (CBS 2000–), forensic science can ostensibly teach scientific lessons to the viewing public. On *AMW*, through the persona of John Walsh, moral lessons can be taught through the forensic spectacles of events such as Katrina, the Oklahoma City bombing, and 9/11. In many ways, catastrophic events such as the attacks on 9/11 and the Katrina event solidified the authority of the forensic and provided another very powerful example of wound culture. Walsh's visual and moral mediation of these forensically framed catastrophes reifies his authority and his tough-on-crime tactics while also staging the appropriate civic response.

Annalee Newitz describes a forensic framing of the postmodern proliferation of images and disappearance of meaning caused by the bombing of the World Trade Center in New York on September 11, 2001: "Into this void of meaning stepped President George W. Bush, whom you might in this narrative situation call the nation's forensic analyst."[12] Newitz proposes that Bush's treatment of the terrorists as deviantly motivated and the attacks as individual acts of violence encourages the public to see them as pathological rather than political. She stresses that this substitution "is fundamentally related to the urge to drain all violent homicidal acts of their political meaning."[13]

This forensic depoliticization of violence extends to the Katrina event of 2005. In an article in *USA Today*, Rick Jervis described ongoing forensic efforts to identify the dead in New Orleans, claiming that "Hurricane Katrina sparked one of the largest and most complicated forensic efforts in U.S. history."[14] Jervis' article highlights the difficulties facing the forensic reconstruction of New Orleans, due particularly to lack of government funding. His description of Katrina as a forensic event is also a key part of the way it is framed on crime television—as a dual process of excavation and reconstruction concluding in absolute pseudo-scientific truths. The Katrina event, however, resists forensic closure because it does not represent an attack on the United States by a human enemy, but signals the failure of the U.S. government to respond appropriately in aiding some of its most vulnerable citizens. The forensic approach of crime television, with its concomitant neoliberal system of checks and balances, attempts to resolve this tension by placing Katrina within existing, familiar narrative and generic structures. In figure 2.1, Walsh stands in front of the ruins of large-scale national disasters, offering moral lessons we can absorb from these events. In a parallel to Newitz's characterization of Bush, he becomes not the nation's forensic analyst but the nation's forensic moralist.

Walsh's interpretation of the forensic process of investigation (and, indeed, his mobilization of the forensic gaze to explain violence) relies on his common sense. In Walsh's recitations there is no techno-speak, and none of the coldness of scientific detachment. His translation of scientific procedures foregrounds the emotional response of an everyman. He embodies the way the (mythological) decent, hardworking American should respond to the forensic spectacle of national tragedy: with outrage, passion, and, a desire for retribution.

In an article about *Law and Order*, Susanna Lee suggests that "the working-through and witnessing of trauma becomes itself a drama, and a crucial element of the modern television drama."[15] Lee discusses the tension between public violence and private pain, concluding that the characters on *Law and Order* "represent a fantasy of psychic intactness and empathetic presence in the face of relentless violence. This intactness is their contribution to society, their act of protection."[16] Walsh's moralizing on *AMW* represents a different kind of fantasy about responding to violence. Rather than respond to violence with stoic compassion, as do the detectives on *Law and Order*, *AMW* prompts us to respond, like Walsh, with righteous rage.

"Doing What the Feds Didn't": Performing Penance for the Traumas of History on *Bones*

The response to trauma imagined in the Fox series *Bones* is, like *AMW*, not limited to witnessing. Where Walsh personifies an outraged response to trauma, *Bones*' lead characters, forensic anthropologist Dr. Temperance "Bones" Brennan and FBI agent Seeley Booth, represent a fantasy of noble suffering. In the course of her many investigations, particularly the episode set in post-Katrina New Orleans, Brennan suffers physically and emotionally. She is frequently involved in fistfights and gunfights, and is kidnapped by at least two serial killers. She also struggles emotionally with the murder of her mother, and the loss and subsequent rediscovery of her father and brother, and grieves over the revelation that her protégée is a serial killer. This is also true of Booth, whose body bears the scars of his military service and his psyche the scars of his past as a sniper. He also struggles to be a better father to his son. Brennan and Booth's personal traumas are a central spectacle of the series. In the post-Katrina episode, "The Man in the Morgue," Brennan is drugged, severely beaten, arrested for murder, suffers temporary amnesia, and is the subject of several voodoo curses. She discovers a colleague's, mutilated and crucified corpse, and may have witnessed his murder.

Channeling the trauma of New Orleans through the body of the female investigator is not only typical of the series, but also of the media coverage of the Katrina event. Repeated reference to (the threat of) rape in the aftermath of Katrina became a particular talking point across news coverage. Frequently this crime was connected to African American men, suggesting a longer American ideological association first, with the suffering female body as standing in for the traumatized national body and second, of the body of the African American man as an alien force threatening the national/female body. The African American voodoo priest who attacks Brennan is an articulation of this longer standing formula of national trauma.

Upon hearing of Brennan's injuries, Booth rushes to New Orleans, risking his job, to investigate the case that Brennan is working on and the assault that she cannot remember. In his position as her concerned partner, Booth articulates larger concerns over the borders of the female body in the face of national traumas such as Katrina. Upon facing these traumas, the characters in *Bones* do not meet violence with blank expressions or vengeance-oriented outrage. They suffer physical injuries, become too involved in cases, and only manage to extricate themselves from victimhood by virtue of their scientific professionalism. Where the long-running *Law and Order* acts out an ideal method of behaving when witnessing violence and *AMW* suggests how to heroically respond to violence, *Bones* imagines how to heroically experience violence.

In the case of the latter this response is framed through the protagonist pair's scientific interventions. This structural device is in keeping with the way that the murder investigations on *Bones* imply a neoliberal necropolitics.[17] Achille Mbembe describes necropolitics, or necropower, as the state's purview to determine which citizens' lives are valuable, and which are disposable. In Mbembe's formulation, necropolitics is the "subjugation of life to the power of death,"[18] which is the ultimate expression of sovereignty. *Bones* puts Brennan and Booth in the privileged position of determining which deaths are more worthy of investigation, and which human remains are disposable. *Bones*' neoliberal necropolitics suggests that the responsibilities of history lie with the individual and (in an imperialist manner) that more "worthy" individuals like Brennan and Booth (middle class, educated, white professionals) must shoulder the burden of responsibility for caring for those less intelligent, less virtuous, and more vulnerable.

The neoliberal intervention into history in *Bones* is emphasized by Brennan's position in a privately funded museum and think-tank clearly modeled on the Smithsonian Institution. Like the Smithsonian, the fictional Jeffersonian has a close working relationship with the Federal Bureau of Investigation, consulting on cases and helping to identify human remains. According to an issue of the *Smithsonian Contributions to Anthropology* outlining the relationship of its forensic anthropologists with the FBI, the Bureau's requests for forensic anthropologists to assist in archeological and criminal cases have risen significantly in the later half of the twentieth century. The report concludes that in most cases murderers do not attempt to conceal their victims, and that the forensic anthropology team is used mostly for archeological remains.[19] *Bones* uses this relationship to suggest that the Smithsonian/Jeffersonian (and its FBI connections) are uniquely positioned to identify those victims forgotten by history and to actively intervene in history in order to compensate for mistakes and traumas.

Brennan and Booth embody this institutional partnership and in "The Man in the Morgue" the strength of this partnership helps them to solve several mysteries associated with the Katrina event, including the murder of one voodoo priest by another and his assault on Brennan. The episode relies on many established tropes of New Orleans' culture including jazz music, Cajun food, and voodoo. In this stereotypical and traumatized version of New Orleans, criminals use both the carnivalesque atmosphere of New Orleans and the confusion of the Katrina event to commit and conceal crimes. In this landscape (as in the urban landscapes of forensic and reality crime television) violence is both personal and decipherable by experts like Brennan. This personalization and deciphering of violence is dramatized in "The Man in the Morgue" through Brennan's volunteering to help identify New Orleans' dead during her vacation time.[20] The man in charge of the identification process, a self-described "southern gentleman," is curious as to why Brennan is giving up her holidays; "are you doing penance for FEMA?" he asks. While Brennan is rather evasive in her answer, the program implies (without much subtlety) that the answer is yes. Brennan, whose week-by-week mission is to identify the remains of those forgotten by time or circumstance, is making up for the mistakes made by her government and her society. She will thus be able to provide explanations for what happened in New Orleans (in forty-two and a half minutes) that the government has failed to give since 2005.

Brennan approaches the Katrina event as an archeological project, identifying victims by reconstructing their bodies, giving them back their names, and thus, facilitating mourning. Over the course of the excavation, Brennan determines which corpses merit investigation and which merit only identification. As previously outlined, both the character of Dr. Brennan and the series privilege certain violent crimes over others, granting them more narrative time and emotional force. Brennan's forensic process works through the trauma of living in wound culture (of which the Katrina event is axiomatic). The findings of her forensic archeology resonate with the neoliberal necropolitics of this wound culture, insisting that certain deaths are more worthy of retribution, certain victims are more disposable than others, and every case hinges on an individual pathology rather than on larger socioeconomic circumstances.

AMW suggests a similar hierarchy of victims. Producer Michael Linder summarizes the approach to choosing cases for the show: "A drug dealer who shoots another drug dealer is not as compelling...as a child molester or murderer...If a man brutalizes innocent children, that definitely adds points."[21] The forensically framed historical disaster on *Bones* and *AMW* presents a version of criminality that is juxtaposed against formulations of innocence. "Innocent" victims are frequently characterized as children, families, and, at times, infantilized adults, like those of many poor African American New Orleans communities. The convention of the innocent victim is reinforced by an almost mythic representation of evil, incarnated by villain figures like the serial killer, the pedophile, and, on *Bones*, the voodoo priest.

In his interrogation of the biopolitics revealed by the Katrina event, Henry Giroux suggests that

> [t]he events surrounding Katrina are about more than incompetence, lack of compassion, and ignorance; they are the consequence of a systemic, violent form of social engineering in which those populations in the United States marginalized by race and class are now considered disposable—that is, simply collateral damage in the construction of a neoliberal order.[22]

While the *Bones* episode acknowledges the failure of the government to respond appropriately on the Gulf Coast, its insistence on Brennan and Booth's personal sacrifices refuses any consideration of the wider issues Giroux highlights. Over the course of the investigation Brennan's assistant, Zack Addy, wonders if their institution's funding covers "Dr. Brennan's vacation work." Computer analyst Angela Montenegro answers that they are "just doing what the Feds didn't" contributing to the "yin and yang of government spending." The necropolitical suggestion here is that virtuous government officials balance out any failings of the system as a whole. Likewise, Walsh's congratulatory "they're doing one heck of a job" and *AMW*'s foregrounding of the tenacity and ethical dedication of the police officers volunteering in New Orleans suggest that these good individuals are more than making up for any mistakes that might have been made (although it must be noted *AMW* never acknowledges that any have been made). In true neoliberal form, it is up to the citizens America values the most (white, privileged, educated, professionals such as Brennan, Booth, and Walsh) to take up the government's slack on an abandoned social contract—expressed in *Bones* as an exchange of scientific expertise for government spending. In the closed system of the episode this exchange is sufficient to generate resolution of the case at hand. However, as soon as this case is solved Brennan leaves New Orleans to identify its own dead and moves on to her next assignment.

Lee's discussion of crime drama concludes with an insistence that crime television reinstates the safety of the screen when representing violence. This is accomplished by addressing us as the spectators of wound culture. She claims that "in the end violence for us is television and living with violence is spectatorship."[23] Witnessing and spectatorship are enmeshed—equally involved in working through the traumas of the everyday and the extraordinary traumas of events like Katrina. The process of watching historical narratives about events like Katrina becomes a civic duty—an important part of memorializing tragedies. To a certain extent *Bones'* forensic framing insists that television viewing can be a process of working through and making up for the traumas of history, especially those that the American government contributed to or did not resolve. In paralleling spectatorship with witnessing, *Bones* reassures us first that television spectatorship is akin to the practice of good citizenship and second that we can trust virtuous professionals like Brennan and Booth to make good in our places.

AMW encourages a much more active, if equally conservative, model of spectator engagement. Because of its format as a crime appeal program, *AMW* urges the public to be vigilant (to surveil neighbors and strangers alike) and to call the show's hotline with any suspicions. *AMW* congratulates and thanks its spectators, as Walsh does with the police in New Orleans. He will announce on air the number of fugitives that have been caught to date thanks to "viewers like you" and the *AMW* website has a permanent counter that lists this number.

Gray Cavender points out the paradoxical nature of the community of spectators fostered by shows like *AMW*, insisting that they "assume and reinforce a traditional sense of community even as their depictions negate the viability of it."[24] Despite Walsh's celebration of the involvement of its viewers and the small triumphs of American communities in the face of tragedies like Katrina, the series' recreations show communities at constant risk—from neighbors who are pedophiles, husbands who try to kill their wives, and contractors who cheat victimized families. Furthermore, the show's interactive format insists that the constant surveillance of its spectators' communities and a concomitant suspicion of those marked as different are the only ways to protect families from such predators. Walsh's paternal authority becomes a way of resolving this paradoxical model of community, and a site for suggesting that the system does work because dedicated individuals, such as the police and Walsh himself, will not give up until the forensic wreckage of events like Katrina or 9/11 has been reconstructed. This representation of the Katrina event within a linear model of apolitical disaster, destruction, and reconstruction negates any governmental accountability and elides the role of systematic prejudices and inequities in American society.

The working-through of trauma so central to crime television (in both its narrative and reality formats) becomes a way of obscuring sociopolitical contexts in order to focus on a wound culture made up of individuals—stereotypical criminals and dedicated professional investigators. *Bones* and *AMW*'s spectacle of forensic reconstruction depends on a neoliberal system of checks and balances. This is produced by redeeming the failures of the government through the virtues of the individual. This neoliberal articulation of responsibility is predicated on the assumption that worthy individuals can atone for the mistakes of the government, and thus that the government need no longer concern itself with the minutiae of its citizens' pain. Deeply conservative texts, both *Bones* and *AMW* raise doubts about U.S. government, culture, and community only to redress those doubts through forensically informed investigative structures. Thus, the Katrina event is slotted into preexisting narrative formats where spectators can watch it being "solved" and, ultimately, dismiss the event as merely one act of violence among many others from which we can learn and move on.

Notes

1. *Serial Killers: Life and Death in America's Wound Culture*, p. 253.
2. Other types of narrative dramas on television also included episodes dealing with Katrina. For example, a 2006 episode of the medical drama *House* (FOX 2004–) entitled "Who's Your Daddy?" followed a young woman rescued from the hurricane repeatedly re-experiencing the trauma of the event. This episode is discussed in detail by Jane Elliott in her essay for this volume. In the thirteenth season of the long-running hospital drama *ER* a Katrina victim turns up in the ER likewise traumatized by her experiences in New Orleans ("Breach of Trust"). After having her leg amputated in an emergency surgery, she is counseled by Dr. Weaver to take her second chance at life and ensure that the Katrina event is not forgotten.
3. I am using the term "Katrina event," following Nicole R. Fleetwood, in order to describe not only the storm and the floods, but "the material and social impact of the storm, as well as the complex set of social, technological, and economic narratives and processes reported by the news media." "Failing Narratives, Initiating Technologies: Hurricane Katrina and the Production of a Weather Media Event," p. 768.

4. *Bourbon Street Beat* focused on two private eyes working in New Orleans. Made in the spirit of *77 Sunset Strip* (ABC 1958–1964), the series tried to capitalize on its exoticized setting emphasizing the bayou, jazz, and colorful local characters.
5. Where the long-running *AMW* fit Katrina into its crime appeal formula, *Bones* used its season one Katrina episode, in part, to establish its successfully continuing formula: combining abject corpses, forensic science, and a close heterosexual partnership that functions to mediate those spectacles.
6. *Tabloid Culture: Trash Taste, Popular Power, and the Transformation of American Television*, pp. 6–7.
7. According to amw.com, John Walsh "is the best-selling author of three books: *Tears Of Rage*, *No Mercy* and *Public Enemies*." The website also celebrates Walsh's partnership with Julie Clark, the creator of Baby Einstein, claiming that they "have been lauded as exceptional resources for parents and kids in dealing with predators in the real world and online."
8. www.amw.com (accessed October 2, 2007).
9. *Law and Justice as Seen on TV*, p. 236.
10. "'Take Responsibility for Yourself': Judge Judy and the Neoliberal Citizen," p. 233.
11. Ibid., p. 232.
12. *Pretend We're Dead: Capitalist Monsters in American Pop Culture*, p. 50.
13. Ibid., p. 51.
14. http://www.usatoday.com/news/nation/2009-01-20-body-id_N.htm?POE=click-refer (accessed January 23, 2009).
15. "'These are Their Stories': Trauma, Form and the Screen Phenomenon of *Law and Order*," p. 83.
16. Ibid., p. 89.
17. Fleetwood makes this connection between the Katrina event and Mbembe's necropolitics: "More important, technological determinism is complicit in producing certain populations as disposable for the state, or what Achille Mbembe theorizes as necropolitics." "Failing Narratives, Initiating Technologies: Hurricane Katrina and the Production of a Weather Media Event," p. 770.
18. "Necropolitics." p. 39.
19. Gretchen A. Grisbaum and Douglas H. Ubelaker, "An Analysis of Forensic Anthropology Cases Submitted to the Smithsonian Institution by the Federal Bureau of Investigation from 1962 to 1994," p. 12.
20. The series frequently refers to Brennan's vacation volunteer work in the war and disaster-stricken areas of the world, for example, excavating the victims of genocide in Rwanda and unearthing mass graves in Guatemala. The program's handling of the Katrina event resonates with its wider neoliberal insistence that political violence can

be remedied through the individual dedication of professionals like Dr. Brennan. Unlike crime dramas such as *Homicide: Life on the Street* (NBC 1993–1999) or, to a certain extent, *Law and Order*, forensic television (like *Bones*) rarely leaves moral questions open ended, unanswered, or ambiguous. The technologies of science and dedicated forensic scientists are there to offer definitive answers, supposedly free from the prejudices of history.

21. Rapping, *Law and Justice as Seen on TV*, p. 243.
22. *Stormy Weather: Katrina and the Politics of Disposability*, p. 11.
23. Lee, "'These are Their Stories': Trauma, Form and the Screen Phenomenon of *Law and Order*," p. 84.
24. "In Search of Community on Reality TV: *America's Most Wanted* and *Survivor*," p. 158.

Chapter 3

The Big Apple and the Big Easy: Trauma, Proximity, and Home in New (and Old) Media

Joy V. Fuqua

> *[a text] is not only a conduit for the circulation of ideas, as knowledges or truths, but a passage or point of transition from one (social) stratum to another. A text is not the repository of knowledges or truths, the site for the storage of information…so much as it is a process of scattering thought; scrambling terms, concepts and practices; forging linkages; becoming a form of action… Texts, like concepts, do things, make things, perform connections, bring about new alignments.*
>
> —Elizabeth Grosz, Architecture from the Outside

The fourth anniversary of Hurricane Katrina passed with articles about the aftermath of the breaking of the levees and flooding of the city appearing in television news, in newspapers, and in magazines from the *New Yorker* to *Newsweek*. Four years ago, New Orleans, the city affectionately called "the big easy," was my home. I spent the fourth anniversary of Hurricane Katrina here in New York City, reading the online version of *The Times-Picayune*, talking to friends in New Orleans, and thinking about what it means to miss New Orleans while living in "the big apple." I wonder about proximity, about shared experiences of very different kinds of trauma, in these spatially distinct but culturally connected places—New Orleans and New York City. In some ways, I feel I am a go-between as I did literally move, for almost two years, in between these two beautiful and wondrous cities before leaving one city for another.

Examining the role of visual artists in the representation of trauma through a focus on the remnants of home, this chapter asks: How do New York City and New Orleans, as sites of national traumas, as material and discursive wounds upon the nation's landscape and citizens, move through each other via the work of visual artists? If television and other media texts have tended to respond conservatively and in ideologically restrictive ways to Hurricane Katrina and 9/11, then I posit that visual arts such as sculpture and the "new media" represented by artists' blogs and websites offer a destabilizing and critical way of imagining disaster and its aftermath. In this context I ask what the cities of New York and New Orleans share symbolically and how public discourse tends to produce *distance* and *dissonance* between them. Two artists, New Orleans-based Jana Napoli and New York-based Takashi Horisaki, embody this affinity between the two places and disasters. Both Napoli and Horisaki work in conventional or "old" artistic media (sculpture and painting), but they also use new technologies to document their work through websites and blogs. Additionally, Napoli's *Floodwall* combines new and old media through mobile installation while Horisaki's *Social Dress* literally makes home mobile.

The affinities between New Orleans and New York and their shared disasters and traumas are represented through Napoli's and Horisaki's mutual appropriation of one of the most taken for granted, oversimplified, and sentimentalized of concepts: *home*. Through multimedia installation and through sculpture both artists are particularly concerned to explore the affective dimensions of domestic space and their work engages with the politics of dwelling at its most basic level and probes the materials and social constructs we refer to under the aegis of "home." Crucially, their work also helps widen the perspective of what counts as "media textuality" after Hurricane Katrina. Visual artists with training in painting and sculpture, Napoli and Horisaki nonetheless call attention to the ways that artistic representation challenges our ideas of what media are. The introduction to this anthology explains that "A chief goal of the essays here is to consider the ways in which Hurricane Katrina and its aftermath have/have not precipitated revision of the narrative and ideological codes of popular film and television." The contribution that my chapter makes is to expand that consideration to other aspects of visual culture not captured within the purview of popular mainstream media forms. Delving into representational forms that preceded film, television, and video, my essay also examines the virtual versions of two artists' websites as an acknowledgment of the necessity of the Internet as a means of documentation of ephemeral art as well as a fundraising and promotional tool.

I am interested in the ways that Hurricane Katrina and its aftermath both challenged and perhaps further stabilized our existing ideas about the parameters of representational and documenting practices, be they in the realm of popular commercial or independent video or the, to my mind, less examined areas of installation, performance, photography, or sculpture. As media (but not "mass media" in the sense of broadcast or cablecast television programs or documentary film), works such as Napoli's and Horisaki's nonetheless should be considered as contributions to the wider discussion of what it means to represent a national trauma. We should note that works such as the photographs of Robert Polidari and the performance art of Paul Chan (*Waiting for Godot in New Orleans*) also count as "media." Do these forms of visual culture work in similar ways to conventional media texts or do they manage to accomplish certain things that conventional media texts cannot? Post-Katrina New Orleans has become a renewed and expanded hub of contemporary artistic production with Prospect 1 Biennale offering proof of the lure of the city's newly emerging status as a go-to destination for not only commercial photographers, but international artists as well. Organized in the spirit of other established international art biennials, such as the Whitney Biennial or the Venice Biennial, Prospect 1 New Orleans was founded by Dan Cameron to provide a forum for different artistic practices—local and otherwise—and to stage an event that would serve as a revitalization gesture for the city of New Orleans.[1] One could argue that it is perhaps a disaster aesthetic or a fascination with the debris of trauma that propels such events as Prospect 1, but that would be too facile an explanation for why New Orleans offers a "particular representational urgency" around and after Katrina. If it is the case, as Diane Negra has observed in the introduction to this anthology, that there is a "strong tendency in mainstream representations related to Katrina" to ascribe "blame and even moral deficiency to the residents of New Orleans rather than to government agencies or corporate interests," then visual artists such as Napoli and Horisaki offer a different take on media textuality from which to view this trauma. Existing as material sculpture and also as virtual representations through their websites, these two artists contribute to a different kind of Katrina archive, one in which feelings and immateriality are as valuable and significant as more conventional documents and representational modes (such as documentary film, television, and video).

While other essays in this collection focus on the representation of Hurricane Katrina in relation to specific media texts such as individual films or narrative and reality television programs as well as radio and Internet sites, my chapter hones in on the artistic productions, and attendant websites, of two visual artists. Placing Napoli's and Horisaki's work within a comparative framework invites us to ponder how the cities of New Orleans and New York articulate complementary, yet divergent, narratives about the relation between nation and citizen, inclusion and exclusion in a wider context of neoliberal practices and policies.[2]

It has often been said that Hurricane Katrina revealed aspects of American life that were, somehow, unseen, hidden, or cloaked by a patina of ideological denial of racism, poverty, and decades of urban neglect. However, in mainstream news accounts that purport to be about how the disaster revealed these facets of daily life, the reports tend to naturalize what was, for decades, an ongoing and officially sanctioned historical trauma (persistent poverty, lack of equal access to quality public schools, safe and affordable housing, consistently corrupt public officials, and neglect of municipal infrastructure and environment). Refusing episodic resolutions to the problems they represent, these visual artists offer challenges to the tendency of commercial television and film to offer tidy solutions to complex problems. While these artists simultaneously condense and challenge ideological constructs about *home*, they manage through their open-ended structures to serve as examples of what it means to be a media artist, or as Dan Streible has discussed in relation to the films of Helen Hill, "outsider activists" working in the contexts of "urban localism."[3]

Napoli's *Floodwall* and Horisaki's *Social Dress New Orleans—730 Days After* take remnants of homes, turn interior to exterior and in so doing open up a symbolic means of visualizing loss and of displaying—in mobile ways—how trauma may be seen in what remains behind, what is discarded or scheduled for official demolition. Of particular importance are the ways these two artists and their work move between New Orleans and New York City and how this movement becomes part of a narrative of trauma, of proximity, and of the permeable tissue of loss. Thus, the places in which their work is exhibited become affective fulcrums upon which shared experiences of national trauma turn and inform each other. Each work articulates a relation of proximity between different experiences of public, national trauma through the enduring symbolic and ideological value, yet impermanent and shifting structure, of *home*. Both artists put an emphasis on *materiality*; the actual process of making these artistic productions is evident in the works themselves and foregrounded in the narratives on each artist's website.

Homemade and Home(un)made

Home, as I refer to it in this chapter, is always more than a structured space; it is, as scholars from a wide variety of disciplines and approaches have pointed out, always more than a material dwelling. It is also an ideological, historical, and affective construct within which and through which ideas about origin, belonging, family, the body, identity, and nation are lived. The interconnection between bodies, histories, and the structured space of the home is exemplified in the common practice of marking the height of growing children on the interior of doorframes or walls.[4] In this gesture, the record of individual lives is literally written onto the material of the home, representing temporality by marking its spatial structures. For feminist theorists, home has been critiqued as a gendered category that constrains and reproduces normative power relations, on the one hand, and also a place in which these same normative patterns may be contested or resisted (female teenagers' "bedroom culture").[5] Depending upon whose home one is talking about, the ideological implications of this material space can have very different meanings. For feminist film and television scholars, analyzing the representation of home through the domestic or family film melodrama or the family-focused television program (including situation comedy, dramas, and soap opera), home has been seen as a site of rupture and also of gendered consolidation. Particularly in relation to feminist television studies, home has also been recognized as *the* place for television. Indeed, one of the core themes in television studies has been the way the medium reproduces, through its programming and physical presence, a certain order in the home as well as the ways that the home, and particularly women's movements within that space, structure television programming. From reception and ethnographic analyses to textual analyses of images of the home in television programming it seems that television and the home were made for each other. By contrast, in Napoli's and Horisaki's work, the idea of mediated domesticity seems to be both destabilized and reframed as a means of coming to terms with loss of "life structures" such as the home.

In typical ways of regarding home, the space is rendered as one of predictability, order, cleanliness, regularity, and control. However, as Mary Douglas observes, the home can also be a scene of chaos, catastrophe, disorder, and pain: "As to those who claim that the home does something stabilizing or deepening or enriching for the personality, there are as many who will claim that it cripples and stifles."[6] While Douglas notes that home is "not necessarily a fixed place" and that it can be a "wagon, a caravan, a boat, or a tent," some version of space is a prerequisite "for home starts by bringing some space under control."[7] Douglas continues: "For a home neither the space nor its appurtenances have to be fixed, but there has to be something regular about the appearance and reappearance of its furnishings."[8] By this definition, the idea that home starts by "bringing some space under control" has unique significance for thinking about home and trauma or home and disaster. Both Napoli's and Horisaki's works foreground what happens when the space of the home cannot be controlled—when the dwellers are trapped by that structure and also the consequences for rethinking the linkages between control, space, and home. Moreover, if it is the case that homes bear the marks of ideas about space and time (organization of rooms, relation of interior to exterior, etc.), and if, for Douglas, "the home is the realization of ideas," then what happens when the home is destroyed? Are the ideas that gave it shape also gone or is there something that remains, that lingers in the debris?

For *Home Territories*, his study of the relations between theories of media and home, David Morley has aptly chosen as cover photograph an image of British artist Rachel Whiteread's sculpture *House*. Turning to other visual artists such as Martha Rosler, Morley sees in Whiteread's cast model of the interior space of a house (that was soon to be demolished) a materialization of the private turned public, inside turned outside, negative space reversed. It is also a visualization of, according to critics, a commentary on homelessness and London's housing policies in the 1980s. Morley refers to Whiteread's *House* as a means of problematizing the ways that home and homeplace have functioned differently for various communities. He acknowledges that the "function and significance of home clearly varies with its context and, in a hostile social environment the importance of 'homeplace,' as bell hooks phrases it, is all the more important."[9] He continues to acknowledge the ways that home can mean differently by quoting hooks' comments about the function of "homeplace" to African Americans' sense of autonomy as part of the foundation for a "wider community of resistance."[10]

Other visual artists who provide entrances into a less fixed and even contingent idea of home that might cast into relief other media narratives about it include, in addition to Whiteread, the late Gordon Matta-Clark and contemporary artists Frances Cape and Do-Ho Suh. While Matta-Clark's work called attention to the spatial and temporal aspects of various kinds of structures including houses and abandoned industrial buildings, Suh and Cape, like Horisaki, fabricate home spaces as sites of affective impermanence.[11] In such works as *Seoul Home, 1999*, and *348 W. 22nd St.*, Suh recreates specific spaces in which the artist has actually lived by using transportable, sewn materials such as silk organza. Viewers of Suh's work walk "through apartments and hallways and see the furnishings, right down to the door knobs and light switches."[12] Frances Cape's domestic installations consist of actual recreations, out of wood and other building materials, of rooms, houses, and furniture. It is in this spirit of domestic reproduction that Horisaki's *Social Dress* can be understood not simply as an exercise in preservation, but as a comment upon the dislocations of homeplace.

If texts "do things," as Grosz maintains, then what kinds of things do the visual cultures surrounding traumatic events such as Hurricane Katrina or 9/11 do? How do they function as conduits, or thresholds that articulate one experience to another? How do, for example, the works of Napoli and Horisaki forge affective articulations across spatial and temporal divides? Specifically, how do Napoli's installation (which combines photography, LED display, and, currently, more than seven hundred flooded household dresser drawers) and Horisaki's latex mold of a shotgun-style house at 1941 Caffin Avenue in the Lower Ninth Ward (a house owned by elderly couple Roosevelt and Billie Johnson) serve as conduits for thinking through the effects of disaster in two American cities?

Napoli's *Floodwall* is first and foremost a text of recovery, of salvage, an expression of loss and mourning gathered from the debris that once was part of the interior of flooded homes; Horisaki's sculpture *Social Dress* is a reverse reproduction of 1941 Caffin Avenue. When Horisaki applied cheesecloth, latex, and paint to the exterior of the house, small bits of the house adhered to the application. Then, when Horisaki peeled away this dried layer, identifying marks such as the address "1941" appeared in reverse. Thus, the work carries material remains of the house within its new skin-like structure.

Both artists' work can be understood as public performances of scavenging and salvaging, mourning and memorializing in relation both to the exterior physical structure of a specific home and the intimate, interior objects out of which we make *houses* into *homes*. While the contents of the drawers that Napoli collected were lost, material evidence of the contents remain in stains or through some of the owners' recorded oral narratives. As 1941 Caffin Avenue was demolished by the city, material parts of the house still exist in the form of Horisaki's sculpture.

Napoli and Horisaki's shared artistic connection (forged through their experience of disaster) is significant because it makes clear what might otherwise be understood as the repressed affinities between 9/11 and Katrina. The fact that many New York-based artists came to New Orleans to perform, to produce work, and to document the disaster's aftermath is highly germane in this context. As Napoli said of the relationship between New Yorkers and New Orleaneans, "New Yorkers are the people who knew."[13] Napoli's *Floodwall* had its first public exhibition on the Liberty Street Bridge, overlooking Ground Zero, while Horisaki's *Social Dress* was on view in New Orleans as he "reconstructed" portions of 1941 Caffin Avenue, but had its official premiere exhibition at the Socrates Sculpture Park in Long Island City, New York. Set against the backdrop of Manhattan, the Socrates Sculpture Park is itself built upon a former landfill.[14] Since the initial exhibition of *Social Dress*, Horisaki has moved the sculpture, in a U-Haul truck, back to New Orleans to be included in Prospect 1 Biennale, 2008. Through the initial exhibition of both *Floodwall* and *Social Dress*, these artists offer ways of complicating ideas of proximity, distance, and trauma both common and distinct in relation to 9/11 and Hurricane Katrina.

About New Orleans and New York: Trauma, Articulation, and Proximity

Two key concepts, proximity and articulation, allow us to more fully consider what might be at stake in a comparison of what, at first glance, might seem to be the very different experiences of trauma represented by 9/11 and Hurricane Katrina. When I use the term "trauma," I recognize that there are multiple ways of responding to and experiencing the events of 9/11 and Hurricane Katrina just as there are different registers or "measures" of trauma. Here, I am reminded of E. Ann Kaplan's approach to trauma in which she argues that just as it is important to "distinguish different types of trauma" and to "analyze different ways people relate to traumatic events," so what is "equally important about trauma is one's specific positioning vis-à-vis an event."[15] Positioning implies a relation, not necessarily a fixed, spatial one, but perhaps an affective relation between the event and the subject who experiences it (in a direct or mediated way). In other words, to refer to the Elizabeth Grosz quotation that serves as an epigraph for this article, we can think about the events of 9/11 and Hurricane Katrina as *textual*, in the richest and most complex sense of the word, allowing for the "circulation of ideas" about what it means to *live* trauma as an individual and national *wound*.

With New York City and New Orleans, proximity is established through shared experiences of trauma and culture. The two have relational proximity through cultural artifacts. However, economically speaking, New York City and New Orleans are vastly different in terms of how neoliberal economic policies—the dismantling of the architecture of the state and the elevation of the idea of the self-reliant individual—impact the two cities. They are further distinguished from each other in terms of how the events of 9/11 and Hurricane Katrina have signified.

We can imagine symbolic and geographic proximity or "nextness" between these two cities and their experiences of trauma, but it is also the case that certain forms of public discourse create distance and dissonance between New York and New Orleans. While cultural and symbolic workers, such as Napoli and Horisaki, seem to forge articulations that connect common experiences of national trauma, at the same time, hegemonic culture works just as hard to specify the "uniqueness" of each event and to distinguish 9/11 from the devastation of Hurricane Katrina. New Orleans and New York, through their shared experiences of trauma as well as through the exchange of symbolic and cultural representations, both lose and maintain particularity in ways that suggest, as Doreen Massey explains, "the particularity of any place is... constructed not by placing boundaries around it and defining its identity through counterposition to the other which lies beyond, but precisely (in part) through the specificity of the mix of *links* and *interconnections to* that 'beyond.' Places viewed this way are open and porous."[16] The histories of personal and community trauma represented by the empty dresser drawers in *Floodwall* or the spectral skin of the empty 1941 Caffin Avenue house point to the ways that experiences, as well as spaces, are "open and porous." 1941 Caffin Avenue, which continues to mark, in a legal proprietary sense, an actual place (now an empty lot in New Orleans' Lower Ninth Ward), becomes mobile, has a second life as a structure that both preserves and negates its original form.

With sea levels rising and with ten square miles of Louisiana wetlands dissolving into the Gulf of Mexico each year, New Orleans is literally floating away from the United States, untethered, spatially and economically; it is peripheral and marginal in relation to the larger nation. Indeed, in its own history, as part of the vast Louisiana Purchase, which brought it into the nation in a legal territorial sense, New Orleans has always figured as a place with tenuous claims to "American-ness." It is described in Herbert Asbury's 1936 "pulp history" *The French Quarter: An Informal History of the New Orleans Underworld* thus:

> Wickedest City in the World!! Two hundred years ago a French Governor began the pattern of gaudy living for New Orleans. But it wasn't until the early 1800s under the United States flag that the city really blossomed into its golden age of sin... For over a century, New Orleans was the gayest and most sinful city on the North American continent.[17]

Asbury, also the writer of the 1927 *Gangs of New York: An Informal History of the Underworld* that provided the basis for Martin Scorsese's 2002 film *Gangs of New York*, saw in both cities this idea of the "underworld," which links the Big Easy and the Big Apple in claims to an unseemly, yet compelling, "informal history." Placing New Orleans and New York together also allows for an examination of how contemporary and historical social and racial injustice is lived in the land of plenty. It is evident that 9/11 and Hurricane Katrina hold different and oftentimes competing positions as symbolic events in terms of cultural meaning or significance. The events of 9/11 have been embraced as a national tragedy; a variety of institutional and governmental entities used it to stoke the flames of nationalism and so-called preemptive war as the preferred response, crafting a narrative of patriotism and national allegiance replete with easily demarcated heroes and villains.[18]

By contrast, Hurricane Katrina *exposed* or *revealed* national racism and poverty and the horrific effects of three decades of governmental abdication of social responsibility for its citizens. But in the time since the flooding and devastation, this very exposure has been covered over by a veneer of "blame the victim" discourse. This discursive frame prevents the type of national embrace, for the most part—and with exceptions—that New York has received. In other words, while people from all over the world wear I "heart" NY t-shirts or "FDNY" t-shirts, it is not common to see "I 'heart' NOLA" or "Be A New Orleanian Wherever You Are," "New Orleans Matters," or Make Levees, Not War" t-shirts and bumper stickers outside of New Orleans. This is not to say that New Orleanians have not been welcomed into generous strangers' homes, given jobs and housing in multiple cities across the United States—including New York—but that the overall national "mood" in relation to New Orleans tends to be characterized by a sense of individualistic responsibility. In addition to the "blame the victim" perspective, there is also the frequently heard mantra of "why would anybody want to live there?" that then gets translated into reactionary insurance policies and reluctance on the part of taxpayers to "foot the bill" for people who "choose to live" in "risky areas."

When thinking about the economic differences between New York and New Orleans, we must note New York City—a world financial powerhouse with Wall Street and the huge Bronze Bull sculpture that draw hundred of tourists each day—represents both conceptually and materially the world of twenty-first-century finance capital. In some ways, one could say New York City represents the national center, while New Orleans represents the national periphery. Along those lines, New Orleans represents more of an early twentieth-century model of extraction capital, where the economy rests on the removal of natural resources (the oil and gas, shrimp and fishing, and rice and sugar cane industries). New York City has consolidated its position as a financial center, while New Orleans has had its riches exploited and extracted by Big Oil and others for decades—revenue that could have been going to Louisiana to fund education, health care, and the state infrastructure, rather than into the pockets of offshore oil companies such as Shell.[19] This extraction and exploitation of Gulf Coast resources, even in the form of disaster, continues in the recovery period with one of the first contracts for hurricane debris clean up going to a subsidiary of energy services and defense contractor Halliburton.

I recognize that New York City is surely not monolithic in its symbolic meanings; while simultaneously a center of financial and cultural power, it has also long been a place for counterculturalism and can connote, at different times and for different interests, the center of elite art or illicit desire, yet it is the case that New York continues to signify globally as a place that visitors come for their "betterment," for theater, museums, and other elite cultural experiences. They come to New York to learn, to acquire cultural capital (however defined). In contrast, visitors go to New Orleans, especially during Mardi Gras, to revel in the city's long and rich history of abandon, indulgence, transgression, and the pleasures of the flesh over the edification of the mind. Visitors flock to New Orleans to let it all hang out, to experience carnality, or its simulation through the mythology of the city, even if this experience of authenticity is confined to the few blocks around Bourbon Street.[20] In other words, the cities are associated with starkly different modes of urban tourism and while they both have bits of center and periphery built into them, they occupy different places on America's meaning map. As George Lipsitz carefully observes, the hegemonic meaning of New Orleans, echoed in some of George W. Bush's statements about the city, describe it as a "place to come to from somewhere else not a place to live in, a spot for revelry that can be smirked about knowingly in retrospect after one's return to bourgeois respectability and domesticity."[21]

In media representation, also, we can see traces of proximity and distance between the two cities and these national traumas. Comparisons of Hurricane Katrina to 9/11 have been and continue to be made, most notably and recently, in the federal government's own "analysis," of the response to the New Orleans disaster in *A Failure of Initiative* and also through the unfortunate and off-the-cuff remarks of, for example, New Orleans mayor Ray Nagin who when explaining the lag in his city's recovery talked about New York City as a "hole in the ground." While relational proximity is established in one area, another area of public discourse severs the connection and produces exceptionalism, competition for resources, or cultural dissonance.

With respect to television's role in the production of a consensus about the meaning of these two national traumas, Lynn Spigel has observed that when television interrupted its regular flow after 9/11, "media corporations and advertisers were compelled to restore business routines and marketing practices of contemporary consumer media culture."[22] However, television's response to Hurricane Katrina was different in that while 9/11 disrupted the commercial flow of television, with Katrina there was more of a sense of forcing the ongoing disaster to conform to conventional modes of production and narration. Even within individual news stories as reporters expressed disbelief at the scenes of suffering people in the days following Katrina, there seemed to be a recuperative movement that closed off further or deeper engagement. For one thing, the conventional flow and segmentation of commercial television was not disrupted as it had been during 9/11. This in itself is telling for how 9/11 was perceived by media as an attack on the entire nation while the effects of Hurricane Katrina were deemed to be local. Nonetheless, these differences, in the response of television as a medium, had significance in shaping or delimiting the kinds of meanings that could be made of these traumas. Yet, as CNN producer Jim Spellman commented about Hurricane Katrina, "I really don't think we have a vocabulary for this... Television brought this horror story—this disturbingly real, violent and deadly version of *Survivor* into our living rooms. It hurt to watch."[23] Even though television did not interrupt programming as it had during 9/11, five networks (NBC, BET, MTV, VH1, and CMT) broadcast fundraising events and Disney, the Weather Channel, and Warner Bros. offered millions of dollars to the American Red Cross. One common observation about 9/11 and Hurricane Katrina is that both traumas "revealed" certain things about the ways that the state values or devalues, protects or endangers the lives of its most vulnerable citizens. Marita Sturken suggests, "using the term 'ground zero' had the effect of wiping clean earlier meaning" and producing "the narrative that 9/11 was a moment in which the United States lost its innocence."[24] Could the same be said for Hurricane Katrina? It is within this tension that Napoli's *Floodwall* and Horisaki's *Social Dress New Orleans—730 Days After* take on mobile meanings as they move between cities.

New Orleans in New York: *Floodwall*

I first saw Napoli's *Floodwall* in early January 2007. The work, consisting of hundreds of ruined and discarded dresser drawers from homes flooded after the levees broke in Hurricane Katrina's wake, had its premiere installation in a space of transition.[25] Now an active (re)construction site, the activity at the World Trade Center provided a powerful backdrop for the ordered disarray represented by *Floodwall*. As a reminder of the disorder of debris, the 350 flooded dresser drawers were positioned to invite passersby to make comparisons between the installation and the World Trade Center site visible from the bridge's large windows.[26]

Collected from flooded homes and displayed horizontally along the floor on top of a 230-foot long plywood platform, the dresser drawers were arranged to expose their interiors. Along the plywood base and in front of the drawers were several LED "tickers"—like the text that appears at the bottom of TV screens in cable news formats. Quotations from some of the drawers' owners were displayed in red on the LED offering such personal commentary as, "This drawer is where I kept my love letters from my husband before we were married" (Honorine Weiss, New Orleans resident). Napoli explained that she was inspired to construct *Floodwall* upon returning to the silence of New Orleans' trash and debris-strewn neighborhoods; as she put it, she found herself "trapped in grief on the street." The artist has said that she wanted to show *Floodwall* to New York because of the affinity between the two disasters; for financial and logistical support, she contacted the Lower Manhattan Cultural Council and Creative Time Inc., a nonprofit arts organization.[27] Because of a sense of affinity, she suggests, "They made a space for us."[28] Napoli posits that New Yorkers and New Orleaneans have a shared understanding of trauma and mourning that might have different meanings for communities that have not endured such disastrous events. *Floodwall* was installed on the Liberty Street Bridge, with one end an entrance into the World Financial Center and the other leading down to Liberty Street and the New York Fire Department's station house for Ladder 10 and Engine 10, called "Ten House." The Liberty Street Bridge offers an elevated view onto the Ground Zero area, which makes this particular location for *Floodwall* all the more significant in terms of linking the trauma of 9/11 to that of Hurricane Katrina.

Marita Sturken, for example, points out that, regarding 9/11 and the Oklahoma City bombing, "there was a common tendency for people to marshal their proximity to the event[s]" as a means of establishing depth of engagement or authenticity of experience. As Sturken observes,

> [e]xperience is the category of engagement that is seen to be the most authentic, a primary mode of being that is longed for. Yet, most Americans' experience of the key events of history are mediated ones...Even many people who were in close physical proximity to these events watched them on television rather than in person.[29]

Floodwall places 9/11 in proximity to Hurricane Katrina—not merely in the sense of geographic proximity, but as the *Oxford English*

Dictionary defines it as a "relational proximity," a "state of being nearest, nextness," two events sharing an affinity. Napoli's piece invites us to draw together two national traumas that are often held apart and in so doing, this articulation mitigates against the kind of easy closure offered by television and other mainstream media narratives.

This proximal affinity is achieved, I suggest, in two ways. First, proximal affinity is activated through each city's historical and symbolic functions as centers of immigration; as ports for the passage of people and things; as tourist centers (despite the different experiential emphases I noted earlier); as exchange points of commerce as well as centers of civil rights struggles; and, as places of vice and temptation. Second, the location for this particular installation of *Floodwall* suggests an affinity between the two traumas. The location also provides a contrasting counterpoint between the two events; while Ground Zero is now an active, ordered site of construction and memorialization, New Orleans remains disordered, interiors exposed, like the drawers without dressers, without structures within which to (re)place them.

That combination of similarity and difference resonates with a second key concept that is integral to this reading of *Floodwall* in relation to Ground Zero: articulation. As Stuart Hall has explained, articulation

> is the form of the connection that can make a unity of two different elements, under certain conditions. It is a linkage that is not necessary, determined, absolute and essential for all time. You have to ask, under what circumstances can a connection be forged or made... The "unity" which matters is a linkage between the articulated discourse and the social forces with which it can, under certain historical conditions, but need not necessarily, be connected.[30]

In this way, *Floodwall* can be a point of temporary yet provocative articulation, a conduit of proximity, of "nextness," between two temporally and spatially distinct disasters.

Napoli's *Floodwall* literally keeps vigil over Ground Zero, and is a powerful reminder of the ways that proximity is more than a spatial measure of intimacy or distance. *Floodwall* invites comparison between these two places through a visual link, a structural connection: a space of transition meeting a space of transition. It is an installation that, in this iteration, materializes and enacts the concept of articulation in that it conjoins two different traumatic sites through the very mundane furnishings of everyday life. Moreover, it does seem provocative that this site was selected for the first installation of *Floodwall*. As a careful arrangement of "debris" positioned so close to a site that has just recently been cleared of debris, *Floodwall* challenges us to realize that while Ground Zero is now a building site, New Orleans, five years after the disaster, is still dismantling structures and disposing of debris. According to one estimate, there was 1.2 million tons of building debris at the World Trade Center Site, with a concentration of debris in a twelve square block radius. An Army Corps of Engineers Report in April 2008 stated that the debris from Hurricane Katrina covered a ninety thousand square mile radius including areas in Louisiana, Mississippi, and Alabama.[31]

Floodwall not only exists as a material structure; its website is also a powerful collection of different media from photography to video and audio. The website for *Floodwall* functions like an interactive archive as well as an active information and documentation center for residents who may have been directly affected by Hurricane Katrina and other visitors seeking information about the project or the disaster. The website for *Floodwall* makes clear that this is a multidimensional work that continues to be assembled as more and more oral narratives are collected and the requests for exhibition challenge the logistics of transportation. Napoli described her work as a means for spectators to "see the silence" that was the aftermath of Hurricane Katrina. Within the intimate and interior everyday furnishings of home life, drawers are something that most of us have: the drawer where we keep special objects; the drawer where loose change rubs up against pocketknives or old wine corks; the drawer that is full of random office supplies or hair pins.

Napoli hoped that by transporting what is now a "piece of furniture" in its own right, *Floodwall* could let "Americans see that silence."[32] Napoli wanted *Floodwall*, through its physical structure with drawers that can be pulled out but that remain empty, to fill the void that remains in the representation of Hurricane Katrina's devastation. The drawers missing their original structure represent thousands of families and individuals missing their homes and the silence of the neighborhoods once filled with sound. Indeed, New Orleans is known for its sounds, mostly musical ones of course, but also the sounds of neighbors, the sounds of people living in proximity to each other and building a lifetime of conversation. As Napoli has observed of the months following Hurricane Katrina when she traversed New Orleans' empty neighborhoods, "You'd hear the sound of a screen door shutting, and turn around and hope someone was there. But there was nobody. It was the wind. It was deathly. It was the one thing journalists, writers and TV couldn't do, show that silence."[33] Through the silence evoked by the empty dresser drawers juxtaposed to the sounds of construction at Ground Zero, and through the proximity of *Floodwall* to this other site of disaster, both public in their display, we are invited to ask under which conditions national trauma can be articulated.

In its virtual form, *Floodwall*, as the website's homepage explains, "restores to us a part of what the levees of New Orleans shattered. A sculptural installation of household drawers by artist Jana Napoli, *Floodwall* stands witness to the magnitude of devastation but equally to the transformative power imbued in the detritus of daily life."[34] Local yet inclusive in its direct address, the website displays that written text over a photograph of part of the sculpture. At the bottom of the page, quotations from various drawer owners appear. The page is organized into various topics, one of which is "Drawers and Personal Stories." This link matches a color photograph of a numbered dresser with the address from where it was collected, along with the neighborhood and zip code, to the name and image (if available) of the drawer's owner. Artist Rondell Crier, working with Napoli, collected video and audio interviews with some drawer owners. A few interviews are included and when one listens to them it seems as if the drawers themselves are talking. Only one interview, at this point, is a short video. However, each interview exists only as a fragment. They are very brief (most are approximately one minute long), but the narratives contain information about the history of the object, what was kept inside the drawer, how and under what conditions the owners found the drawer, stories about being stranded in a home, rescued from a home, and other descriptions of loss and trauma.

Visitors to this portion of the documentary interactive website may search for drawers and stories by postal zip code. The organization of the drawers by number and by address balances the idea of neighborhood specificity with an awareness of the enormity of the flood. The website directly addresses a visitor with questions such as, "Is your drawer a part of *Floodwall?*" This direct address suggests an involvement with the disaster and encourages recognition of the personalized dimensions of loss. Even as drawers and owners are "matched" and the drawer is (re)placed in the wall sculpture, the narratives underscore the impossibility of easy endings. *Floodwall* simultaneously maps and destabilizes loss and home.

The project's interviews (such as the video of Norma Jackson from 4601 Saratoga Street, New Orleans, 70115 [Freret Neighborhood]) attest to survivors' experiences. Jackson appears centered in the frame, sometimes directly addressing the camera, sometimes turning her gaze to the side, as she recounts the moment of her and her family's rescue by the National Guard. Near the end of her story, she says that a National Guardsman arrived in a boat. While carrying a rifle, he told her that her family had to leave. Ms. Jackson looks at the camera and asks, "Where were we gonna go?" The video testimony ends here with the question unanswered. Her image appears to the right of a color photograph of her dresser drawer, "No. 032—Norma Jackson." Identified like a piece of evidence from a crime scene, the drawers appear as material remains that cannot be filled and cannot be filed away. Under the "Neighborhood" link on this same page, can be found historical information about the specific neighborhood in which the drawer was found along with descriptions of this neighborhood's place in relation to other parts of Orleans Parish. A map of the neighborhoods is also provided. This part of the website—incorporating still and moving images, audio, and text—gives voice to the inanimate dresser drawers so that each one seems to tell its own story. Material culture speaks, after all.

Refusing neat and tidy closure, these oral histories, along with the remaining fragments of home, work against narratives that privilege a discourse of renovation and recuperation. The drawers remain fragments, as do the oral histories that accompany them. As such they resist maneuvers that attempt to preclude ongoing mourning as they reinforce the open-endedness of the project. *Floodwall*, in other words, is, like the levees in New Orleans, an active construction site.

In May 2007, I was living in my house in New Orleans, having coffee and reading *The Times-Picayune*. In the middle of an ordinary, domestic ritual, I came across an article, "Artist's Plan for Disaster Art May Fall to Wrecking Ball," by Katy Reckdahl. The newspaper article described how New York-based artist Takashi Horisaki was trying to create a scale-size mold of a flood-damaged house at 1941 Caffin Avenue in the Lower Ninth Ward. Horisaki was in a race with the U.S. Army Corps of Engineers who had scheduled the house for demolition. Then in his second month of work on the project, Horisaki was trying to prevent the Army Corps from demolishing the already severely damaged house before he completed the casting. Intrigued by Horisaki's project, a friend and I drove over to 1941 Caffin Avenue to see what this New York artist was up to. We brought him some Popeye's chicken and biscuits for lunch and talked to him about his project as his assistants, art students from Loyola University (where he had received his BA in fine arts in 2003), applied latex and pigment.[35] Originally from Japan, but now living in New York City, Horisaki said that he felt compelled to return to New Orleans as a "neutral observer, not exactly an outsider, but with some distance and perspective on the situation." While not actually a neutral observer, but an artist with knowledge of New Orleans and a desire to call attention to the lack of progress in the city's recovery effort, Horisaki wanted to figure out a way to "make this tragedy tangible to those far removed from the disaster." *Social Dress New Orleans* articulates the trauma of Hurricane Katrina through the framework of domesticity and the reproduction of an actual home (figure 3.1). While *Floodwall* collected the remains of numerous and different

Figure 3.1 Visual artists such as Takashi Horisaki represent trauma through a focus on the remnants of "home." *Social Dress New Orleans—730 Days After*, Socrates Sculpture Park, Long Island City (August 2007, photograph by author).

home interiors, Horisaki's *Social Dress New Orleans* is a physical, scale model of a specific house, with a specific address.

The process of making the mold of 1941 Caffin Avenue began with securing consent from the property's owners, Roosevelt and Billie Johnson, who were living in a trailer on their other Hurricane Katrina damaged property in Pontchartrain Park. Horisaki estimated that he would produce forty sheets of latex, each coated in baby powder to prevent the layers from adhering to each other, and then transport the sheets back to New York City for assembly at the Socrates Sculpture Park. This process of production from destruction provides a corollary to Napoli's *Floodwall* in that both artists were attempting to reinvest emptied out spaces with meaning. Or perhaps it is the case that the spaces were only perceived as empty, as ready for demolition. The photograph of Horisaki at work at 1941 Caffin Avenue that accompanied the newspaper story I read shows the artist applying the latex and pigment to the front of the house, framed by two large pecan trees, with a sign (made by Horisaki) that says "Please Do Not Demolish." Yellow "caution" tape is strung between the trees to warn passersby of the danger that the structure might pose. It is, of course, a crucial request that Horisaki's sign "Please Do Not Demolish" appears in front of a home that, to an ordinary observer, appears to have already been demolished by floodwater from the broken levees. Yet, upon closer inspection, the structure preserves, like the individual drawers in *Floodwall*, the marks of life that once animated its site. Moreover, the mold that was produced retains some of the physical remnants of the house—bits of wood from the frame, pieces of wallpaper, impressions of paneling, nails, and windowpanes.

Horisaki's Internet home page features a single large color photograph of the sculpture, *Social Dress*. Links along the left side of the page offer a list of Horisaki's projects. The link for *Social Dress* calls up a series of photographs that document the production process. These production photos are presented in a way that exposes the artistic process as dirty, sweaty, and also a collaborative effort with several volunteers helping Horisaki apply latex and cheesecloth. These photographs describe stages in the production of *Social Dress* while they emphasize the original structure as a kind of fragile, material signifier of loss and devastation. Some of the photographs that feature the application of latex and cheesecloth make it seem as if Horisaki is administering first aid to the injured, frail home. Recognizing that the home was just days away from being demolished by the city, this project becomes all the more striking as a means of literally reversing that process. More than a mere exercise in preservation, Horisaki's *Social Dress*—both in its actual and virtual forms—evokes the presence and absence of home.

When 1941 Caffin Avenue was rebuilt in New York City it consisted of a series of cloth panels representing the shotgun-style house. Its "walls" and "doorways" blew in the breeze and one could feel the ridges of the original structure. As a reversal of conceptual artist Matta-Clark's planned "cuts" into domestic as well as industrial structures, Horisaki's *Social Dress New Orleans* encouraged examination of the physical aspects of home while, at the same time, noting its fragility not only as a concept but also as a space. In transporting 1941 Caffin Avenue to New York City, Horisaki's sculpture begs the question of home, set against an urban background of skyscrapers—home and industry, domesticity and commerce. It also suggests, by its presence in New York City, that the national traumas of 9/11 and of Hurricane Katrina quite literally brought home the tenuous claims citizens have to a most basic human need: shelter from a storm, succor in a disaster. As homes became traps due to rising floodwaters and with roofs becoming sites for the rescue of New Orleaneans, what remains are the bits of debris that link the experience of disaster through a flooded dresser drawer, a sculpture of a demolished home, and a desire to comprehend national trauma.

So what is to be gained by the juxtaposition of 9/11 and Hurricane Katrina, of New York City and New Orleans? Comparative theoretical and historical maneuvers that anchor New Orleans to the nation as an economic center prevent an easy dismissal of New Orleans as an expendable American city. Horisaki's sculpture and Napoli's installation can be considered public *reckoning texts*, conduits for the examination of shared cultures of trauma. Both Horisaki's sculpture and Napoli's installation are public space projects—they take place in plain sight (or did originally); both pieces are fragile, made of ephemeral materials that will eventually disintegrate; both artists share a personal history of New Orleans.[36]

Writing about mourning following 9/11, Judith Butler has described some forms of grief as being about the "loss of First World presumption," which is a "loss of a certain horizon of experience, a certain sense of the world itself as a national entitlement."[37] For Butler, loss of this sense of entitlement, for some, becomes a form of productive mourning, one that, Butler hopes, provides a space for social transformation; where mourning becomes productive of something larger than the self in pain. Proximity and distance merge through people crossing geographical boundaries to flow into New Orleans, to help, to do the work that needs to be done and that neoliberal governmental policies have abjured. Cities and cultural representations speak to each other across trauma, across distance, and exchange narratives about what it means to live through and in proximity.

Notes

The author wishes to acknowledge the Research Foundation of the City of New York and PSC-CUNY, which provided research support for this chapter.

1. Before accepting this position at the CAC and also becoming the chief curator of "the largest biennial of international contemporary art ever organized in the United States, *Prospect 1* (from November 1, 2008 through January 15, 2009)," Cameron was the Senior Curator at the New Museum in New York City from 1995 to 2006. See http//www.prospectneworleans.org (accessed September 15, 2009).
2. Napoli has installed *Floodwall* in other spaces such as in Baton Rouge, Louisiana, and Austin, Texas, but I am most concerned with the installation that appeared within direct visual proximity of Ground Zero during 2007. This installation on the Liberty Street Bridge was the first public exhibit of *Floodwall*.
3. See Dan Streible's essay in this book.
4. In a broad conceptual sense and no doubt in many literal ones too such growth charts were replaced by another sort of line measurement, the distinct water lines that marked the accumulated level of water in and around New Orleans.
5. Angela McRobbie and Jenny Garber. "Girls and Subcultures: An Exploration," pp. 209–222.
6. "The Idea of Home: A Kind of Space," p. 289.
7. Ibid.
8. Ibid.
9. *Home Territories: Media, Mobility and Identity*, p. 29.
10. Ibid.
11. Gordon Matta-Clark's *Splitting* (1974) involved the actual cutting or "building cuts" performed on an abandoned suburban home at 322 Humphrey Street in Englewood, New Jersey. The house was split in two and further destabilized using a series of foundational lifts. See Pamela M. Lee, *Object to be Destroyed: The Work of Gordon Matta-Clark*.
12. Seehttp://www.brown.edu/Facilities/David_Winston_Bell_Gallery/suh.html.

13. Megan Gillin-Schwartz, "Still Life in a Series of Open Drawers."
14. In 1986, "a coalition of artists and community members, under the leadership of artist Mark di Suvero, transformed [Socrates Sculpture Park] into an open studio and exhibition space for artists and a neighborhood park for local residents." As such it represents the effects of reclamation of heretofore-disposable land transformed into a public space for artistic production and community use. http://www.socialdress-neworleans.blogspot.com (accessed September 14, 2009). Socrates Sculpture Park is located at 3201 Vernon Boulevard (at Broadway) in Long Island City, New York, along the East River.
15. *Trauma Culture: The Politics of Terror and Loss in Media and Literature*, pp. 1–2.
16. *Space, Place, and Gender*, p. 5; emphasis in the original.
17. *The French Quarter: An Informal History of The New Orleans Underworld*, p. 1.
18. See Susan Faludi, *The Terror Dream: Fear and Fantasy in Post-9/11 America*.
19. Even as Wall Street is also seen as the epicenter of the contemporary financial crisis, it is nonetheless still a hegemonic signifier of capital.
20. "Authenticity," or its promise, is also very much at stake in New York as well where, in the area around Union Square, "big box" chains such as Home Depot, Old Navy, and the Olive Garden have moved in to displace local merchants.
21. "Learning from New Orleans: The Social Warrant of Hostile Privatism and Competitive Consumer Citizenship," p. 451.
22. "Entertainment Wars: Television Culture after 9/11," p. 629.
23. "The Big Hurt."
24. *Tourists of History: Memory, Kitsch and Consumerism from Oklahoma City to Ground Zero*, p. 311.
25. As a "co-presentation of the World Financial Center and the Lower Manhattan Cultural Council, the site-specific artwork was designed by the Manhattan-based exhibition company Whirlwind Creative and brought to the city after L.M.C.C. President Tom Healy heard about the project and went to New Orleans to assist Napoli in her collection." Working with Napoli was her partner Rondell Crier (who designed the wall structure for the drawers), along with Tatiana Clay (who has collected oral narratives of some of the drawers' owners). The drawers are organized by zip code and are now arranged in a thirteen-feet-high wall built by Crier into which the drawers slide in and out. This construction design allows for the wall to be assembled and disassembled for transport to other exhibition locations. It is still a work in progress as people recognize their drawers and contribute their stories to the database. Napoli's and Clay's goal is to

collect at least fifty oral histories that will then be housed at Louisiana State University.
26. The creation and installation of *Floodwall* was a collaborative project between artists and cultural workers in New York City and New Orleans. While it was Napoli who originally began collecting the drawers and had the vision for the work, other artists, photographers, carpenters, and creative personnel facilitated its installation on the Liberty Street Bridge in Lower Manhattan. Tom Healy, president of the Lower Manhattan Cultural Council, and Anne Pasternak, executive director of Creative Time Inc., flew to New Orleans and helped Napoli collect drawers. Also, David Lackey, owner of Whirlwind Creative, "designed the installation so it would fit in Liberty Bridge." The majority of the funding for this installation of *Floodwall* came from the Lower Manhattan Cultural Council and the World Financial Center. See Millie Ball, "Empty Vessels."
27. Personal interview with artist, August 3, 2009.
28. Gillin-Schwartz, "Still Life in a Series of Open Drawers."
29. *Tourists of History: Memory, Kitsch and Consumerism from Oklahoma City to Ground Zero*, p. 29.
30. "On Postmodernism and Articulation: An Interview with Stuart Hall," p. 53.
31. Linda Luther, "Disaster Debris Removal after Hurricane Katrina: Status and Associated Issues," p. 4.
32. Millie Ball, "Empty Vessels."
33. Ibid.
34. See http://www.floodwall.org.
35. While my friend and I were visiting with Horisaki, a second group of visitors arrived. They started talking to Horisaki and then we were introduced to them. Among the visitors was Paul Chan, another New York artist who, a year later, would produce *Waiting for Godot in New Orleans* in the Lower Ninth Ward, outdoors on a city street. It was an interesting moment as Chan, a recognized artist in his own right, met Horisaki for the first time, and talked with him about the project at 1941 Caffin Avenue.
36. Both artists' works are ephemeral in choice of materials and in terms of the trauma they document, if trauma can be understood as fleeting and not located and place bound. Upon walking through Horisaki's *Social Dress* assembled in New York City, I was reminded of temporary, tent-like structures children build with the knowledge that they will be gone the next day. I was also reminded of the work of Eva Hesse whose *Schema* (latex, September 1967) and translucent *Aught* (latex, canvas, polyethylene sheeting, metal grommets, 1968) appear to be on the verge of disintegration and collapse before your eyes. Both Horisaki's and Hesse's works call attention to

impermanence, of the inability to fix time and space even as we experience and live within them. Perhaps it is this recognition that provides an articulation between the ephemeral works of Horisaki and Napoli vis-à-vis the traumas of Hurricane Katrina and 9/11.
37. *Precarious Life: The Powers of Mourning and Violence*, p. 39.

CHAPTER 4

EXPANDED MEDIUM: NATIONAL PUBLIC RADIO AND KATRINA WEB MEMORIALS

Maria Pramaggiore

As commercial news and entertainment media in the United States become increasingly visually oriented—with cable television news and opinion programs taking design cues from the webpage—commercial and public radio broadcasters also have begun to embrace multimedia strategies to deliver news stories, music, and entertainment programming across multiple platforms. Don Imus simulcast his CBS radio show on the cable network MSNBC (before being fired in 2007 for making racist comments on air) and, after a short stint hosting a television show in 1992, Rush Limbaugh made his conservative talk radio show available *as* a radio show on the Internet through his live "Ditto Cam." Liberal radio and television talk show counterparts include Rachel Maddow, whose radio show has been broadcast on Air America and whose political commentary show is aired on MSNBC. Although the specific forms of cross-platform programming that will emerge as dominant amidst the corporate consolidation and vertical integration of the U.S. mass media remain to be discovered, the fact that the same news information and entertainment programming will become accessible across television and radio broadcasting and Internet streaming is unquestionable.

The reality that media convergence has caused numerous independent sources of news and information to vanish, as media corporations replace expensive investigative reporting with tabloid journalism and garrulous opinion-meisters, has incited journalism professors and labor organizations to describe convergence as both alarming and inevitable, using terms such as "brave new world" and "incestuous corporate couplings"[1] to characterize the "ever-growing digitalized unity [of media and entertainment industries]."[2]

Amidst all the talk about the revolutionary changes wrought by the information superhighway, radio remains a somewhat forgotten media form, despite its persistent popularity. Whereas traditional music formats have experienced a steady decline in listeners,[3] often attributed to the growth of MP3 formats and iPods, talk radio has been booming since the mid-1980s, when the Federal Communications Commission dispensed with the Fairness Doctrine mandating balanced coverage of controversial issues. According to SABOMedia, between 1983 and 1998, the number of talk radio stations increased twenty-fold, while the total number of radio stations remained constant.[4] Experts acknowledge the surprising strength of traditional AM/FM formats, but predict that the Internet will continue to make inroads since radio is "unusually well suited to the digital transition."[5] The growth of digital radio—whether in the form of satellite or Internet—may prove to be the most "successful" digital transition story, yet it is a narrative that has been woefully neglected by scholars. Elisa Cohen and Sharon Willis have examined the role that radio played in helping to memorialize the tragedy of 9/11 and observed, "[the aural experience] as a site of digital multimedia convergence [...] has been an understudied area of scholarly concern."[6] Critical examinations of the potentially pernicious influence of talk radio culture on American political discourse have been published,[7] yet radio's ability to give voice to public concerns while moving through stages of multimedia convergence has been virtually ignored, particularly in relation to the scholarship on television and print journalism.

With its very specific aural and oral capabilities, radio has been utilized in important ways to manage several national tragedies, including Hurricane Katrina. The manner in which one ostensibly public radio network—National Public Radio (NPR)—has approached the memorialization of Katrina through the timeframe of the anniversary and the technology of the web memorial is the primary focus of this essay. It is both useful and relevant, however, to first examine the social and institutional contexts for "public" broadcasting in 2005, when this local event that bore such significance for U.S. national identity occurred. Therefore, I briefly examine NPR's institutional history before turning to an exploration of the importance of radio broadcasts in the days immediately following Katrina's landfall, which involve fascinating attempts to objectify sound and voice to produce what film theorist Christian Metz termed the aural object, as opposed to the visual one.[8] This process is, in turn, critical to NPR's ongoing efforts to manipulate sound waves and visual information on anniversary websites on the Internet in order to preserve the space and time of Katrina, with significant implications for the shaping of early twenty-first-century U.S. national identity.

NPR and its Publics: The Storm before the Storm

It's a fair question to ask why NPR should be the focus of a discussion about how radio has been conscripted to shape the work of memorializing national tragedies. A first response might be that NPR is our most recognizably public radio entity—perhaps merely by virtue of its name. Yet the functioning of the terms "public" and "national" in National Public Radio are far from transparent. In the context of media convergence, the motivation to reap financial benefits from circulating the same information across many media might appear to be the province of profit-driven corporations, but, in fact, NPR, as a government and listener-supported public radio network, has never been immune to commercial pressures facing the industry. From its inception during the Nixon administration, the network's parent company, the Corporation for Public Broadcasting (CPB), has served as a lightning rod for political wrangling, perhaps most famously during the Republican revolution of the mid-1990s when the CPB's meager subsidy became a contentious political issue because such government support flew in the face of the conservative mantra of market deregulation. Federal budget cuts forced both the Public Broadcasting Service (PBS) and NPR to increase their reliance on corporate sponsorship and listener contributions, with, as Robert McChesney argues, catastrophic effects on content.[9]

When Republican revolutionaries led by Representative Newt Gingrich challenged public funding in 1995, those defending public radio and television broadcasting attempted to forward the claim of "audience inclusiveness," with data suggesting that the audience for public television was a mirror of American society as a whole.[10] Ten years later, however, a book-length history of NPR characterizes the network's audience of the previous two decades in decidedly different terms. In his sympathetic study, Michael McCauley argues (without any trace of irony) that NPR truly found its way after it dispensed with the notion of functioning as a public radio network that would speak to everyone. McCauley compares NPR's listeners to characters on ABC's *thirtysomething* (1987–1991), in terms of their baby boomer status, their idealism, and their desire to create community.[11] "[T]he American public radio industry began to soar, " he writes, "when its leaders realized that people who were very much like this program's characters—highly educated, socially conscious, politically active—were most likely to listen to their brand of broadcasting."[12] This realization—using McCauley's terminology—retrospectively explains NPR's aggressive courting of a "nationwide" audience rather than a national community of listeners.[13] The difference in these terms is telling, if not downright chilling, and it makes manifest the way that notions of the public sphere were impoverished by successive conservative and neoliberal government administrations during the 1980s and 1990s, not to mention the (de)regulatory and corporate environment for broadcasting in the United States since the 1970s. A community of affluent listeners physically distributed across the geographical United States, sharing an aurally implied space, is a curious and degraded stand-in for an engaged citizenry debating within a public forum.

The nationwide audience model suspends listeners between the local and the national, allowing them to choose fluidly between the two: this model may have worked so well for NPR because of the medium's ability to function on both levels. "In less than a century of existence," Robert Hilliard and Michael Keith observe, "radio has gone from local to national to local and national again."[14] Radio emerged as a community phenomenon in the 1920s, but within a decade it had established itself, with nearly six hundred stations, as a national medium. This shift was prompted in large part by the Radio Act of 1927, which gave the Federal Radio Commission the power to reassign frequencies, a move that favored larger, commercial operators. By the 1950s, the tides turned as television asserted its dominance over the national airwaves (and poached some of the most talented and popular radio genres and performers) and radio once again embraced specialized, local programming, this time as a means of survival.

The subsequent demise of community oriented radio in the 1980s and 1990s was the result of several factors: in addition to the deregulation mentality of the Carter and Reagan administrations, which culminated in the Clinton-era Telecommunications Act of 1996, the rise of talk radio played a critically important role in recasting community or public radio as nationwide broadcasting. According to nationally syndicated, self-professed libertarian radio host Rollye Cornell "For a long time the prevailing logic, particularly with talk radio, was that to be successful a show needed to be local." Yet "Rush Limbaugh single-handedly proved this axiom false," she asserts. "In order to succeed, a show needs to be relatable, and while local content can go far to that end, it is not absolutely necessary. Relatability is not necessarily linked to geography."[15] It was precisely this nationwide model, based on an entertaining "relatability," buttressed by Limbaugh's unprecedented success, and assisted by the consolidation of station ownership, that eclipsed the functions of local radio that were most needed at the time of Katrina: local reporting on traffic, weather, and other civic matters of urgent importance within a relatively small geographical radius.

NPR's successful cultivation of a narrowly defined cultural and lifestyle mission must also be scrutinized against the backdrop of a longer historical evolution of its audience. From its earliest incarnation as the heir to educational radio, NPR was defined in its founding document, William Siemering's *National Public Radio's Purposes* (1970), in terms of an explicitly national, if sometimes contradictory, institution whose mission encompassed melting pot diversity and humanist coherence. Siemering argued against treating listeners as a unitary mass market and championed a network that would "celebrate the human experience as infinitely varied rather than vacuous and banal."[16] He also forwarded the idealistic view that "NPR's public affairs and cultural programming could, at once, highlight American pluralism and help reintegrate a fragmented society."[17]

But the best laid plans often go awry, and the network's business practices often failed to reflect the values of the mission statement. For example, its method for acquiring and supporting affiliate stations resulted in the subsidization of the strongest stations and the marginalization of smaller local entities. A corporate reorganization in 1976 centralized authority within national headquarters in Washington, DC, saw the merger of the news and cultural programming divisions, and created a corporate relations division. By the 1980s, amidst Reagan era budget cuts, NPR had clearly distinguished itself and its calling from other public, and often explicitly progressive, radio networks such as Pacifica Radio, which was founded in 1949 with KPFA in Berkeley, or the more commercially oriented American Public Radio, which successfully competed against NPR in the 1980s and 1990s and changed its name to Public Radio International in 1994.

By the early 1980s, NPR turned to corporate underwriting—with a third of its news budget provided by thirty foundations and corporations— to such an extent that its own board and news staff began to criticize the fact that the practice was "compromising independent new judgments."[18] This shift to corporate sponsorship was accompanied by the inevitable focus on listener demographics: as early as 1977, NPR had begun to gather data on its audience and found that its listeners overwhelmingly inhabited major urban centers such as New York, Boston and Washington, and smaller university towns (a vestige of the university homes of many of NPR's earliest affiliates). By 1990, NPR's disproportionately college educated, white-collar professional audience was deemed "highly business influential" and was therefore deployed as a lure for potential underwriters who benefited from the FCC's endorsement of rules that permitted public broadcasters to identify a company's products on air rather than simply their names. As a result, former NPR correspondent William Drummond derided public broadcasting as "an entitlement program for the middle class" with its "steady din of upscale boomer blues."[19]

Indeed, McCauley's comparison of NPR's target audience to the economically upscale, emotionally self-involved characters from *thirtysomething* bears examination in light of NPR's shifting audience address and cultural status. Just as the commodification of museum culture quickened with the emergence of museum stores, and the market for tie-in products such as action figures and DVDs has come to dominate the film industry, the increasingly frequent and sometimes desperate appeals for listener donations to supplement or replace dwindling government funds have provided an occasion for NPR to begin marketing its own ancillary commodities, from mugs to tote bags to CD compilations of its programs. One recent fundraising tactic reflects the presumed tastes of the affluent, educated target audience as well: a local affiliate in North Carolina, where I live, offers a chance to win a giveaway of trendy merchandise (iPods), books tied into specialty programs (*The People's Pharmacy* and *Car Talk*), entertainment events (a "Carl-abration" honoring droll news anchor Carl Kasell), and exotic trips (to Paris, Rome, and Australia) to those who call in.

In the early 1990s, NPR had begun to brand itself by constructing the ideal listener as an identity, not merely through specific programming or fundraising tactics. The network acquired a certain cachet within the developing genre of the personal ad, where presenting oneself as an NPR fan carried the mark of intellectualism and an appreciation for the finer things, if not wealth and professional status. Geek chic began to assert itself in 1987 with the broadcast of interactive game segments with the puzzlemaster Will Shortz (who succeeded Eugene Maleska as the editor of *The New York Times* crossword puzzles) on "Weekend Edition Sunday" and, more recently, with the anarchic news quiz show *Wait Wait...Don't Tell Me*, which began airing in 1998.

In transitioning from the 1980s into the 1990s, NPR became a culturally important, visible, and successful radio network: with more than four hundred affiliates, 86 percent of the American population was able to receive a public radio signal. Over this same period, the balance of local to national programs on public radio stations shifted from more than 60 percent to less than 50 percent.[20] Its growth in size and influence during a period in which it was politically embattled inside the Washington Beltway was due in large part to its increased centralization, its more precise targeting of an affluent demographic, and, most important to this study, to the fact that it usurped so many functions of local radio. For example, NPR opened news bureaus in major cities. It frequently rejected submissions to *All Things Considered* from local affiliates in favor of broadcasts with higher production values from the BBC.[21] It is particularly ironic that Siemering had initially conceived of *All Things Considered* as a news program that would not "substitute superficial blandness for genuine diversity of regions, values, and cultural and ethnic minorities which comprise American society."[22]

By 2008, NPR had not only made clear its commitment to marketing itself as part of a contemporary, urban, commuter lifestyle, but also its plan to replicate the convergence strategies of commercial media networks when it named Vivian Schiller as CEO. Schiller's credentials included a successful tenure as chief operating officer at NY Times.com, the largest newspaper website, and a stint as vice president at the Discovery Times cable channel, a short-lived joint venture between Discovery Channel and *The New York Times*.

In light of this broad historical overview, it is hardly surprising that NPR joined commercial news organizations in adopting a multifaceted, multimedia approach to covering Hurricane Katrina, making use of its strengths in conveying information visually as well as aurally and seeking to convey the gravity of the tragic situation to its upscale listeners far removed from the geographical and social mélange that is the Gulf Coast. NPR's coverage of the storm and its immediate aftermath exploited the digital capabilities of the

Internet, as well as radio's ability to capture events through recorded sound and interviews. After briefly characterizing NPR's reporting of the story, and assessing the importance of local radio during and after Katrina, I will turn to the question of NPR's continuing investment in reporting Katrina, and, specifically, its predominant method for keeping the story in the public eye: the Katrina memorial website. In creating web memorials, NPR has staked out new territory as a representative of the American public, likening Katrina to other national traumas including, most importantly and immediately, 9/11, and employing the formal properties of radio and the Internet to temporalize and spatialize American national identity with what I would argue is a Bush-era inflection.

Covering Katrina

In late August and early September 2005, NPR relied upon both traditional radio broadcasts and photographs to convey the unfolding Katrina disaster. NPR's long form news programs, including *All Things Considered*, *Day to Day*, and *Morning Edition*, acknowledged the power of the visual image by cross-referencing radio broadcasts with the NPR website (www.npr.org), where still and moving images became available along with podcasts of interviews and news reports.

After the hurricane made landfall on Monday, August 29, NPR used familiar techniques associated with documentary reportage: broadcasts included on-the-spot reporting by Russell Lewis, John Burnett, Greg Allen, and Scott Horsely. Early accounts from commercial network reporters (many of them located near and/or reporting from the city's higher elevations) suggested that New Orleans had "dodged a bullet," and NPR did not deviate from this mischaracterization. On August 29, Greg Allen reported that the city had avoided a catastrophic hit and that one million people had evacuated, leaving the city center uninhabited. Later that day, on *Day to Day*, Alex Chadwick interviewed John Burnett, who, according to the broadcast, was "hunkered down in a hotel room"—on the twenty-third floor of the Hilton Riverside Inn on Poydras Street—for a story entitled "New Orleans Misses Worst of Hurricane Katrina." (The fact that NPR relied upon interviews with its own personnel is another hallmark of low-cost reporting strategies ushered in by media convergence. This trend is also manifested tangibly in the practice of double booking recognizable broadcast journalists Juan

Williams [NPR, Fox News], Mara Liasson [NPR, Fox News], and Cokie Roberts [ABC News, NPR] who opine on politics on both commercial and public radio and television programs).

In this particular instance of that dubious practice, Chadwick and Burnett's conversation focused on the fact that Katrina had been downgraded from a Category Five to a Category Four hurricane before slamming into the Gulf Coast. They emphasized that the city had largely been spared. By Tuesday, August 30, however, it became apparent that the breach of the levees was contributing to massive flooding, and Allen filed a story on the flooding and looting taking place in the city. (Journalists who reported from New Orleans in the aftermath of Katrina, including Allen, make a distinction between people taking essential supplies such as water and food versus those exploiting the tragedy to acquire speciality footwear and electronics. Most admitted, in retrospect, that the vast majority of the "looters" fell into the first category and expressed regret over the way their initial responses fed racist stereotypes about New Orleans residents.)[23] During its early coverage of Katrina, then, NPR's content was virtually indistinguishable from that of the major commercial radio and television networks.

In the weeks to follow, NPR began to shape human interest narratives around named individuals whose experiences were tracked in follow-up segments, a move that the organization employed to distinguish itself from commercial media: in other words, NPR burnished its credentials as the voice of the public because it stayed with the story on a long-term basis. In addition to formal anniversary websites created in 2006 and 2007, which are explored in greater detail later, examples of the NPR commitment include a September 2008 story entitled "Three Years After Katrina, Family Preps for New Storm" that followed up on Donald and Colleen Bordelon, a St. Bernard Parish couple that reporters had met during Katrina. The Bordelon story typifies NPR's investment in "human interest" coverage, which simultaneously foregrounds voices of individuals in the region while containing them within a predetermined narrative of progress that elides progressive community activism in favor of hard won individual success stories. In 2009, no official webpage was created, but a portal page offers links to recorded broadcasts of ongoing stories, including an update on the Bordelons and reporting on the recent ruling by a federal judge in New Orleans that the Army Corps of Engineers had been negligent and was required to pay damages of more than seven hundred thousand dollars to four New Orleans residents and one business.

In order to monitor the recovery in a consistent and ongoing way, NPR established an office in New Orleans in December 2006, managed by one permanent staff member, Russell Lewis, who was named southern bureau chief. His responsibilities include editing stories from fourteen southern states. One additional reporter has rotated in and out of New Orleans, spending three-four weeks at a time, and a few freelance reporters contribute Katrina recovery stories. Lewis's stated goal was to present one-two in-depth Katrina stories each week.[24] Clearly the expenditure of resources to continue to report on Katrina is compromised by a cost-saving strategy—the bureau chief position was relocated to New Orleans in order to establish a presence in the city, and the transient nature of the reporters' assignment undoubtedly hampers the development of personal relationships with local officials, residents, savvy insiders, and self-appointed community historians.

If the decisions made regarding the deployment of personnel for its continuing coverage of Katrina seem disappointing, at least the sheer volume of information compiled on its website attests to NPR's commitment to reporting the disaster as an ongoing crisis. As of December 2009, news stories on the NPR website that mentioned Katrina numbered 4559. An indication that Katrina has assumed the status of an ongoing story is the fact that 634 new stories were posted in 2008; half that many (306) new entries were posted during 2009.

The continuing reportage and, especially, the decision to return to New Orleans on each successive August after Katrina, represents a process of consolidation through which NPR has not only reported on the hurricane and recovery efforts but has also sought to shape their larger meaning. Perhaps, not surprisingly, the critical nodes for collecting and organizing the vast amount of information on Katrina are two anniversary webpages, the first was "Katrina One Year Later," a week-long series of broadcasts in September 2006 (www.npr.org/news/specials/katrina/oneyearlater/), and the second "Katrina's Legacy" appeared in September 2007. One hint that temporal displacement, which I discuss more fully later, is key to the anniversary project is the term "legacy," which implies the passage of an entire generation in only two years. The third anniversary in 2008 garnered less coverage by comparison; ironically, the threat of Hurricane Gustav caused the cancellation of memorial events in New Orleans, such as the burial of the last seven unclaimed victims of the storm, and also led to the suspension of high profile events at the Republican National Convention, including President Bush's appearance. In 2009, a total of six stories were filed that marked the anniversary, two on *Talk of the Nation* and two on *All Things Considered.*

Whereas NPR chose to play a role in the ongoing memorialization of Katrina, local radio stations and ham operators used radio's "old school" broadcast practices and its potential for integration with new media technologies to play a critical role in the unfolding drama of Hurricane Katrina.

Ham Radio and Political Operators

When Katrina hit the Gulf Coast, local and community radio played a key role in disseminating information and effecting rescues. After the storm knocked out the power and communications infrastructure that supported cell phones, land lines, and even the Internet in some areas,[25] low-power FM (LPFM) broadcasters, also known as pirate, low-fi, microstations, or ham operators, many of whom are trained in emergency procedures, provided weather reports and facilitated the rescue of trapped residents, while 911 lines and other resources were breaking down as documented in the award-winning documentary film *Trouble the Water* (2008). One operator, cognizant of radio's unglamorous status within mass media, wrote, "The geek down the block with all the antennas on his property could turn out to be your best friend someday. Because sometimes, old trumps new."[26]

Community radio operators are insistent about taking credit for their participation, mainly because LPFM broadcasting has become a subject of contentious policy debate in the wake of media convergence, particularly since the Telecommunications Act of 1996 and the FCC's elimination of all ownership restrictions in 2003. In fact, illegally broadcasting on microradio has become a political movement, with early vanguard stations such as Black Liberation Radio (now Human Rights Radio) in Springfield, Illinois, in 1986, and Radio Free Berkeley, established in 1993. Despite the fact that NPR is publicly supported, and might be expected to support the local information, education, and cultural focus of microradio, in fact, the organization has increasingly aligned itself with commercial media. NPR joined with the Disney Corporation to support legislation that would limit the access of LPFM community broadcasters to the airwaves, citing the (highly unlikely) possibility of frequency interference as the basis for its position.

Along with LPFM broadcasts, better-known genres of radio secured a place of importance throughout the Katrina experience. Nationally syndicated talk show host Tom Joyner was called "the voice of Katrina" because of his dedication to reporting the story. As far as local broadcasters were concerned, Garland Robinette's reporting through the night on the WWL-AM has been singled out as heroic. As Judith Sylvester suggests, "In catastrophes such as Katrina, radio often is the lifeline because when power fails battery operated radios may be the only way to get information."[27] Robinette served precisely this lifeline function as he broadcast throughout the storm, even as Katrina's winds blew out the windows in the building in which the WWL studio was located. During the flooding, WWL offered solace to stranded residents, inviting them to call in if they could, providing information to rescuers, and helping to facilitate communication among displaced New Orleanians. Their dedication led to successful rescues—"rescuers told [Robinette that] many, many times that they were listening as people would call in and give their locations"—yet Robinette soberly acknowledges that "[w]e know for sure that a number of [people] died as we were talking to them on the phone."[28]

In fact, a moment that transformed the intangibility of the aural object into solid iconicity occurred during the radio interview that New Orleans mayor Ray Nagin gave to Robinette on WWL-AM on Friday, September 2, 2005. Nagin's heartfelt and salty expression of frustration at the lack of assistance from state and federal governments was re-broadcast across the country. The emblematic status of Nagin's verbal assault—and, notably, his exhortation for officials to "get their asses moving to New Orleans"—led one New Orleans native to produce a souvenir that endorses the continuing relevance of the aural object—in this case, the human voice.

This novelty toy, a key chain called "Da Mayor in Your Pocket," (figure 4.1) was created by Steve Winn, a Katrina evacuee who listened to the Nagin broadcast in a Memphis hotel room. Winn had previously created and marketed similar key chains, including "Cajun in your Pocket," "Mr T in Your Pocket," "Triumph the Insult Dog in Your Pocket," and "Scarface in Your Pocket." These inexpensive novelty items, made possible by digital recording technologies and Chinese manufacturing, capture and reify the ubiquitous sound byte of advertising, the evening news, and the political campaigns. They transform individual and culturally marked human speech, distilling the familiar catchphrase of a star or character ("I pity the fool") into portable commodities that permit the owner to replay catchphrases and perhaps serve as ventriloquist's dummy, re-embodying the meaningful statements they seem to "contain" within them. In short, they represent aural style: in a culture that places high value on an individual's ability to

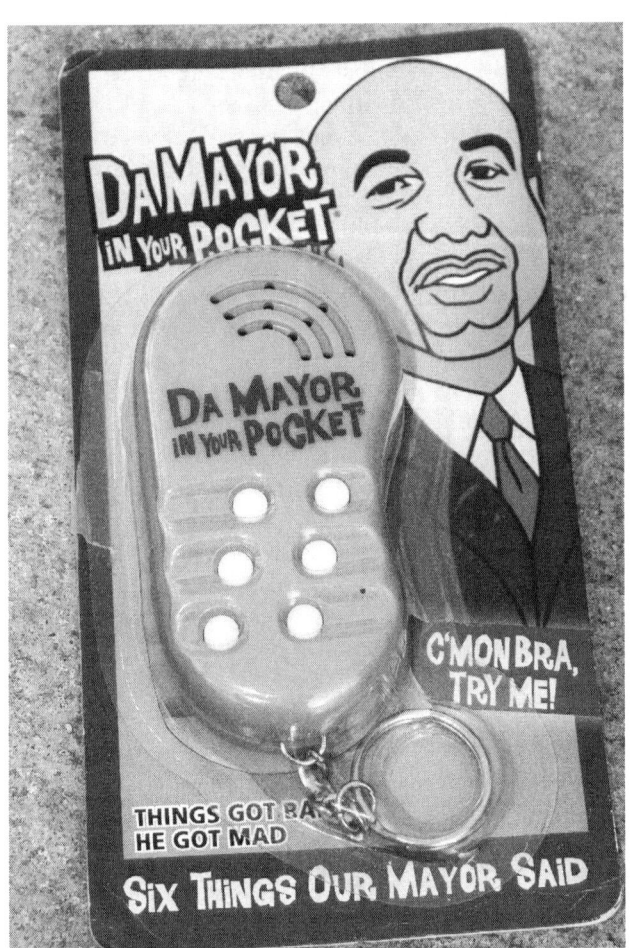

Figure 4.1 A novelty keychain transforms New Orleans mayor Ray Nagin's bold complaints about the lack of government action, first broadcast on radio station WWL-AM, into an aural object. With kind permission of Steve Winn. Photo credit: Melinda Pfeiffer.

associate with a celebrity, the toys permit a form of impersonation that moves beyond physical resemblance to a new level of authenticity and a new realm—that of the sound wave. The key chain captures the voice and makes it portable, capable of redeployment in any new spatial context. In an uncannily postmodern moment of self-reflexivity, Nagin held up "Da Mayor in Your Pocket" at a press conference during his mayoral reelection campaign in May 2006. Perhaps the toy's very specific framing of Nagin as a rebel, fighting on behalf of his city against the uncaring, white Establishment in the form of Governor Katherine Blanco and President George Bush helped secure his subsequent reelection.

For the record, six of Nagin's statements, originally broadcast on WWL radio, were parsed and recorded on "Da Mayor in Your Pocket": "You gotta be kiddin' me!"; "Get their asses moving to New Orleans"; "Excuse my French, everybody in America"; "This is a national disaster"; "Now let's fix the biggest goddamn crisis in the history of this country"; and, finally, "But I am pissed." Three of these six passionate sound bytes emphasize the historical and national dimensions of Katrina, offering a useful segue to a discussion that more directly theorizes the relationship between radio and Katrina: one that examines the way in which NPR's memorialization of Katrina through anniversaries attempts to expand the phenomenological characteristics of radio as a mass medium, laying claim to temporal and spatial coordinates, with specific political implications. As it sought to represent and then to memorialize the chaos of the storm, the breach of the levees, and the lack of appropriate government response, with the presumption that it could speak to a shared national interest in post-Katrina New Orleans, NPR, paradoxically, further marginalized voices of witness and dissent that might help to make evident the possibilities and challenges for variously defined national communities. Perhaps unwittingly, the memorial project spoke to NPR's nationwide audience and may have contributed to the sequestering of political speech that characterized the George W. Bush era.

The Sound and the Fury: Katrina and Web Memorials

If Mayor Nagin's voice crystallized the sound and the fury of Katrina victims, survivors, and observers, its circulation in the key chain ensured its presence in an ongoing way. The ephemeral quality of sound can instantaneously return listeners to that moment in a kitschy version of Freud's repetition compulsion, the urge to repeat in order to master the traumatic event.

Similarly, NPR's web memorialization of Katrina represents an attempt to fix a moment in space and time—to compile diverse ongoing narratives (in the form of radio broadcasts) in one virtual space. As scholars of both physical and virtual memorials have argued, these sites are epideictic: they do the work that we expect eulogies to do.[29] The spatial and temporal attributes of such memorials imply a peculiar stasis: the anniversary is a gesture for both marking distance (turning time into space) and also for collapsing time. The annual cycle explicitly references the year before in order to remember, commemorate, and to measure one's spatial and temporal distance from the rite of passage (birth, marriage) or the trauma (death, battle). The anniversary is thus an exercise in suspension: it invites us to spatialize time by moving backward in order to move forward and recognize the time and place of the present.

The webpage is a form that similarly evacuates temporality from narrative by refusing linearity and additionally confounds the positions of author, narrator, text, and reader, according to Mark Poster.[30] And yet, NPR has embraced the anniversary webpage as a way of organizing the chaotic time and space of Katrina—seeking to produce a national narrative that could encompass the destruction of coastal Louisiana and Mississippi and the flawed process of human decision-making that marked its traumatic aftermath. The public anniversary framework not only shores up NPR's dubious claim to be a representative of the broader American public (a claim belied by data on listener demographics and the fact that it has touted statistics on its highly educated, white-collar listeners to potential sponsors since the 1980s), it also links the events of Katrina, and the reporting of it, to other national disasters that require memorialization, including wars and the terrorist attacks of 9/11. Media scholar Andrew Hoskins has argued that "the media operate as a framework of memory as they assist continuously in the reconstruction of our past by dominating the present."[31]

Aaron Hess emphasizes the peculiar power of the website memorial to open a space for communal memorializing, one that can provide a forum for the expression of the vernacular voice.[32] The voice would seem particularly crucial to NPR's attempt to create a site that could perform memorial work. Yet the site offers nothing but broadcast interviews and news stories. The Katrina weblog ends in

2005. Despite the fact that NPR's audience members have "a greater opportunity to form *communities of interest* that transcend geographical boundaries" because of satellite and digital media outlets, the possibility of actively creating content is nonexistent; McCauley observes as late as 2007 that "public radio organizations should create more space for user generated content."[33]

The most significant virtual precursor to the Katrina memorial websites is NPR's 9/11 memorial, which differs enormously from the Katrina memorials in terms of its approach to mourning, its design, and its approach to user created or supplied content. The prototypes for both of these efforts are two memorials based in physical rather than cyber space: the Vietnam and Pearl Harbor Memorials. The larger framework of public memorialization is relevant to this discussion because the striking differences between and among these memorials (and the discourses around them) point to the profound difficulties that Katrina poses for the concept of national community in the United States.

NPR's Katrina anniversaries are occasions through which the radio medium arrests time and converts it into space, which is necessary for the erection of a national memorial. Theories of and research on memory from psychological and political science perspectives posit a close connection between memory and place.[34] French sociologist Maurice Halbwachs argued that collective memory requires that a shared sense of time be created: "the precondition for any kind of memory is the creation of an external, shared, form of duration that is abstracted from the flow of individual consciousness."[35] After 9/11, a national collective memory has been organized by the shared duration of the annual cycle—in part because political leaders seek to remind us each year that we have not been attacked since 9/11. Michael Kammen argues that such political anniversaries have grown in prominence because "we increasingly tend to measure how we are doing (in terms of collective knowledge) by how well we commemorate anniversaries."[36] And yet the fact that the anniversary is a construct is, paradoxically, underscored and undermined by the fact that the annual cycle associated with Katrina involves the weather conditions that instigated the crisis in the first place. The fact that third anniversary events—and, concomitantly, a third anniversary website—could not be realized because of Hurricane Gustav simultaneously recalls the conditions at the time of Katrina and also displaces the human attempts to reanimate Katrina in order to lay her to rest. Ironically, memorializing the tragic events of Katrina annually may also lay the groundwork of emotional investment that will insure high ratings for mediathon coverage of subsequent hurricanes as well.

Radio must convert its temporality as a medium into space in order to provide a location for memory. Constructing memories and commemorating apocalyptic physical events over the radio clearly pose challenges. Radio is often described as the most personal and also the most intangible of the mass media. Sound, transmitted in waves that act upon the human body, seems to enter the listener rather than maintaining the distance of the image, hence sonic experiences may seem more personal. Devices that transmit sound (such as speakers) often blend into the environment so as to produce the illusion of unmediated access. With its duration and potential for rhythm, sound has a far more tangible relationship to time than it does to space, however, and thus may fail to provide the sense of complete totality that visual representation can provide.

One strategy that NPR in particular has used to address the odd spatiality of radio broadcasting is to overtly refer to the location of audition, citing the fact that listeners are often in their cars and making a social institution out of the much vaunted "driveway moment" (in which engrossed listeners pause in their cars before getting out on arrival at home). NPR certainly participates in Americans' pervasive automobile culture, not only by acknowledging its own importance to commuters in the private space of their cars during drive time, but also through programming (*Car Talk*) and listener giveaways (travel coffee mugs). This creates a shared perception among individual listeners of membership in a community of people who are doing the same thing—not merely experiencing the same sound waves. Yet even that tactic of simultaneously lamenting and celebrating the car, which, ironically, supports the industries that, in part, made the New Orleans ecosystem so vulnerable, does not focus attention on a shared public space.

Marking time through repetition in the anniversary broadcasts and websites creates a shared aural pause—time removed from the everyday that offers a space for listeners removed from the events to occupy. This is particularly relevant in the case of Katrina, whose devastation was not visually witnessed as a discrete event or with the global simultaneity that marked 9/11. The sentimental place of remembrance that NPR creates through the anniversary attempts to organize an unmappable place—or, at least, one that is difficult to visualize using the techniques of radio reportage—and may help to obscure the real territorial disputes over the reconstruction of New Orleans. Furthermore, the framework of the public anniversary may undermine the listener's or website visitor's ability to conceive of, much less analyze, the racial and class politics of the disaster as everyday occurrences across the United States. The anniversary website polices the social and psychological disruptiveness of events such as Katrina by converting time into space in the service of crystallizing and controlling collective memory.

I have drawn comparisons between Katrina and 9/11, although, of course, there are important differences that the Katrina anniversary sites seek to obscure. The events of 9/11 have been figured symbolically as unified—taking place on one day—and this has demarcated the American national body (as the territory of the mainland Unites States, if not the real estate represented by the World Trade Center) and the existence of enemies attacking the homeland in air attacks. The single-minded focus on the World Trade Center as the locus of those events and the relative neglect of the events at the Pentagon and in Pennsylvania, where United 93 went down, is indicative of the move toward symbolic consolidation. The 9/11 anniversaries function as occasions for displays of national unity aimed at endorsing the War on Terror. While the Katrina anniversaries follow in the wake of 9/11, there are critical differences that suggest the ways that Katrina cannot be forced into that same frame of national identity, despite Ray Nagin's protestations.

The marked differences in NPR's Katrina and 9/11 memorial websites suggest the problems that Katrina poses for American national identity. NPR's 9/11 site is not based upon spatializing time, but on collapsing the events of 9/11 into a single, now fantasmatic space: that of the World Trade Center. The memorial project, called the Sonic Memorial, was created by one hundred individual NPR affiliates, working in conjunction with independent producers. The sonic memorial is an audio archive that commemorates the World Trade Center itself as a structure and a place of social interaction by compiling recorded sounds, music, interviews, and testimonies not only from 9/11, but from the World Trade Center prior to that date. Examples include recordings of music that was played on New Year's Eve in 1999; music played by undocumented Latino workers who cleaned the buildings and were killed on 9/11; and phone messages from individuals who did and did not survive the terrorist attacks in 2001.

The fact that 9/11 encompassed other physical sites—that is, the hijacked planes crashed into the Pentagon and rural Pennsylvania—is acknowledged by NPR correspondents Noah Adams and Leanne Hansen on the website. The sonic memorial invites contributions from individuals wishing to speak about those locations, yet, as Noah Adams puts it, "the Trade Center represents an American commons of grief"[37]. It's easy to speculate on the reasons why the WTC can be understood as a site of remembrance—not least of which are the television images that captured the second plane crash and the collapse of the North and South towers, the designation of the site as Ground Zero, the long months of clean up, visits by politicians and dignitaries, and the contentious process of designing a memorial to be built on the site.

But I suspect that the WTC can be designated a commons of grief in ways that New Orleans and the devastated Gulf Coast region never can be, partly because of New Orleans' problematic position as an un-American space prior to the hurricane—expressed in designations such as "the northernmost Carribean city"[38] and its association with repressed American histories of slavery, Catholicism, and voudoun—and partly because the Katrina disaster has as much to do with breaches of race, region, and class within American culture as it does with the breach of the levees. Without a clear story of national unity, the practices of memorialization are jeopardized.

Several other differences between the 9/11 Sonic Memorial and the Katrina anniversaries are telling. The Sonic memorial is interactive; it invites anyone to participate by submitting sound clips, reinforcing the idea that 9/11 is a shared, democratic, national tragedy and one whose plethora of stories do not need to be recuperated as a narrative of anniversary. The sonic memorial references a tangible, easily mapped geographical space—a set of buildings—and perhaps because of that apparent clarity, the sound clips are organized without editorial commentary—they speak for themselves, telling us what we already know about American exceptionalism, an ideology that imbues the descriptions of the WTC (pre-9/11) and victimization (on 9/11). By contrast, on the Katrina anniversary sites, commentators narrativize all the entries—all of which are earlier broadcasts—as if the meaning of each segment must be explained to the audience because the exceptionalism of New Orleans has always been seen as un-American.

Memorialization is "a highly politicized process that reflects the will of those in power."[39] As the broadcast bastion of educated, white, middle-class liberals, NPR might not seem to represent the will of those in power between 2000 and 2008. Yet its process of anniversarizing Katrina parallels similar strategies for shaping and, indeed, confining public discourse that were perfected over the course of the Bush presidency. Two prominent examples of the latter are the construction of so-called free speech zones at public events and the stepping up of enforcement of the permit process for gaining access to public space. These strategies, much like the Katrina websites, squelch the local, the diverse, the participatory by imposing an official framework for the work of political expression and public commemoration. As such, NPR's anniversaries—and the way they create some new public spaces and disallow others—must be closely examined in light of the national public culture of denial that surrounds the Katrina experience.

Notes

1. Joe Saltzman, "The Brave New World of Multimedia Convergence."
2. "Symposium on Media Convergence."
3. Alex Mindlin, "Perhaps iPods aren't Replacing Radio."
4. Rebecca Pirto Heath, "Tuning In to Talk—Popularity of Talk Programming."
5. "The State of the News Media, 2009: An Annual Report on American Journalism."
6. "One Nation Under Radio: Digital and Public Memory after September 11," p. 594.
7. See, e.g., David Christopher Barker, *Rushed to Judgment: Talk Radio, Persuasion, and American Political Behavior.*
8. "Aural Objects."
9. *The Political Economy of Media: Enduring Issues, Emerging Dilemmas*, p. 241.
10. Laurie Ouellette, *Viewers Like You?: How Public TV Failed the People*, pp. 4–5.
11. *NPR: The Trials and Triumphs of National Public Radio*, p. 2.
12. Ibid.
13. Ibid.
14. *The Quieted Voice: The Rise and Demise of Localism in American Radio*, p. 9.
15. Ibid., p. 16.
16. Ralph Engelman, *Public Radio and Television in America: A Political History*, p. 90.
17. Ibid., pp. 90–91.
18. Ibid., p. 104.

19. Ibid., p. 116.
20. Ibid., p. 127.
21. Ibid., p. 108.
22. Ibid., p. 94.
23. See Judith Sylvester, *The Media and Hurricanes Katrina and Rita*.
24. Ibid., p. 168.
25. Chris Gaither and Matea Gold, "Web Proves Its Capacity to Help in Time of Need," p. 4.
26. David Maliniak, "In Katrina's Wake, Ham Radio Triumphs."
27. *The Media and Hurricanes Katrina and Rita*, p. 91.
28. Ibid., p. 95.
29. Carole Blair, "Contemporary U.S. Memorial Sites as Exemplars of Rhetoric's Materiality," p. 17; Aaron Hess, "In Digital Remembrance: Vernacular Memory and the Rhetorical Construction of Web Memorials," p. 813.
30. *Information Please: Culture and Politics in the Age of Digital Machines*, p. 135.
31. "Television and the Collapse of Memory," p. 110.
32. "In Digital Remembrance: Vernacular Memory and the Rhetorical Construction of Web Memorials," p. 813.
33. *NPR: The Trials and Triumphs of National Public Radio*, p. 123; emphasis in original.
34. Jens Bartelson, "We Could Remember It for you Wholesale: Myth, Monuments, and the Constitution of National Memories."
35. David Middleton and Steven Brown, *The Social Psychology of Experience*, pp. 44–45.
36. *Mystic Chords of Memory: The Transformation of Tradition in American Culture*, p. 667.
37. *All Things Considered*, Sonic Memorial website
38. "When the Painter Met the Creoles," p. G3.
39. Judy Barsalou and Victoria Baxter, "The Urge to Remember: The Role of Memorials in Social Reconstruction and Transnational Justice," p. 1.

Chapter 5

Life Preservers: The Neoliberal Enterprise of Hurricane Katrina Survival in *Trouble the Water*, *House M.D.*, and *When the Levees Broke*

Jane Elliott

> *I've seen some flotation devices that you would not believe. But I mean we got some geniuses in our race who don't even know it. I mean, you'd be surprised, empty barrels, telephone posts that's fallen down, they'd ride them, you know. There's things that before then you would never have even thought they had use for.*
>
> —Henry Armstrong, Quoted in "Henry Armstrong and Dorothy Griffin Remembering Katrina"
>
> *People were inventive. Look at that. Forget about boats. If you didn't have a boat, you had to find something. Container, mattress, refrigerator. Look at that, using a broom as a paddle. People were being inventive. People were trying to save their necks.*
>
> —Spike Lee, Audio Commentary, When the Levees Broke

Certain images of Hurricane Katrina have come to be ritually repeated when the storm and its aftermath are represented in the visual media: white flags and SOS signs being waved from rooftops, thousands massed in the heat outside the New Orleans Convention Center, an elderly African American woman dead in her wheel chair. For critics such as Henry Giroux, these images have inscribed in visual terms the imprisoning and lethal nature of neoliberal "biopolitics," which corrals those who are unproductive as workers and consumers into zones marked out for death.[1] In this reading of the intersection of governmentality, race, and poverty, neoliberalism positions the poor, particularly the nonwhite poor, as a constitutive outside in two related ways: on the one hand, neoliberal policies result in the creation of a disposable and often unacknowledged class living in unrelieved poverty, while on the other neoliberal rhetoric blames those persons for their fate by presenting them as lacking the characteristics required for successful, self-enterprising neoliberal subjectivity.[2] While this account of the racialized poor as failed neoliberal subjects has considerable explanatory power in relation to many aspects of what Nicole R. Fleetwood terms "the Katrina event," it is less useful in coming to terms with another set of frequently repeated images from the aftermath of the storm: the ingenious actions of "inventive" citizens in the process of "sav[ing] their necks," as Spike Lee puts it.[3] It is hard to imagine a better or more chilling example of neoliberal self-responsibilization than citizens and communities in the act of saving themselves from imminent death in the absence of government support.[4] If, as Nikolas Rose and others have argued, neoliberal subjects must be "self-entrepreneurs" of their own lives, maximizing their "human capital" in a fashion that allows them to fulfill all their own needs within a fully privatized economy, the resourceful and determined actions of individuals engaged in self-rescue seem to express these principles to a degree previously unimaginable.[5]

In addition to images of biopolitical death zones and conservative narratives of African Americans engaged in out-of-control violence and looting, the Katrina event thus offers another version of the intersection of race, poverty, and neoliberal governance: the implementation and performance of the ideals of neoliberal subjecthood by poor Americans, particularly African Americans, in a fashion and on a scale never before registered by the national media.[6] In this set of images and narratives, Katrina survivors appear not as failed bearers of neoliberal subjectivity but rather as avatars of the perils of functional, even hypostasized, neoliberal personhood—subjects whose attempts to save themselves epitomize the extreme demands placed on citizens under the guise of self-responsibilization. Turning to Tia Lessin and Carl Deal's documentary *Trouble the Water* (2008), the episode of the television series *House M.D.* entitled "Who's Your Daddy?" (2006), and Lee's monumental four-part documentary *When the Levees Broke* (2006), I explore the ways in which these texts engage with the neoliberal enterprise of Hurricane Katrina survival, presenting very different arguments regarding this phenomenon and appropriate responses to it. For left-leaning documentaries such as *Trouble the Water* and *Levees*, the association of positive, agential actions of survivors with the imperatives of neoliberal self-governance presents significant challenges to the usual Left practice of uncovering or agitating for an increase in agency by oppressed subjects. The more conservative *House* embraces the association of self-preservation and enterprise that accompanies the Katrina event, but uses this association to turn its survivor character into a stand-in for all the series' usually disavowed fears regarding the horrific aspects of neoliberal hegemony, or what I term "catastrophic neoliberalism." Despite their differences, all three texts indicate the way in which moments of self-preservation encapsulate the peculiar trap of neoliberal subjectivity, which can increase agency at the same time as it increases suffering, suggesting another crucial means by which the nightmarish by-products of catastrophic neoliberalism were laid bare by the Katrina event.

"Success... The Only Option"

In the opening scenes of *Trouble the Water*, we see Kimberly Roberts entering a Red Cross shelter for Hurricane Katrina evacuees. In a brief exchange with the filmmakers, Roberts begins promoting some as yet undefined object, declaring, "Nobody ain't got what I got" and "This need to be world wide." After a cut to what seems to be the same space on the same day, she and her husband, Scott, introduce themselves to the camera as from the Lower 9th Ward of New Orleans, "under water." The screen goes black, the words "two weeks earlier" appear, and we find ourselves watching handheld footage of the couple's neighborhood on the eve of the storm, shot and narrated by Kimberly Roberts under her rap moniker, Black Kold Medina. The "what" that Roberts wants to take "world wide," it now becomes clear, is the footage she shot just before and during Hurricane Katrina—footage that, along with interviews with the Robertses and their friends and family, is the subject of the film we are watching. The black screen between the Robertses' self-introduction and the start of the Black Kold Medina footage thus does more than take us back in time to the brink of the storm. It also takes us ahead to the point at which an agreement has been reached between Roberts and the filmmakers that allows this unique footage to receive the exposure Roberts desired. While the actual discussion takes place off-screen, the pause of the black space seems to remind us that there is a piece of this story missing, encouraging us to imagine that agreement being hammered out. What allowed the film to come into being, we come to understand, is a transaction, possibly financial, that took place between a Katrina evacuee, a poor African American woman from New Orleans, and a couple of documentary filmmakers from New York.

In foregrounding this transaction, my point is not to impugn the documentary ethics of Lessin and Deal. Although we don't see it unfold, the necessity of this transaction—the way in which Roberts must sell herself and her experiences if she wants to try to improve her life—is in fact an element of the status quo that Lessin and Deal consistently critique throughout the film. That the existence of *Trouble the Water* arises from this transaction is less a fault than the central means by which form mirrors content in the film: *Trouble the Water* both arises from and materially embodies a transaction based in Kimberly Roberts' self-entrepreneurship, and the film is fundamentally about what it means to live in a neoliberal world in which such individual enterprise is offered as the only possible avenue of transformation or uplift. In both its usage of Roberts' footage and the way it encourages us to read her self-presentation, I want to argue, the film suggests that Kimberly Roberts, her husband, and her friends are all hostages to a form of contemporary neoliberal selfhood that intertwines experiences of agential action, self-reliance, and profound suffering.

Roberts' association with neoliberal discourses of enterprise and self-entrepreneurship is evident from her first moments on camera. Not only do we first see her selling herself ("nobody ain't got what I got"), but also the very existence of Roberts' footage resonates with neoliberal capital's injunction to make profit from risk. In a through-the-looking-glass version of what Naomi Klein terms "disaster capitalism," Roberts attempts to capitalize on her own hurricane experience, cannily predicting that the footage she gets may be of some value: as she presciently tells one of her neighbors, "If I get some exciting shit, I can sell it to the white folk."[7] Enacting the sort of lemons-into-lemonade narrative dear to the heart of American neoconservatives, Roberts sets out to turn the very elements of her oppression into a moneymaking opportunity. In effect trapped in the city—she recounts in her voiceover that she was unable to "get a rental"—Roberts turns this imprisonment in the path of the coming hurricane into an opportunity for on-the-spot reporting: "I ain't going nowhere, I'm going to be here to give you this live and direct footage." If, as Lisa Duggan points out, neoliberalism masks its underlying racist and sexist agendas by promoting goals such as "self-esteem," "independence," and "personal responsibility" among the poor, this is a perspective that Roberts seems to have internalized.[8]

Although the storm footage is in effect focalized entirely through Roberts—she is both cinematographer and narrator—*Trouble the Water* itself raises immediate doubts about the efficacy of her commitment to self-entrepreneurship. Because the film as a whole begins with news reports of the storm's aftermath and locates Roberts within that trajectory through her introduction at the Red Cross shelter, Roberts' footage is subject to considerable dramatic irony. We already know that the levees will break and that the children she interviews, who argue that there is no reason to be afraid since a hurricane is "nothing but water," will unfortunately soon have every reason to change their minds. From the moment we begin to watch Roberts' footage, in other words, we are placed in a position in which her own account of her situation begs another level of interpretation, in which we weigh her reading of events against what we know will come to pass. This sense of meta-interpretation is intensified by the brief interaction we have seen between her and the filmmakers. We know that this is not Roberts' film but instead a film that employs her footage, and that the documentarians occupy a very different class position than Roberts does—one that makes them the "white folk" that Roberts hopes will purchase her film. Thus, when we begin watching Roberts' footage, we do it in effect over the shoulders of filmmakers who seem unlikely to live in or ordinarily visit neighborhoods like the one Roberts inhabits and documents.

This class difference—"gulf" might not be too strong a word—creates a kind of bifocal view of Roberts' footage, one that overlays an outsider's curious, almost ethnographic gaze over Roberts' own, contemporaneous perspective. Because of the film-within-a-film effect, Lessin and Deal remain framing presences whose own view of this footage we know has preceded our own, and, given their assumed unfamiliarity with Roberts' milieu, part of what is spotlighted by their imagined gaze on this footage is the sheer information it conveys regarding what it is like to be a poor African American woman living in New Orleans. Thus, at the same time that Roberts is adopting a journalistic tone that works to underscore the on-the-spot, historic nature of her storm footage, the presence of this second view draws our attention not to these momentous events but rather to the details of daily life among African Americans in the 9th Ward, as exemplified by Roberts: buying smoked neckbones, joking with drunks on the corner, waking up an uncle passed out on a porch. That is, while Roberts presents herself as embarking on a project of individual enterprise designed to improve her lot, the framing view of her footage underscores instead the undertow of a daily life spent in poverty in a fashion that both shows the necessity of transformation and calls into doubt—almost ironizes—her optimism regarding the ability of any individual action to bring about that transformation. In effect, this doubled perspective on Roberts' footage both uncovers and enacts the pernicious juxtaposition of a neoliberal discourse of self-empowerment with a life systematically denied access to resources and opportunities.

As when the camera later lingers on a t-shirt worn by Scott Roberts, which reads "Success... The Only Option," *Trouble the Water* consistently focuses on what happens when such neoliberal discourses of individual self-empowerment are taken on by those who are most oppressed by them. While it is clear, since after all we are watching Roberts' footage, that to some extent her self-entrepreneurship has been successful, the film's approach to Roberts' own artistic efforts makes equally clear the limits of this process.[9] As the film shifts from long segments of Roberts' hurricane footage to later footage of her life after the hurricane recorded by Lessin and Deal, Roberts' attempt to record her life is in turn recorded by the *Trouble the Water* film in a fashion that creates a hierarchy between these two artistic projects. In the first such scene, we see the Robertses and their friend and fellow Katrina survivor Brian Nobles in a car, while Brian films and Kimberly Roberts talks on the phone, telling a friend that she has met some "people who are making a documentary, a real documentary. And all in the same minute, I'm teaching Brian [Nobles] how to be a director." Although Roberts' description indicates the persistence of her own ambitions, the phrase "a real documentary" seems to acknowledge a kind of downgrading of her own efforts (particularly as earlier Roberts describes her hurricane footage as "the documentary '05" in her voiceover). Underscoring the existence and ranking of these competing projects, the image track in this scene cuts between long segments of footage of the Robertses shot by the filmmakers' cameraperson, much briefer and more washed-out segments of footage shot by Nobles, and then footage of Nobles filming. The effect is to encapsulate Roberts' and Nobles' efforts within a larger and more polished product, which orchestrates and controls the viewer's access to Roberts—and vice versa.

Again, I am less interested in censuring Lessin and Deal than in untangling *Trouble the Water*'s argument about neoliberal subjectivity in relation to survivors of Hurricane Katrina, which unfolds in large part through its complex and subtle positioning of Roberts. It is evident that the filmmakers took pains to acknowledge Roberts as an artistic collaborator, giving her pride of place as one of the film's directors of photography and showcasing her music as the central performer on its soundtrack. However, these efforts sit side-by-side with an approach that simultaneously foregrounds, contains, and offers its own perspective upon Roberts' artistic and interpretive efforts. In a confluence of form and content similar to that encoded in Roberts' originating transaction with the filmmakers, the hierarchy of interpretive visions at work in *Trouble the Water* stages in artistic terms the power dynamics in which Roberts is ensconced in the world at large: all of her self-affirmation does not give her the power to prevent her footage from being framed and reinterpreted once she has transacted with the filmmakers, nor does it give her the power to offer an on-screen interpretation of Lessin and Deal that would compete with or question their interpretation of her. The limitations placed on her artistic agency within *Trouble the Water*, which we see unfold even as Roberts continues her own film project, intimate the way in which Roberts' fierce commitment to herself and her achievements may have a similarly delimited effect in the face of the pernicious racism, sexism, and classism that have shaped her life.

It is within the context of this critique of self-empowerment that we see and hear Roberts' account of her rescue, a perspective that creates a link between neoliberal discourses of individual enterprise and the heroic efforts of residents of the 9th Ward to save those left to die by their government. *Trouble the Water* goes beyond exposing neoliberalism's structural role in creating this situation to focus on the way in which individual rescue efforts reflect the specific burden of neoliberal subjectivity for the poor. This dynamic unfolds particularly in relation to Roberts' neighbor Larry Sims, who ferries those stuck in the Roberts' attic to a taller house, using a punching bag as a flotation device. When Sims first appears as a rescuer in Roberts' footage, she describes the bag's appearance with some amusement and zooms in on it, and when Larry appears later without it, he is asked "Larry, where the punching bag?" Sims' choice seems humorous precisely because it is so incongruous, but it is also this fact that makes it so ingenious—exactly the sort of inventive and resourceful approach to a problem that defines the word "enterprising." Roberts suggests just this connection between rescue and capitalist enterprise when she praises Sims' efforts during the storm: "Give it up for my brother Larry, bro, cause he really handled his business, man."

Although we learn later in the film that the rescue efforts of Sims, Scott Roberts, and Brian Nobles also involved a boat, the boat is at that point outside a school that has become a government base, and Scott Roberts and Nobles only approach it gingerly after gaining permission from the surrounding soldiers. The boat, a proper instrument for water rescue, seems to belong to the authorities, while the punching bag is both a makeshift raft and uncontested neighborhood property. Like the globe that Scott Roberts and Nobles use to plan their drive to Memphis, the punching bag and the other improvised objects of self-rescue function as metonyms for the twin burdens neoliberal subjectivity places on the poor: the insistence on self-empowerment and self-care, and the radical diminishing of material resources with which those living in poverty undertake this project. If the classic injunction to "pull yourself up by your own bootstraps" epitomizes neoliberal governance, then these makeshift tools suggest the efforts of those who have been systematically denied both boots and straps, but who still strive to fulfill the requirements of neoliberal citizenship, demonstrating their fitness for survival precisely by inventively employing the few scavenged and substandard resources to which they have been allowed access.

While the examples I have discussed thus far register a struggle to achieve the ideal of individual agency required for neoliberal self-responsibilization, moments of successful self- and community rescue in the film indicate the way in which achieving this agential ideal fails to result in a reprieve from structures of domination. Usually, of course, we consider agency to be an index of freedom, assuming that the more effect one can have on the world the more free one is, but this perspective founders when we consider the rescue experiences represented in *Trouble the Water*. In comparison with the tedium and stasis of life in the 9th Ward as demonstrated by Roberts' pre-storm footage, the sort of dramatic rescues Sims undertakes—as when we see him carrying a little girl on his back through rising waters—represents a veritable explosion of agency. Overnight, he moves from a landscape in which young African American men are given scant meaningful opportunities for positive action in their communities to one in which he is literally making life and death decisions that will determine the fates of those around him. At the same time, however, it seems cruelly unjust to describe this transformation as one that somehow either increases Sims' freedom or decreases his interpolation in profound structures of domination. Such moments suggest the way in which neoliberalism puts pressure on the conventional association of agency and freedom, intertwining experiences of intense agential activity with circumstances of intense suffering and profound structural inequities. The film stages precisely this conjunction when it pairs dramatic footage of Sims' rescues with audio from 911 calls in which drowning New Orleans residents are told that no rescue services are available. Saving one's own life and the lives of others in the absence of governmental intervention may mean that one has decisively escaped political controls on one's actions, but this is hardly a form of freedom most of us would choose.

This tragic confluence of intense domination and neoliberal discourses of individual achievement comes to a climax in *Trouble the Water* in Roberts' performance of her song "Amazing." While Roberts testifies to her strength and commitment to survival in extended speeches at two earlier points in the film, the song takes these claims to a new level, offering an arresting account of Roberts' life history that seems to occupy a different, heightened register from the rest of the film. In part, this sense of intensity arises from the relationship the song constructs between Roberts and the film's creators and audience: when she insists that "I don't need you to tell me I'm amazing," Roberts' performance seems to punch through the frame that has been constructed around her by the filmmakers, issuing a direct challenge to those who are engaged in recording, watching, and evaluating her life. If part of Roberts' loss of artistic agency came from the way in which she and her footage were framed and interpreted by the filmmakers, her lyrics push pointedly back on that process of interpretation, insisting that she doesn't need anyone else to explain her life to her. As Rob Nelson suggests, much of the pleasure in this scene, which is often described as the highlight of the film by reviewers, comes from seeing Roberts at last achieve some of the artistic control she so clearly craves throughout the film, a sight that Nelson justly describes as bringing on goose bumps.[10]

At the same time, however, when Nelson goes on to argue that this scene offers "a brief moment [in which] socioeconomic adversity is transcended," he seems to have missed the other half of the scene's point.[11] The song makes clear Roberts' achievements in a fashion that fully endorses her self-assessment, but it also calls into question the possibility of "transcending" the socioeconomic through artistic agency. For example, while her performance is indeed stunning, Roberts' lyrics are notably repetitive, ("Trying to swallow me up but I was determined to make it/Had enemies everywhere but I was determined to make it"), violating the usual hiphop convention of avoiding identical rhymes in favor of clever and surprising ones that

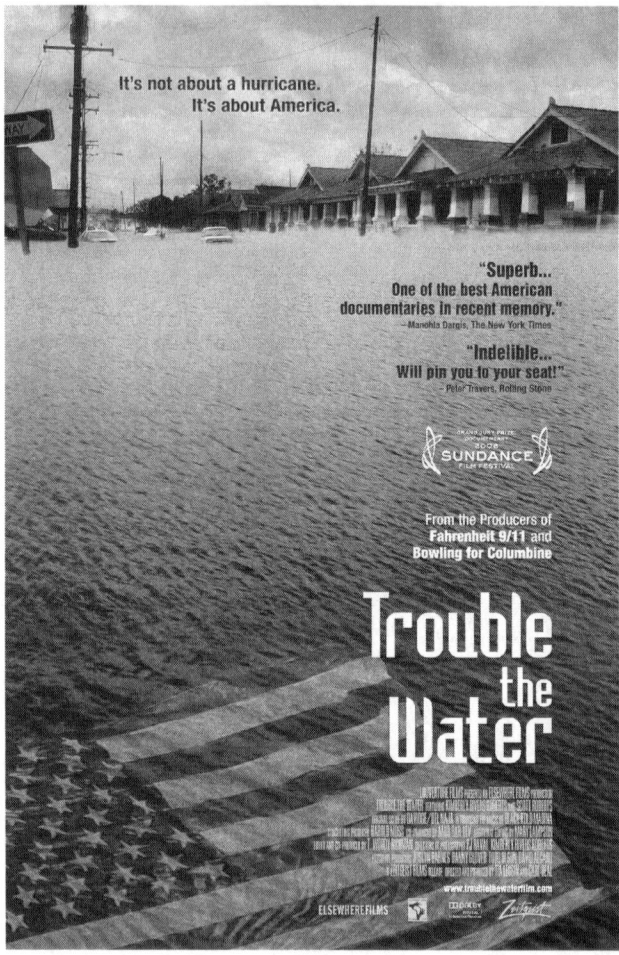

Figure 5.1 Documentaries such as *Trouble the Water* and *When the Levees Broke* associate the positive, agential action of survivors with the imperatives of neoliberal self-governance.

showcase the artist's flair. The appearance of repetition where one would expect difference suggests an artistic struggle to break with the given that reflects the thwarted attempts at transformation at work in the lives of the Robertses as a whole throughout much of the film. That Roberts raps along with a recording of her own voice brings together the stasis of repetition with the burden of self-help in all its meanings: as when Roberts recalls that she wrote the song to cheer herself up "when [she] was depressed," Roberts' self-accompaniment registers the sterile tautology of even "amazing" efforts at self-empowerment in a climate in which doing everything for oneself is the very form of domination. *Trouble the Water* does enact the process of uplift through art, sharing its artistic cachet with Roberts in a way that seems to have had materially transformative effects on her life off-screen. But its climactic scene also questions that very process, calling on us to resist the seductive idea that the increase in agency suggested by successful neoliberal self-empowerment is a genuine step toward freedom—even when that idea comes to us in the well-beloved guise of the *sui generis* artist whose talent and belief in herself triumph against all odds (figure 5.1).[12]

"Because of what's she's been through…because she's still alive"

If the adoption of neoliberal principles by Hurricane Katrina survivors is depicted as a form of cruel and unusual punishment in *Trouble the Water*, it becomes a crime that merits just such punishment in the television series *House, M.D.* In general, *House* offers an ongoing paean to neoliberal subjectivity in the person of its hero, the brilliant diagnostician Dr. Gregory House. Coming off like a particularly abrasive spokesperson for Chicago School neoliberalism, House routinely argues that people always act in their own interests and that human behavior can be accurately predicted based on this fact—and his own reliably scandalous activities constitute a veritable personification of this maxim. A leg injury associates him with that most Benthamite of interests, physical pain, while his shameless addiction to painkillers enacts the neoliberal axiom that every individual has the right to pursue his or her own interests, provided no one else is harmed.[13] House's other major interest, diagnosing unusual medical illnesses, gives this neoliberal fantasy a markedly utopian cast: fortuitously, House's consuming and entirely self-centered desire to solve puzzles just happens to save lives. In a fashion reminiscent of Adam Smith's infamous invisible hand, the maniacal pursuit of individual interest somehow results in benefits to all. Although his clash with a profit-obsessed boss in Season One demonstrated that House employs neoliberal rationality in the service of locating "the answer" rather than improving the bottom line, even this commitment to truth finds a reflection in the neoliberal tendency to boil every employment decision down to performance metrics: whenever House's shenanigans get him into trouble, he need only point to his high success rate in solving cases to stymie his critics.[14]

It is into this milieu that the series introduces its Hurricane Katrina episode, which features an old friend of House's from college, Crandall, and Leona, a sixteen-year-old Katrina survivor who lost her mother in the storm and claims that Crandall is her father. Having had an affair with Leona's African American mother while he was writing a book about Leona's grandfather, a famous jazz pianist, Crandall, who is white, accepts Leona's claim and brings her to House for treatment after she suffers from hallucinations and a heart attack on their flight out of New Orleans. House, knowing his friend for an easy mark, immediately decides that Leona is scamming Crandall and decides that he will prove that she is not Crandall's daughter and diagnose her illness at the same time. On one level, this plot line offers a straightforward if revolting national allegory: Leona represents the destitute Hurricane Katrina survivors desperate for assistance after the storm, while Crandall represents the decent if overly gullible American public, who allow themselves to be conned into thinking that it is somehow their responsibility to provide this help and are thereby positioned (as House puts it) as the "Katrina victim victim[s]."

In the transposition of the word "victim" from a poor black woman to a middle-class white man who is providing assistance to her, we can hear echoes of the infamous "welfare queen" rhetoric of the 1980s, which positioned white middle-class Americans as the victims of scheming black female con artists who bilked the system at the expense of hardworking white people; in both cases, the oppressed and suffering are transformed into the aggressors against the white middle class, who appropriate the mantle of innocent victim for themselves. Yet Leona retains her own victim status to an extent that sharply distinguishes her from the imagined welfare queens of Reaganite lore. Rather than questioning the extent of her suffering, House's medical team describes Leona as having been "stuck in hell" because "New Orleans was a third world country."

The hellish nature of her experiences is ratified for the viewer via Leona's harrowing hallucinations of the storm, and ultimately we learn that it was an infection related to the storm that has caused her illness. The episode never blames Leona for her "choice" to stay in the city in a fashion that would raise doubts about her status as a self-responsibilized neoliberal subject, nor does it imply that she disdained other, more ethical or arduous means of self-support in favor of latching on to Crandall. Instead, "Who's Your Daddy?" takes a very different and ultimately more disturbing approach: accepting that Leona was "in hell," that Crandall was her only way out of hell, and that, in keeping with neoliberal principles, only irrational individuals fail to act in their own best interests, the episode nonetheless presents Leona's rational and self-interested attempt to escape hell as utterly repulsive and unconscionable. Rather than criticizing Leona as failing to merit neoliberal citizenship, the episode positions her bid for survival as a logical outcome of rational neoliberal subjectivity but reviles her nonetheless.

Obviously, this is an oddly laborious and contradictory way to go about vilifying Hurricane Katrina survivors, particularly when the tools for painting them as failed neoliberal citizens are so ready to hand. But this approach makes sense if we view maligning survivors as a by-product or side benefit of a more overarching narrative project: distinguishing neoliberal hegemony from the desperate, chaotic struggle for survival associated with New Orleans after the storm. While in modern political theory the drive for self-preservation is more commonly associated with the extra-political state of nature—a lawless realm devoid of normative standards of behavior—than with modes of political rule, neoliberalism's constant war on any sense of a shared communal public life has seemed to position the state of nature less as a long-abandoned past or philosophical hypothesis than as a swiftly approaching future.[15] By associating Leona with the problem of self-preservation, the episode presents her as a stand-in for this chaotic, violent state of self-interest run amok. When Crandall asks House how he can doubt Leona with "what she's been through," for example, House interrupts him to say that it is "because of what she's been through" that he doubts her, in particular "because she's still alive." Because Leona's self-preservation was threatened, House can argue that her necessary self-interest led to desperate and hence nonnormative and unprincipled behavior; self-preservation equates to an unacceptable incarnation of the philosophy of interest, a vision of "catastrophic neoliberalism" as an anarchic realm in which nothing at all is held in common and people are merely vessels for the amoral engine of self-interest.

This association between Leona and catastrophic neoliberalism is underscored by her hallucinations of Katrina, the first of which features a life-threatening flood. In the episode's opening scene, while Leona has a quiet conversation on a plane with Crandall, she notices a trickle of water that soon explodes into a filthy tidal wave that submerges her, an occurrence we quickly realize took place only in Leona's mind. Like her later hallucination of the dead and maggot-ridden body of her mother, this scene verifies the reality of the threat to Leona's life experienced during and after the storm, but it does so through a vision at odds with external empirical experience, creating a single-occupant "reality" that is at once intensely individual and fiercely motivating. In a fashion that mirrors House's assertions regarding the non-normative quality of the interest in life, Leona's hallucinations of the storm enact both the fevered pursuit of her interest in survival and the radical loss of a shared, consensual social realm in which such normative standards might be enforced.

It is as proof and reminder of this nightmarish vision of neoliberal hegemony that Leona is condemned and punished by *House*. The remainder of the episode assembles the case for differentiating House's own version of neoliberal existence from Leona's catastrophic Katrina experience, in the process rejecting Leona in a fashion so violent and overdetermined that it would be amusing if it weren't so pernicious. Pain is the key means by which this process unfolds, an approach that makes sense given that the pain/pleasure calculus plays such a crucial role in codifying human interests under neoliberalism. In both scenes in which Leona has hallucinations regarding her awful experiences during and after Katrina, the episode cuts directly from her screams of horror to a shot of House struggling to withstand his leg pain. In both scenes, House is shown enduring his pain in order to pursue his other, more socially beneficial interest, finding the truth about a medical illness, thereby indicating that self-interest serves the social fabric rather than destroying it. The second phase of the episode's deployment of the pain trope is the transformation of Leona's suffering from mental to physical anguish. Gathering from various medical clues that Leona has a neurological condition in which physical pain results in hallucinations, House decides to prove his theory by systematically hurting Leona while her brain is being scanned. After feeble protests from his staff, we watch as House straps Leona down, mendaciously informs her that

"This isn't going to hurt at all," and then begins to drive a needle into her body while demanding that she tell him the truth about her parentage. When this doesn't work, he bends back her finger until it breaks, and this more intense pain brings on a hallucination, proving House's diagnosis right.

As even this brief summary will suggest, this scene is so nakedly sadistic as to almost beggar belief. Given House's status as a hero in the series, viewers are apparently expected to look on with approval and enjoyment as a towering white man deliberately inflicts pain on a literally helpless, weeping teenage African American girl. In its recourse to torture, this scene indicates both the intensity of the threat that catastrophic neoliberalism represents, and the means by which this threat comes to be contained: the re-regulation of self-interest. As hallucinations, Leona's pain indicated the individual, extreme, and hence problematic quality of self-interest. As a physical sensation, however, her interest in avoiding pain becomes the means through which she can be governed and controlled. Torture ceases to be scandalous under neoliberal hegemony precisely because it is only an acute example of neoliberal governmentality more broadly: as in neoliberal governance at large, subjects under torture are compelled to make individual choices between options that have been predesigned to appeal to their self-interest through the presence of certain incentives and disincentives.[16] In torture scenarios, the choice regarding whether or not to talk is seemingly left up to the individual; not talking just happens to carry the disincentive of extreme pain. When House tortures Leona, he turns the same rational interest in avoiding suffering that has led her to scam Crandall against her; he transforms her self-interest from a hyper-individual, anarchic force to a means by which she can be subdued. In the process, the specter of catastrophic neoliberalism is likewise subdued, replaced with a vision of individual self-interest as a potent, almost omnipotent technology of control. Completing the differentiation between Leona and House, House argues that his own role in this process is innocent because, like his other interests, his desire to torture Leona happens to result in benefits for others besides himself: "Diagnostically, she needed to be hurt. I wanted to hurt her. Win, win."

The success of this containment strategy is proven by the utter eradication of Leona as an active subject from the remainder of the episode. Breaking with the series' own conventions, the episode presents no scenes in which House's underlings chat with Leona, and, in fact, after the torture scene, she never speaks another line.

While many of House's patients enter comas or become otherwise unresponsive in the course of an episode, Leona's status is rendered rather more specific when her digestive system becomes blocked and feces ooze from her mouth—a notably abject and revolting mixing of consumption and excretion. If Leona's self-preserving behavior brought to mind the dangers of extreme, chaotic interest, this reduction of her to an inert abject body gone awry seems to suggest that this chaos has now been confined to her body, leaking out only enough to let us know that it is ensconced and raging within her. As she is immobilized, silenced, and rendered an object of disgust, the horror of Leona's experiences seems to be compressed into her physical being, safely cordoned off below the surface of a body that is then itself symbolically ejected from the social through the process of abjection.

Having decisively dealt with Leona, the episode directs our attention to Crandall in order to promote its own version of post-Katrina neoliberalism. House at first attacks Crandall's desire to "manufactur[e] responsibility" for Leona but revises his opinion when Crandall argues that believing he is Leona's father "feels good" and "feels good is a good enough reason." This reasoning is endorsed by the episode's final shot, which shows House's morphine syringe next to test results that prove Crandall is not Leona's father, information House never shared with Crandall. If helping Katrina victims makes you "feel good," the juxtaposition implies, then it is reasonable to be allowed to pursue this interest, just as the physical interest in avoiding pain makes it reasonable to shoot morphine if you are in agony. In a corollary to *House's* long-standing argument that self-interest has the side effect of helping society, we now learn that social benefits should *only* arise as side effects to self-interest. Meanwhile, the key to diagnosing Leona's illness turns out to lie in Crandall's book about her grandfather, Jesse Baker, entitled *Genius Destroyed*. The book blames Baker's drinking for his deterioration into madness, but House gleans from the accompanying performance CD that Baker was not crazy and drunk but suffering from an obscure illness that Leona has inherited. Crucially, House's exoneration of Baker arises from the intersection of truth and performance metrics: House can tell Baker was ill because he played too well to be intoxicated. Instead of having destroyed himself through ungoverned attachment to what "feels good," Baker turns out to be a sick man who nevertheless performed admirably—rather like House, in other words. The subplot attempts to persuade us that African Americans won't necessarily be excised from a stable neoliberal future, provided they avoid Leona's association with self-preservation and match House in marrying self-interest to measurably valuable performance.[17]

"We place a great importance on culture"

I want to conclude by examining briefly the way in which *When the Levees Broke* negotiates the problematic of self-preservation I have been exploring thus far. Assembled primarily from talking-head interviews and archival footage, *Levees* frequently intercuts interviewees' description of events that they witnessed or that relate to their professional expertise with footage of the same or similar events, such that the interviewee's account becomes in part a voiceover for the film's chronology of the storm and its aftermath. Because it avoids including Lee's questions as much as possible, this approach serves to make the interviewees the film's primary narrators, in a fashion that Lee in his audio commentary describes as allowing survivors to "testify."[18] When it intercuts interviews and archival footage, the film both illustrates and authenticates Katrina survivors' testimony, which is proven to be accurate via the indexical record of the film footage that accompanies their description.

However, the use of this practice is varied in a fashion that gives it resonance beyond its value as authentication. In general, *Levees* relies on intercutting when interviewees are providing general accounts of developments and events that they witnessed or opinions about various causes and effects during the Katrina event, but it rarely employs this practice when its interviewees are describing their own individual experience and actions. For example, Mike Seelig's dramatic interview account of watching the sewer system in the process of failing is intercut with footage of the same event; Phyllis Montana LeBlanc's account of being stuck at the New Orleans airport is not, although such footage is provided for the immediately proceeding interview, an airport director's account of the same period and events. The effect of this approach is to foreground the interviewee's role as narrator and observer rather than as suffering participant, even when he or she is describing personal experience and actions. Because LeBlanc took part in the events in the airport as an evacuee rather than a government official, intercutting her account with footage of evacuees stuck in the airport would in effect identify her with or interpolate her within those archival images, recreating her participation in these earlier events. By avoiding the inclusion of footage to accompany LeBlanc's account, *Levees* ensconces her outside of and at a level above her past experience—a position underscored by the location of her interview on a balcony overlooking the floor where she and her husband were packed in with thousands of others, awaiting a flight out of New Orleans.

Tellingly, the film's major deviation from this practice arises in the sequence focused on self- and community-rescue efforts, which consistently intercuts between the interviewees' accounts of individual action and archival footage of people undertaking the same or similar actions.[19] For example, when LeBlanc describes how she and her family waved SOS signs and then evacuated themselves using refrigerators as rafts, her account in part overlays aerial footage of people undertaking similar actions with empty plastic tubs and other makeshift flotation devices—the only one of LeBlanc's many interviews in the film proper to be intercut in this fashion.[20] This technique foregrounds the link between self-rescue and agential activity by turning its narrators back into protagonists: when we hear the interviewees' descriptions of their actions as voiceover accompaniments to images of similar actions, the effect is to place the narrators within the footage, to associate them with the bodies depicted taking those actions. In so doing, these sequences in effect synchronize the interviewees' past acts of self- and community rescue with their present narrative account, linking them through both content and form to the presence of agential action in the midst of suffering and domination.

If moments of self-preservation indicate something of the problematic quality of agency under neoliberalism—the way in which neoliberalism's eradication of a shared social realm can increase agency and deprivation simultaneously—*Levees*' intercutting practice both acknowledges and attenuates this connection. The film registers the interfiliation of agency and suffering in its use of intercutting in the self-preservation sequences, but it more often presents its interviewees as narrative authorities over an experience of suffering from which they have been distanced, both temporally and formally. By foregrounding narrative authority in this fashion, *Levees* pries apart and reconfigures the relationship between suffering and agency through the addition of a third term: cultural practice. Through the emphasis on interviewees as narrators, agency becomes associated with an act of *describing* an experience of suffering—an experience that is simultaneously honored and located as an object of contemplation lodged within the past. This transfiguration of the link between agency and suffering through artistic practice is further developed in the film's reliance on diegetic musical performance—for example, Wynton Marsalis' *a capella* rendition of "St. James Infirmary," which serves as the soundtrack for a montage of still photos of people enduring the aftermath of the storm. Because these are still images, all activity of the bodies within them is halted, while Marsalis' recorded-live performance of a New Orleans jazz classic enacts a present tense, ongoing tradition of African American cultural agency, into which the suffering caused by Katrina seems to be transmitted directly. Instead of the intercutting process that peopled Katrina footage with subjects we have come to know through interviews, we view images of stilled, unnamed bodies in distress while the performance of a renowned musician brings a cultural artifact to life. In effect, the agency that accompanied suffering in the survivors' accounts of self-evacuation is replaced here by jazz musicianship, which both preserves the experience of suffering and becomes itself an object worthy of preservation.

Of course, the historical importance of New Orleans to African American cultural history, particularly jazz history, has made the linkage between culture and storm in films such as *Levees* seem only to be expected, a sense of inevitability intensified by Lee's own connections to the jazz community. Because of this history, it seems equally inevitable that the film would deploy New Orleans' cultural heritage in a canny attempt to prove that the poorer areas of the city deserve to be rebuilt. If New Orleans residents "place a great importance on culture," as actor Wendell Pierce puts it in the film, this is a valuation shared with what Jodi Melamud calls "neoliberal multiculturalism," a late twentieth-century variant of multiculturalism that draws on the idea of a culturally diverse nation in order to position the United States as morally superior to "monocultural" regimes abroad.[21] In its emphasis on New Orleans' unique culture *Levees* seemingly plays to the logic of neoliberal multiculturalism, in effect offering cultural specificity as a reason why the 9th Ward should be rebuilt. Yet the intercutting patterns I have been tracking in the film suggest something else may be at work as well. If moments of self-preservation indicate the way in which agential action in one's own best interest does nothing to release one from neoliberal structures of domination—quite the opposite—then we might understand the film's preference for artistic practice as an attempt to retain some sense of agency for its interviewees without simultaneously endorsing the tainted version at work in neoliberalism. In effect, *Levees'* focus on the artistic agency necessary to represent suffering seems to offer something of a utopian alternative to the particular dynamic of neoliberal domination; in both cases, suffering and agency coexist, but in the moments of artistic practice featured by *Levees*, they are separated into two bodies, the one whose life was under threat and the one who tells the tale.

In its attempt to produce this alternative, *Levees* draws on the longstanding and highly contested association between art and resistance, redeploying art's utopian pulse in an attempt to resist new neoliberal forms of domination. Whereas earlier incarnations of art's utopian promise highlighted art's ability to wrest agency from ideological closure, *Levees* instead attempts to replace a problematic version of agency with an artistic form that seemingly, and perhaps wishfully, is presented as safe from neoliberal associations. In so doing, *Levees* indicates the way in which the reconfiguration of agency under neoliberalism is placing new demands on our ability to both comprehend and represent domination and resistance, a shift that is registered by each of the texts I have been discussing. In a sense, *House*'s virulent attack on its Katrina survivor, Leona, underscores this shift most emphatically. While the representation of Leona is almost unbelievably racist and castigatory, it relies on none of the Reaganite tropes that depicted African American subjects as either secretly living in comfort or too lazy to improve their circumstances by non-fraudulent means. Instead, *House* positions Leona's drive for self-preservation as an incarnation of neoliberal principles and then condemns her for her association with an event that showed the worst effects of those principles. Even *House*, a veritable paean to neoliberalism, is unable to deny fully the searing reality of catastrophic neoliberalism inscribed by the Katrina event, but it concedes this threat only to expel it through a new racialized politics of blame.

Although their politics are diametrically opposed to that of *House*, *Trouble the Water* and *Levees* display a similar shift: both documentaries demonstrate the way in which acts of self-preservation by African American survivors resonate with the neoliberal ideal in which actions in one's own best interest are undertaken in a governmental vacuum. For *Trouble the Water* and *Levees*, however, the resulting challenge to their representation of Katrina is rather different: once the heroic reclamation of agency from tragedy becomes itself a sign of neoliberal citizenship, the long-standing Left project of augmenting agency for the oppressed is itself called into question. *Trouble the Water* handles this challenge by making the question of agency its central concern, ultimately demonstrating the way in which the limitations on agency and the limitations *of* agency are fundamentally and disastrously intertwined for Roberts and her community. In contrast, *Levees* attempts to resist the problematic nature of neoliberal agency by reconfiguring agency as a form of artistic practice, an approach that both acknowledges and displaces the neoliberal confluence of suffering and agency. Taken together, these texts suggest the way in which racialized narratives of the Katrina event at times exceed the paradigm of the biopolitics of disposability, producing new configurations of neoliberalism, race, and domination that do not require the eradication of agency to produce unspeakable domination.

Notes

1. See *Stormy Weather: Katrina and the Politics of Disposability*, p. 22.
2. Although it is specifically focused on the Katrina event, Giroux's polemic resonates with pre-Katrina analyses of the relationship between neoliberalism and identity politics such as Lisa Duggan's important assessment in *The Twilight of Equality?: Neoliberalism, Cultural Politics, and the Attack on Democracy*. Both readings underscore neoliberalism's tendency to attach the worst effects of its policies to the racialized bodies of the poor, and to circulate images of those bodies as examples of failed neoliberal citizenship.
3. Nicole R. Fleetwood, "Failing Narratives, Initiating Technologies: Hurricane Katrina and the Production of a Weather Media Event."
4. On neoliberalism and self-responsibilization, see, for example, Bilge Yesil, "Watching Ourselves: Video Surveillance, Urban Space and Self-Responsibilization," and Mitchell Dean, *Governmentality: Power and Rule in Modern Society*, p. 163.
5. *Powers of Freedom: Reframing Political Thought*, p. 142. Rose's work is grounded in Michel Foucault's influential account of liberalism and neoliberalism in *The Birth of Biopolitics: Lectures at the Collège De France, 1978–79*.
6. I am indebted here to Kimberly Springer's illuminating analysis of the relationship between neoliberalism and African American figures such as the hiphop entrepreneur. See Springer, "Hate the Game, Not the Playa: Unmasking Neoliberal Articulations Amongst the Black Power Elite." For an important and related reading of reality TV and self-responsibilization, see Anna McCarthy, "Reality Television: A Neoliberal Theater of Suffering."
7. Naomi Klein, *The Shock Doctrine: Rise of Disaster Capitalism*.
8. *The Twilight of Equality?: Neoliberalism, Cultural Politics, and the Attack on Democracy?*, p. 14.

9. For a review of *Trouble the Water* that examines Roberts' loss and recovery of artistic agency in the film, see Rob Nelson, "Screenings: *Trouble the Water*."
10. For example, Nelson terms the performance "an old-school show-stopper" in his review, while Legacy Lee describes it as "uplifting" and "the film's only resolution." See Nelson, "Screenings: *Trouble the Water*," p. 69, and Legacy Lee, "Trouble the Water," p. 18.
11. Nelson, "Screenings: *Trouble the Water*," p. 69.
12. In her incisive account of "situated testimony" in *Trouble the Water*, Janet Walker raises important questions regarding the utopian ending of the film, particularly in relation to Scott Roberts' new employment by a kindly white boss. See "Rights and Returns: Perils and Fantasies of Situated Testimony after Katrina."
13. On the relationship between Jeremy Bentham and contemporary neoliberalism, see Stephen G. Engelmann, *Imagining Interest in Political Thought: Origins of Economic Rationality*, pp. 52–55.
14. This plotline involved an African American millionaire who attempted to rationalize hospital operations in a way that would maximize profits and benefit his own pharmaceutical company, a process that led him to try to fire House. The casting of an African American in this role is in keeping with the series' association of the business of medicine with House's female boss; in both cases, minorities/women ventriloquize the elements of neoliberalism that serve corporate interests, a tendency that the series desires to disavow. Regarding House's commitment to truth over profit, see E. Rich Leigh et al., "The Afterbirth of the Clinic: A Foucauldian Perspective on 'House M.D.' and American Medicine in the 21st Century." On neoliberal governance through performance metrics, see Rose, *Powers of Freedom: Reframing Political Thought*, pp. 151–153.
15. See Thomas Hobbes, *Leviathan*. On self-preservation, normativity, and liberalism in Hobbes, Locke, and the war on terror, see Yaseen Noorani, "The Rhetoric of Security.."
16. For a related argument regarding torture and governmentality, see Dean, *Governmentality: Power and Rule in Modern Society*, p. 15.
17. This emphasis on the cultural value of Katrina survivors in terms of music history was reflected in real-world media attention to the rescue of Fats Domino. I discuss New Orleans' music culture, agency, and Katrina survival in greater detail in the next section.
18. On *When the Levees Broke* and "situated testimony," see Walker, "Rights and Returns: Perils and Fantasies of Situated Testimony after Katrina."
19. Exceptions include footage produced by Lee's crew regarding the return to New Orleans and the long-term effects of the storm (e.g., Terence Blanchard's return to his mother's house) and footage shot

by interviewees, in which they appear as narrators and cinematographers (e.g., Shelton "Shakespeare" Alexander's footage from the Superdome). In the first case, temporal distance removes survivors from the extremity of physical suffering associated with the flooded city, while in the second, artistic agency is emphasized through the presence of the interviewee as narrator and filmmaker. I discuss the role of cultural agency in greater detail later.

20. There is significantly more intercutting in the ancillary Act V in interviews with LeBlanc and others; for the most part, the intercutting occurs in an extended segment focused on self- and community-rescues.

21. See "The Spirit of Neoliberalism: From Racial Liberalism to Neoliberal Multiculturalism." On *Levees'* own investment in monocultural experience, see Walker, "Rights and Returns: Perils and Fantasies of Situated Testimony after Katrina."

Chapter 6

Discovery Channel's Nature-Reality Hybrid Shows: Representing Survival in the Wake of Katrina

Andrew Goodridge

A series of natural disasters at the beginning of the new millennium have heightened the cultural presence of anxiety about humanity's relationship with the forces of nature and our (in)ability to respond effectively. On December 26, 2004, an earthquake in the Indian Ocean set off a series of tsunamis that would reach the coasts of Indonesia, Malaysia, and Thailand. The recorded death toll for Indonesia was over one hundred and fifty thousand. Less than a year later, Hurricane Katrina, one of the strongest Atlantic hurricanes on record, made landfall as a category three storm on portions of southern Louisiana and Mississippi. The storm was the costliest natural disaster in U.S. history, with estimates of over eighty billion dollars of damage. Just weeks later, Hurricane Rita hit the Texas and Louisiana coasts, substantially delaying the recovery efforts in Louisiana. In October 2007, wildfires destroyed over five hundred thousand acres of land in Southern California and prompted both Governor Schwarzenegger and President Bush to declare a state of emergency in seven Southern California counties. Recent research shows that there is cause for continued alarm regarding natural disasters: a 2007 study conducted by the Centre for Research on the Epidemiology of Disasters (CRED) found that the number of natural disasters has quadrupled over the last two decades, going from an average of approximately 120 per year in the 1980s to nearly 500 per year in the early 2000s.[1]

Television and film programs have reacted to these and other natural disasters in a number of ways. Narrative programming has incorporated disaster events, as is the case with the Fox police drama *K-Ville* (2007). Set in "Katrina-ville," the local name for post-hurricane New Orleans, the show's title stresses the ability of natural disasters to change the landscape of civilization and insinuate themselves into regional and urban identities. Other series have dedicated episodes to addressing the aftermath of Katrina and the tsunami, such as the 2006 episode of *Extreme Makeover: Home Edition*, "After the Storm: New Orleans," which was centered on rebuilding homes destroyed by the hurricane. Event miniseries, such as Spike Lee's 2006 documentary *When the Levees Broke: A Requiem in Four Acts*, present a mix of individual survival stories and examinations of governmental failures and missteps. The third-highest grossing documentary of all time, *An Inconvenient Truth*, helped Al Gore to win the Nobel Peace Prize for his "efforts to build up and disseminate greater knowledge about man-made climate change." The film's inclusion of Katrina in its discussion of global climate change has merged the topics of global warming and natural disasters.

The media response to growing anxieties regarding natural dangers has been vast and varied, with the result that our uneasy relationship with the forces of nature has become a "cultural presence," a part of the fabric of American cultural life.[2] This essay investigates how Discovery Channel's new nature programs participate in the cultural presence of natural disasters in the wake of Katrina. This new wave of nature programs incorporates the dangerous, even cataclysmic, side of nature into reality programming. *Man vs. Wild* (2006–present), *Survivorman* (2005–present), and *I Shouldn't Be Alive* (2005–2007) present stories of individuals surviving amid the challenges of the untamed wild. These hybrids of nature and reality genres attempt to reposition our relationship to nature in the wake of heavily publicized natural disasters. By examining nature in a post-natural disaster environment, these shows explore and define nature in a very specific way. Contrary to previous modes of nature programming, these shows frame nature as unsafe, unwelcoming, and unreceptive to human life. Yet, against all odds, Discovery Channel tells us, we can survive.

The analysis of cultural presence has previously been articulated by Jeffrey Sconce in *Haunted Media: Electronic Presence from Telegraphy to Television*. Sconce looks at the cultural response to electronic media (the invention of telegraphy, wireless communication, radio broadcasting) and identifies the cultural presence created by various forms of discourse as these media became integrated into American life. For Sconce, a cultural presence is a pervasive social reaction located in a wide array of discourse that is felt through regulation, popular discussion, entertainment, public policy, and the media.[3] Sconce creates a social history by contextualizing these technologies in terms of "historically specific intersections of technological, industrial and cultural practices."[4] In Sconce's study of electronic media, cultural presence is revealed in public reaction to anxieties created by electronic technologies as outlined in newspapers, popular fiction, and scientific debates.

Natural disasters such as Katrina, the California wildfires, and the tsunami have developed a similar cultural presence, traces of which can be found in media such as film, newspapers, magazines, the Internet, and, in particular, on Discovery Channel's nature-reality hybrid shows. This study of three Discovery Channel programs demonstrates how these new nature series draw upon post-disaster anxieties as well as stylistic, thematic, and narrative conventions from both reality and nature genres. In using reality conventions, Discovery Channel inflects nature programming with cultural anxieties about nature and produces a distinctive fusion of nature and reality that is set apart from previous nature genres. The conventions of Discovery Channel's nature-reality hybrid illuminate the cultural presence of natural disasters as well as Discovery Channel's larger industrial motivations in a post-network era where the profile of niche programming has increased significantly. Emerging from the de-regulated media environment of the 1980s to revive television documentary forms that had come to be seen as unpopular and commercially unviable, the Discovery Channel currently maintains a strong "public service" brand image that heightens its authoritative discursive position.[5]

The Cultural Presence of Disasters in Post-Katrina America

Millennial American culture has shifted to a position of heightened disaster awareness with natural disasters continuing to resonate in everyday life after they have ended, and exposing our (in)ability to prepare for them. They shed light on the government's recent history of insufficient response to cataclysmic events. They raise questions regarding social equality and the lack of immediate support to low-income minority neighborhoods. Environmental issues have become important in political debates, and these events have provided contexts to new environmental policies and regulations.

Popular discourse, law and regulation, and political debate have contributed to the presence that feeds Discovery Channel's nature-reality programs. A search of "Hurricane Katrina" on YouTube leads to nearly six thousand hits. The diverse range of postings include home videos of the hurricane, news footage of its aftermath, and clips of rap star Kanye West's now-famous assertion that "George Bush doesn't care about black people." There are eighty-four Facebook groups dedicated to the 2004 tsunami, and eighty-five MySpace groups that focus on Hurricane Katrina. A Google search of the phrase "2004 tsunami" returns nearly half a million responses. Sites include personal blogs telling stories of survival, scientific debates about the tsunami and global warming, and discussions of the World Bank's "Disaster Risk Management Framework" that was revamped in response to the sudden and unexpected devastation caused by the tsunami. Popular magazines have also fostered a sense of disaster-mindedness. Between 2006 and 2008, *Time* magazine devoted six covers to Hurricane Katrina and its aftermath, and two more to the tsunami. A search of *Newsweek* finds that Hurricane Katrina was mentioned in one hundred and sixty-three articles in just over two years. The phrase "Indian Ocean Tsunami" has been used in over two hundred and sixty articles in *National Geographic*.

The cultural presence of these events is defined not solely by the quantity of discussion that has taken place, but also by the wide range of discourse that has arisen. Natural disasters have spurred new discussions and debates on policy regarding public health, urban planning, toxic waste disposal, coastal protection, energy security, and global warming. A search within the FEMA website finds over seventy-four hundred returns for the word "Katrina." The ability of Katrina and other natural disasters to raise new concerns, influence policy, and invade our everyday lives has solidified it as a cultural presence. For example, FEMA has undertaken a national remapping of flood planes and flood zones in the wake of Katrina. For some, this has diminished property values and made flood insurance either expensive or impossible to obtain.

Popular magazines such as *Time, Newsweek*, and *U.S. News & World Report* have all reported on the government's inability to handle natural disasters and unwillingness to take steps to prevent similar situations in the future. Furthermore, all have run articles with specific information about what individuals can do to prepare for the dangers of the cataclysmic side of nature. First-person narratives of post-Katrina responses have also begun to appear in popular nonfiction. Neil Strauss' *Emergency: This Book Will Save Your Life* chronicles the author's pursuit of personal preparedness for any foreseeable disaster after the government's failure to respond to Katrina "shattered every last illusion about my country that remained."[6] Strauss' book emphasizes individualism as the only certain method of self-preservation in the wake of Katrina. As Strauss puts it, "something changed in me, as it did for many people, in the aftermath of Hurricane Katrina. In that moment, I realized that...I had to take care of myself."[7]

Post-Katrina cable television reality programming turns on such neoliberal credos of self-sufficiency by appealing to anxieties regarding survival and the powerful force of nature. In the Discovery shows, an individual is stranded and left to fend for himself against the elements. These shows capitalize on the isolation felt by many citizens, fearing that the government would not be able to respond adequately in the event of another disaster. By isolating a single person (the host) and teaching survival skills to the viewer, the Discovery Channel nature-hybrid shows capitalize on this anxiety promulgating what are presented as pragmatic tips for dealing with disaster.

Crikey!: Early Nature Television Styles, Narratives, and Pedagogy

Discovery Channel incorporates aspects of nature programming that date back over fifty years, creating a hybrid nature-reality genre that does not appear in the same form on other nature-oriented channels such as Travel Channel, Animal Planet, or The Learning Channel. Television's nature-oriented programming has evolved in distinct patterns, and I see this nature-reality hybrid as the fourth "wave" of nature programming. The notion of "waves" of reality programming has been presented by Anna McCarthy, who distinguishes among such waves based on content, narrative, and special goals finding that the first wave of reality television occurred in the late 1940s and early 1950s. The first wave began with programs such as *Candid Camera* and then developed with similar series such as *Person to Person* and *See it Now*.[8] McCarthy describes the early genre as trading in a concept of reality that is "understood as unequivocally good, instructive, and socially progressive through its association with social science."[9]

McCarthy's study provides a useful framework for charting the waves of nature programming and is worth detailing here. Historicizing and subdividing a genre that dates back to the earliest days of television is difficult, though the nature genre has consistently been educational so creating waves based on ideological distinction is most useful. The first wave of nature programming comprises programs such as *Zoo Parade* (1950, NBC), *True-Life Adventures* (1951), and *Mutual of Omaha's Wild Kingdom* (1963–1988, NBC). In the first wave, nature was presented as exotic and fun, and these nonfiction programs focused on the basics of animals and animal behavior. *Zoo Parade* was filmed live at various zoos across the country with a host who explained and narrated animal actions. First wave nature shows were marketed in ways that attempted to draw a family-friendly audience using kid-friendly footage and educational content.

The second wave of nature television argues for the necessity of environmentalism, wildlife conservation, and scientific research. Early examples of these shows include programming such as *The Undersea World of Jacques Cousteau* (1966–1976, PBS) and *The Cousteau Odyssey* (1978, PBS). This second wave of nature programming continues today mostly on Animal Planet with examples including *Nature* (1982) and *The Crocodile Hunter* (1996–2006). Steve Irwin's persona as "The Crocodile Hunter" explored the dangerous side of nature, but the spirit of the show and the host created an atmosphere of entertainment and wonder rather than fear. Irwin's enthusiasm and eagerness to interact with potentially deadly animals mitigated the danger of nature (until his death caused by a sting ray while filming the show). Irwin's popular catch phrase "Isn't she beautiful?" (referring to any animal, but typically a crocodile) captures the essence and heart of the second wave of nature programming: nature should be respected, treasured, preserved. Irwin's second wave show did not fear nature in the way that the nature-reality hybrid does. Thus, Irwin's death makes sense within the second wave paradigm: he was not focused on survival.

Second wave shows all use nature programming as a platform for arguing the necessity of preserving nature. When Irwin picks up a poisonous snake or swims with a dangerous shark, the series is not attempting to teach survival skills or how to avoid a hazardous encounter. Rather, Irwin is attempting to get in for a closer look, to admire the natural world, and to show audiences exactly why the environment is worth saving. While these programs acknowledge that nature can be potentially dangerous, they invite the viewer into a conservationist's role by immersing the audience in nature and encouraging them to admire the wild, though Irwin's death—caused by literally and figuratively getting "too close" to nature—becomes retroactive proof of the danger of becoming complacent about nature.

The third wave of nature programming includes shows such as those described by Adam Fish in "Television, Ecotourism, and the Videocamera: Performative Non-Fiction and Auto-Cinematography." Ecotourism shows are represented by programs such as *The Jeff Corwin Experience* (2001–present, Animal Planet), *Going Tribal* (2005–present, Discovery Channel), and even reality game shows such as *Survivor* (2000–present, CBS) and *The Amazing Race* (2001–present, CBS). According to Fish, ecotourism shows are reality-based programming focused on exploration of little-seen locations. Ecotourism shows are somewhat similar to early ethnographic film, as they aim to explore local people, wildlife, and culture. Their focus is not on the dangers of nature or the need to learn survival skills. Survival skills are generally at the forefront of early episodes in each installment of *Survivor*, though the series does not present the skills in a pedagogic manner, which is a key distinction in contrast to post-Katrina series. There are brief narratives about building fires or catching fish, but as viewers we never learn how to do these things for ourselves. Further, narratives about surviving nature are quickly pushed to the side in favor of storylines about surviving the social climate as the series advances.

These three waves overlap and coexist rather than conform to a specific timeline in which one wave chronologically gives way to the next. Contemporary nature programs variously adhere to the conventions of first, second, and/or third wave nature programming. However, the fourth wave is a recent trend in nature programming that had not been seen before the mid-2000s. This wave shuns "trivialities" from both genres—such as reality show social survival or ecotourism cultural lessons—in favor of a presentation of nature as a threat that cannot be overcome but merely survived, and only with the proper skills, education, self-reliance, and respect for the wild.

Merging Nature and Reality in Popular Television

As previously mentioned, Discovery Channel has premiered three of these prime-time nature-reality hybrid shows since 2005. *I Shouldn't Be Alive* addresses real stories of survival in the wake of natural disasters such as tornadoes, floods, earthquakes, and blizzards. *Survivorman* and *Man vs. Wild* are hosted by survival experts who are abandoned in the middle of nature and forced to fend for themselves against the elements and wildlife, all the while teaching the audience how to survive on our own in a similar situation if the need were to arise. Nature-reality shows are easily identifiable by their common themes of educating the viewer about the survival skills needed in the wake of natural disaster and encouraging a wary respect for nature and its unpredictability. A far cry from Jeff Corwin using an elephant's trunk as a megaphone on *Going Wild with Jeff Corwin*, this new breed of nature shows suspends notions of play and ease in favor of the drama of survival.

A cursory analysis of the content of these shows would suggest they could easily be classified as either exclusively nature or exclusively reality programming. However, a closer look at their fusion of aesthetic, narrative, ideological, and structural traits from both genres necessitates the formation of a new category. Nature-reality hybrid shows can be separated from traditional nature programming in many ways. First, these shows foreground their artificiality in the setup of the narrative structure. As opposed to first and second wave shows such as *Nature, Mutual of Omaha's Wild Kingdom*, or *The Crocodile Hunter*, nature-reality programs are centered around some sort of perceived or stated "goal." There is a constructed and inevitable finality to the end of each individual episode, and the rigid deadlines are in line with the far harsher tone that these series sustain: *Survivorman*'s Les Stroud must outlast the elements for seven days; *Man vs. Wild*'s Bear Grylls attempts to find civilization within five days. *Survivorman* outlines the goal during the opening credits, while Grylls introduces his objective during an opening monologue. Further differing from first, second, and third wave nature programming, *Man vs. Wild* and *Survivorman* adhere to a strict narrative structure with a stated outcome that is worked toward over the duration of each episode. *Man vs. Wild* begins with Grylls being stranded and assessing his living situation in the first act; trying to find food, water, and shelter in the second; then making his progression toward civilization in the final act. Both shows find resolution in the final moments when the hosts have conquered nature. By contrast, a third wave show such as *The Crocodile Hunter* is not structured in acts, and ends almost arbitrarily after thirty minutes.

The nature-reality genre further distances itself from previous modes of nature programming by positioning nature and humans in a struggle. As its title suggests, *Man vs. Wild* positions Grylls as a challenger to nature's dominance, defiantly venturing outside of civilization in an attempt to conquer the wild. First, second, and third wave nature programs tend to portray nature as a source of excitement, beauty, and adventure. Nature and wilderness are presented as something that the host can navigate with ease. While Corwin and others in earlier waves may (or may not) briefly discuss the potential trials of surviving the wild, this struggle is not explicitly shown on screen. Corwin handles venomous animals, meets with fierce weather, and crosses dangerous terrain, and he does it all with a smile on his face. His journeys are not treated with the sense of dread and imminent death that seem to accompany Stroud or Grylls.

The nature-reality hybrid show draws its sense of drama and struggle from the reality genre. While reality television encompasses a wide array of programming and is difficult to define, at minimum scholars agree that the label applies to any program that features nonactors and minimal scripting. Susan Murray argues in an article on the origins of reality TV that the genre can best be described as an "unabashedly commercial genre united less by aesthetic rules or certainties than by the fusion of popular entertainment with a self-conscious claim to the discourse of the real."[10] The three nature-reality hybrid shows analyzed in this essay vary greatly in terms of aesthetics, but they are all united by their "claim to the discourse of the real." Each show tells real stories of real people surviving even though, in the case of *Man vs. Wild* and *Survivorman,* the setup is manipulated. These shows use nonactors and unscripted dialogue to appeal to the audience's senses of reality.

The claim to the discourse of the real is a vital aspect of nature-reality survival programs. The hosts of these programs consistently ground their situations and experience in the real by pointing out, literally, the dangers inherent in surviving in nature. In addition, the hosts sometimes explicitly address actual contemporary natural disasters, such as Katrina and the 2004 tsunami. Nature-reality series foreground nature while some reality shows push it to the background. Series such as *Big Brother* and *The Real World* heavily emphasize the enclosure and entrapment of their participants. These series create an artificial indoor "bubble" of life for contestants, whereas nature-reality series situate real people outside the safety and comfort of a controlled environment. Though some shows such as *Survivor* or *The Amazing Race* do portray the struggles of surviving in nature and also provide some educational content, more time is spent on the competitive and social interactions of the contestants. The focus of the nature-reality hybrid is on surviving and negotiating nature as opposed to a game.

The nature-reality hybrid shows are explicitly educational. While *Survivor* may employ footage of contestants building a shelter, the series is more likely to show scenes of contestants failing at survival, fumbling their way through building a fire or being unable to catch fish. Nature-reality programs are extremely clear in their educational aims, directly addressing the audience and warning the viewer of common mistakes in the effort to survive.

The ultimate goal of the nature-reality hybrid is survival and the successful negotiation of the untamed wild. Explicit hopes for financial gain and reality stardom are not a focus of these shows. Stardom for Stroud and Grylls seems more like a marketing strategy than an attempt to garner mass appeal: the hosts and the series' ideologies differentiate themselves with a somber tone that makes the pursuit of fame seem trivial. The post-Katrina nature-reality hybrid show takes on a focused and serious tone, situating nature's harshest elements as the primary, and often the sole, source of conflict for the hosts of the series.

Nature-reality shows differ ideologically from ecotourism shows, as culture gives way to nature, and ecological optimism yields to harsh realizations—predominant by the latter half of this decade—that man and nature are in competition. *Survivorman* and *Man vs. Wild* are emphatically non-ethnographic series unconcerned with native cultures or people, and resolutely focused on the survival skills needed for these new locations. Like first and second wave nature shows, the nature-reality hybrid focuses on education, but the nature of entertainment is vastly different in fourth wave nature-reality hybrid. This progression of the nature show genre has drastically changed the cultural meaning of the genre. No longer is there anything to be "won," except for life itself.

Education on these fourth wave shows is dispensed exclusively from experts, such as Grylls and Stroud, who are categorically white males (much like predecessors such as Corwin and Irwin) with a unique "encounter" remit. The practical, real-world survival lessons on these shows are never presented by natives of the area, though Grylls and Stroud regularly venture outside of wilderness areas in the United States. Stroud and Grylls are depicted as rugged survival experts but their presentation is never entirely straightforward. Stroud allows himself one luxury item, a harmonica, which he plays for the audience during each episode. Grylls will routinely address the camera and admit that he wishes he could have a cup of chamomile tea. In this way, Grylls and Stroud are positioned as relatable educators, able to relay information in a way that seems relevant for the audience at home. Both hosts have an "everyman" quality that is necessary when teaching the audience these skills. They do not look like grizzled, unshaven recluses who shun the modern world. Rather, they are both educated and articulate (Grylls holds a degree in Hispanic studies from the University of London, and he also works as a motivational speaker). Even the rough-sounding name "Bear" is only a nickname for Grylls who was born Mitchell Winston Grylls.

The series I am discussing offer examples of a widespread contemporary cultural mode that Matthew Ferrari has identified as the "masculine primitive" in which isolation is crucial to the staging of a natural self and the accessing of a "primal potential."[11] That mode, as Ferrari notes however, is often dependent upon a privileged mobility. It is important for the ways these series speak to audiences that their fourth wave hosts seemingly could be anyone and the skills they teach are for everyone, but they do share important similarities based as they are around white males who carefully refrain from excessive displays of machismo. Implicitly, femininity and minority group membership are associated with dependency, which brings to mind tensions immediately following Katrina as racial minorities waited for governmental assistance and black neighborhoods were decimated. Though Stroud's and Grylls' performances of masculinity are tempered, the lack of a female or minority presence and the isolated host predicate these shows on a neoliberal individualism and heroic masculinity in which the ability to survive disaster is conceived as a male trait.[12]

Fourth Wave Ideologies, Aesthetics, and White Male Machismo

The nature-reality shows address the anxieties of an uncertain post-disaster existence. Without electricity, a stable living area, or grocery stores, these shows ask: How can one obtain the basic necessities for survival? How can you start a fire in the rain? How do you build a shelter that can protect you from the cold of night and the heat of day? Which part of the rattlesnake is safe to eat? Nature-reality programs elaborately detail the experience of survival in the wild while seeming to avoid any glamorizing or mitigating of the duress of their hosts' travails, framing nature as a force that one might have to confront in a time of emergency.

Man vs. Wild premiered in November 2006, making it the most recent of the Discovery Channel nature-reality programs. Though it aired only for two months that year, *Man vs. Wild* was the fourth highest rated program on Discovery Channel in 2006, averaging over 3.5 million viewers.[13] Its success prompted the network to renew the series for two additional seasons. In *Man vs. Wild*, host and survival expert Grylls is dropped off in a popular tourist destination that often has a high death toll due to accidents and nature-related complications. Each episode is named for a radical terrain or wilderness that Grylls must survive. The dangers he faces include the extreme temperatures in "Iceland," poisonous and deadly animals in "African Savanna," and the lifeless and unpredictable terrain of "Mount Kilauea." In all these settings Grylls must adapt to the local environment, climate, and wildlife.

At the beginning of each episode, Grylls explains the hazards of the location he will be surviving. In "The Rockies," Grylls is dropped off in the middle of the mountain range. He explains, "millions of people visit every year, and 2000 don't survive... I'm going in to show you how to be the ultimate survivor." In this instance, Grylls warns that even recreation activities such as tourism are unsafe. Here, he stresses that the audience cannot assume that a natural disaster is the only threat from the wild—the next family vacation could end in tragedy unless everyone is equipped with survival skills. The audience is reminded of the presence of nature and its dangers during the voiceover, as images of frozen rivers, poisonous snakes, and unmanageable environments play under the narration. During each episode, Grylls will tell numerous stories of individual survival to frighten, to reassure, and to educate. In the "Hawaii: Desert Island" episode, Grylls makes a direct connection between his survival techniques and the struggles faced in post-cataclysmic disasters by telling the audience how survivors from the 2004 tsunami lived for over twenty-five days on coconuts alone.

On *Man vs. Wild,* safety is found in civilization, away from the wild. The challenge for Grylls is to find his way back to civilization within the course of the hour-long episode. He is accompanied by a camera crew, but, as he explains in each episode, the crew are only to intervene in a life or death situation. Grylls does not rely on the help of anyone else while trying to find his way back to safety, addressing anxieties about how to carry on when one does not know whether help is coming. Grylls spends little time attempting to alert potential rescuers to his whereabouts by using signals from smoke. Instead, he teaches the audience how to survive on our own.

Emblematic of Discovery Channel's commitment to educational and informational programming, *Man vs. Wild* focuses heavily on teaching the audience survival skills, as well as entertaining them. Grylls not only describes the process of building shelter and fire, he also explains in detail why each step is important. He teaches the audience the proper method for creating a "debris shelter" and explains precisely how much warmer one can expect to be while inside. He alerts the audience to potential threats from local animals and explains proper methods for avoiding any dangerous encounters. Grylls teaches us how to find local food sources, as seen in "African Savanna" when he bites the flesh directly off the half-eaten carcass of a zebra that was recently killed by a lion. For less dire circumstances, he explains how to forage for fallen avocados in "Costa Rican Rain Forest."

From the show and its accompanying website, it is clear that Discovery Channel intends for *Man vs. Wild* to serve as an educational tool for audiences, whether we wish to be prepared in the event of being unwillingly thrust into the wild or whether we enjoy the spectacle of wilderness struggle. The official *Man vs. Wild* webpage on the Discovery Channel website provides links for users to "Buy Emergency Gear." Such emergency gear includes rechargeable batteries, a solar-powered lantern, a first-aid kit, and the first season of *Man vs. Wild* on DVD. There is some evidence to suggest that Discovery's attempts to teach audiences how to survive nature successfully may be having a positive effect. In January 2008, three teenage boys were playing on a frozen pond in Binghamton, New York, when the ice broke, sending the youths into the water. After help arrived, the three claimed they were able to get out of the ice and stay warm because of survival techniques they learned while watching Grylls jump into a frozen lake on *Man vs. Wild*.

Survivorman, which premiered in August of 2005, is slightly different from *Man vs. Wild* because the host, survival expert Les Stroud, is completely alone without a camera crew during his survival period and he does all the filming himself. Similar to Bear Grylls, Stroud (who often refers to himself in the third person as "Survivorman") is stranded and must survive on his own for seven days. Like *Man vs. Wild, Survivorman*'s main focus is on educating the audience on proper survival skills in a variety of geographic landscapes.

Rather than visit popular tourist destinations such as the Rockies, an Alaskan mountain range, or the Sierra Nevada, Stroud centers each episode on a survival theme. In the episode "Winter Plane Crash," Stroud is stranded in a forest in the winter, as if his plane had crashed. He demonstrates how to secure the plane for shelter and disassemble the mechanics for useful spare parts. For the entirety of "Lost at Sea," Stroud lives on a small life raft attempting to find an island, as if his boat had sunk. He demonstrates how to build a canopy out of clothing to protect himself from the sun and how to fish using primitive tools. Like Grylls in *Man vs. Wild*, Stroud emphasizes self-reliance. His "goal" of outlasting the elements for seven days does not include searching for help or waiting for rescue. Playing on the anxieties of being isolated in nature, Stroud teaches the audience how to survive nature for as long as is necessary. Whereas Grylls is constantly on the move trying to reconnect with civilization, Stroud teaches how to build a sustainable camp that can serve as a home until help arrives.

In October of 2005, Discovery Channel premiered *I Shouldn't Be Alive*. Although this program differs from *Man vs. Wild* and *Survivorman* in both aesthetic and narrative terms, it shares the fourth wave focus on survival skills in the wake of disaster, education of the audience, and the capitalization on cultural anxieties that result from cataclysmic disasters. *I Shouldn't Be Alive* does not feature a survival expert, but rather allows real people to recount stories of survival, featuring reenactments and interviews with the people involved. *I Shouldn't Be Alive* shows the practical application of the skills related by Stroud and Grylls. Each episode presents the viewer with "The Dilemma," such as "Could you survive a helicopter crash into an inferno?" "Could you survive a fall off North America's highest peak?" and "Could you leave your dad alone in a wilderness full of grizzlies to save his life?" In the episode "Shipwrecked," the dilemma is "Could you survive on a deserted island?" In this episode, two cousins are shipwrecked off the Sea of Cortez while on a fishing trip and find their way to a deserted island where they fend for their lives against the elements and wildlife. They learn to live off the island as they begin catching and eating raw crabs and drinking the juice from local cacti. In the end, guests on the series relate their stories of surviving disaster as character-building experiences. As we watch these people attempt to survive in the wilderness, *I Shouldn't Be Alive* indirectly confirms the importance of the skills taught on *Survivorman* and *Man vs. Wild*.

Conclusion: Surviving On Television

Though these programs represent Discovery Channel's position that we can overcome the forces of nature, the production conditions of these shows might reflect a different standpoint. Allegations that Bear Grylls stayed at hotels in Iceland and received help from survival experts and production staff during the filming of the show cast doubt on the idea that survival in the wilderness can be reliably achieved by an individual's preparation and knowledge of the wild. By not including Grylls' shortcuts in the show, it becomes more obvious that Discovery Channel manipulates these situations to reflect a particular ideology—that, with knowledge, we can all discover how to overcome the threats of nature. Central to the ideological problematics of the series I have discussed is an ongoing suppression of structural support in favor of the drama of individual survival.

The Discovery Channel's mission and corporate context suggest the source of the discourses and ideologies presented on the shows. According to the Discovery website, the channel's mission is to bring "stories and experiences that share knowledge, satisfy curiosity and inspire the joy of discovery" to audiences. Since debuting in 1985, Discovery Channel has accumulated a history of educational and informational programming and an emphasis on science and nature documentaries. The schedule changed over the years, but a commitment to educational programming remained. Discovery Channel's parent company, Discovery Communications, also owns knowledge-themed channels such as The Learning Channel, Animal Planet, Travel Channel, Discovery Science, Discovery Health, and Discovery Kids. The nature-reality hybrid exhibits continuities with Discovery's educational mission and brand identity. Further research might investigate why nature-reality hybrid shows do not air on other channels with similar lineups and corporate motivations, such as TLC, Animal Planet, and Travel Channel.

It has been my argument here that Discovery Channel's nature-reality programs are heavily informed by popular memory of Hurricane Katrina. All premiering in the mid-2000s, fourth wave nature shows have met with considerable success. Discovery Channel has seen a 13 percent increase in ratings since revamping its lineup to focus more on educational shows, which consist largely of nature programming. *Survivorman* and *I Shouldn't Be Alive* both have contributed to this large jump in ratings. The most-watched nature-reality show, *Man vs. Wild*, is the fourth most-watched show on Discovery, right behind *American Chopper*, *Mythbusters*, and *Dirty Jobs*. Other fourth wave nature shows on Discovery Channel include *Deadliest Catch* (2005–present), *Going Tribal* (2005–2008), and *Everest: Beyond the Limit* (2006–2007). Discovery also programs second wave miniseries such as *Blue Planet* (2001) and *Planet Earth* (2006).

Nature programming on television draws from and contributes to the widespread cultural presence of anxieties about natural disasters, and they support cable channels' corporate motivations in an era of intensified niche cable competition. There is a financial stake in nature programs that address current issues regarding climate change and cataclysmic natural disaster. Even after the allegations that *Man vs. Wild* is staged, Discovery Channel renewed the show for a third season. *Survivorman* continues to draw large audiences, and other male-oriented shows such *Lobster Wars* (lobster fishermen survive the challenges of the sea) and *Deadliest Catch* (crab fishermen survive the challenges of the sea) continue to reflect Discovery Channel's stock response to cataclysmic nature: the mantra that with preparation, knowledge, and insight, we can survive the threat of the wild.

Notes

1. *Disaster Risk Reduction,* Center for Research on the Epidemiology of Disasters, 2007.
2. Jeffrey Sconce, *Haunted Media: Electronic Presence from Telegraphy to Television*, p. 6.
3. Ibid., p. 6.
4. Ibid., p. 199.
5. Ole J. Mjos, *Media Globalization and the Discovery Channel Networks*, p. 55.
6. *Emergency: This Book Will Save Your Life*, p. 92.
7. Ibid., p. 93.

8. "'Stanley Milgram, Allen Funt and Me:' Postwar Social Science and the 'First Wave' of Reality TV," p. 20.
9. Ibid., p. 22.
10. "'I Think We Need a New Name for It:' The Meeting of Documentary and Reality," p. 2.
11. "Primal Giggles: Thoughts on Reality Television's Recent Pieties and Parodies of the 'Masculine Primitive.'"
12. In this regard Discovery very much plays to its audience, which as Ole J. Mjos has noted is heavily male-skewing. In *Media Globalization and the Discovery Channel Networks* Mjos reports Neilson research that consistently ranks Discovery among the top ten networks for delivery of male adults aged eighteen-forty-nine and twenty-five-fifty-four (p. 37).
13. "'Man vs. Wild' host Grylls lives to tell about it."

CHAPTER 7

EXILE, RETURN, AND NEW ECONOMY SUBJECTIVITY IN *LAST HOLIDAY*

Diane Negra

Last Holiday (2006) tells the story of a working-class black woman who after a traumatic and unexpected development, leaves her home city of New Orleans for the first time, finally returning to it at the conclusion, a homecoming the film celebrates in a tableau sequence of community cohesion and female entrepreneurial success. Filmed before the storm, released in spring 2006, and publicized with the tagline "Enjoy yourself... Time is running out!," *Last Holiday* stands in uncanny relation to the (heavily African American) population dispersion from New Orleans after Hurricane Katrina. In this discussion I want to explore how an otherwise conventional chick flick empowerment narrative acquires unexpected resonances of cultural trauma.

It is important to consider a popular narrative of this kind because it generated understandings and fantasies about New Orleans at exactly the time when a set of governmental policies that would decisively shape the experience of storm survivors were being put in place with hardly any transparency, consultation, or even much national public concern. The acceptance of such governmental actions depended heavily on a consensus about what recovery should look like, whose concerns it should address and how healthy social and business climates are defined in the contemporary U.S. mindset. As George Lipsitz notes, "Policies implemented at the highest levels of government depend on the ideological legitimation they receive from cultural practices, stories, images, and ideas deeply rooted in the quotidian activities of life in the United States."[1]

Last Holiday's heroine Georgia Byrd (Queen Latifah) is a New Orleans shopclerk who has always lived cautiously and fully within her means, shirking romance with a fellow clerk out of reticence and engaging in symbolically maternal activities such as cooking for a young neighborhood boy named Darius. When mistakenly informed that she has a serious disease and only a short time to live, Georgia liquidates her bank account and travels to a luxury hotel in the Czech Republic where she undergoes a makeover, indulges her appetite to her heart's content, and finds herself mingling with a set of wealthy guests that (improbably) include the owner of the store where she used to work and a New Orleans politician. While imparting lessons to these characters about the psychic and communal costs of corporate greed and political duplicity, Georgia also bonds with French celebrity Chef Didier (Gerard Depardieu) whom she has always idolized. When Georgia's mistaken belief about her fatal illness is corrected, she finds love with her fellow shopclerk, returns to New Orleans and opens a restaurant, setting a scene of hometown rejuvenation sadly at odds with the actual status of New Orleans in 2006. In one respect however Georgia's concluding actions are entirely apposite; they are wholly even remarkably consistent with the recovery of the city imagined by George W. Bush who in his meretricious prime-time address to the nation from Jackson Square on September 15, 2005, promised that "the passionate soul of a great city will return" and expressed his belief that expanded commercial activity would be the salvation of the region saying "When the streets are rebuilt there should be many new businesses, including minority-owned businesses, along those streets."

In terms of its surface plot, *Last Holiday* initially appears a straightforward example of a variant of the contemporary "chick flick" Kimberly Springer has identified as the contemporary "black women's film" in which black women axiomatically "suffer, but are ultimately triumphant, having returned to a place from which they drifted and black family and community are regained."[2] Yet I want to show that the film in fact only nominally adheres to that definition and I want to stress that the peculiar way in which *Last Holiday* stages a fantasy of exile and idealized return is well suited to the post-Katrina moment. Crucially, Georgia emerges as an Old Economy figure registering a protest against the brutalities of the New Economy. Over the course of the film she collides with a store manager in thrall to the dubious wisdom of a financial self-help guru, an HMO administrator who tells her a life-saving surgery wouldn't be covered by her insurance plan, and airline staff who rebuke her for failing to let the man in front of her fully recline his seat into her lap. After this last incident, Georgia's decision to trade up to a luxurious first-class "capsule" mid-flight is indicative of the ways that the film's economic protest dies out (and is in fact replaced by a New Economy endorsement). A financially conservative, coupon-clipping woman all her life, Georgia's sense of empowerment after her diagnosis fuels a foray into the New Economy that the film paints as energizing and essential to the development of the right kind of female selfhood. This facilitates a conclusion that symbolically re-secures the hospitality industry in New Orleans and suggests a post-traumatic scene in which the city is economically refreshed, moving from outdated commercial models to newer entrepreneurial ones.

Central to the meanings of *Last Holiday* is the fact that the film is consistently and thoroughly informed by the acutely body-conscious persona of its star Queen Latifah (born Dana Owens). Discourses of race pride have worked throughout Latifah's career to "explain" her status as a voluptuous black woman. Yet as Cindy Childress points out "although Latifah is more full-bodied than a typical cover model, she has a traditional hourglass shape."[3] In this regard, she emblematizes the fact that "the right kind of body reinforces not only privileged social locations, but types of moralities and the performance of citizenship."[4] Although more generously proportioned than heavily sexualized celebrities such as Jennifer Lopez and Kim Kardashian, Latifah is nevertheless connected to such stars whose conspicuous or diffuse ethnic personae are validated by body types that are more curvaceous than the prevailing ideal.[5] A heavyset (yet shapely) black female body moreover has come to operate as a particular marker of racial authenticity as can be seen in the popular rhetoricizing of "realness" as an adjectival euphemism for black female pulchritude.

For my purposes, it will be useful to bear in mind how Latifah becomes a model minority in terms of her body, which is so often framed, as Childress puts it, as "an exotic interlude" from white, extremely slender body norms.[6] As she reminds us, "'Fat' is a feminist issue near the core of body politics and what it means to be a valuable woman in our society."[7] In *Last Holiday*, as we shall see, an emphasis on the body and its stability/mutability is suggestive in a post-Katrina context, when so many of those impacted by the storm sought to use their own bodies to assert their survivorhood, sense of affiliation with their battered city, and/or affinity with historical precedents to Katrina. These impulses took particular form in body art, which was so in demand in post-Katrina New Orleans, as Marline Otte has documented, that it required an influx of tattooists from elsewhere to accommodate the city's expanded clientele.[8]

Linda Mizejewski has pointed out that Queen Latifah "has achieved stardom with a physique that is unconventional in star culture, but her films—with one exception—have so far resisted centering her as part of a romantic couple."[9] Mizejewski's observation that in a film like *Bringing Down the House* (2003) Latifah's character "functions as a racial signifier rather than a romantic heroine" is equally applicable to *Last Holiday*. Here romance is shunted aside in favor of the heroine's other obligations. Her task is to sound a moral warning to the film's politicians and for this her reward is to (re)become the provident black mammy figure superficially updated as entrepreneur. Georgia infiltrates the world of class-based affluence and privilege but the film's conclusion emphasizes that she will not linger there. In this sense her moral reproach is analogous to the function of Katrina victims themselves who permeated the national consciousness, issued rebukes to power, and then receded. Clearly, part of the energy of the film is derived from the fear of an underclass black woman unmoored from her standard geography and let loose in the world. However, that energy is always already held in check by the film's status as a Queen Latifah star vehicle; here as elsewhere Latifah briefly ruptures white hegemony in order to make a limited socially therapeutic intervention upon it. Georgia's blunt common sense, habit of speaking truth to power, and ultimate rejection of cosmopolitanism in favor of the comforts of home are all consistent with Latifah's persona and cinematic track record.[10]

George Lipsitz reminds us that at the start of her career twenty years ago Latifah's racial signification worked in quite a different register.[11] Calling particular attention to Latifah's rap video "Ladies First," he points out that "During a decade when politicians and journalists in the USA regularly depicted Black women as unwed mothers and 'welfare queens' Latifah's video presented them as 'queens of civilization' and 'mothers' who 'give birth' to political struggle."[12] Linking Latifah to Paul Gilroy's notion of "diasporic intimacy," Lipsitz generates an account that helps us to perceive how a persona once rooted in post-diasporic affirmation has been recalibrated to elide the diasporic features of the post-Katrina experience. *Last Holiday* fits into a broader trajectory of recuperation in which the racial and class components of Latifah's persona are put in service of racial repression and fantasy entrepreneurialism. It is my aim here to investigate how and why the film goes to such lengths to reinstate its protagonist's economic citizenship.

The chick flick, dedicated as it is to reforming and emancipating women under duress, turns out to present an apposite generic form for exploring the concerns I have detailed. *Last Holiday* conforms to a number of recognizable chick flick narrative strategies; in its use of the false death threat to catalyze self-examination it resembles films such as *Life or Something Like It* (2002); in its use of the female cook as a figure of repressed emotion it stands alongside a range of films from *Like Water for Chocolate* (1992) to *No Reservations* (2007); in its conclusive emphasis on the emotional value of "home" and sense of pleasure in the transformative aesthetics of luxury consumption it can be linked to other similarly preoccupied chick flicks too numerous to count. Like a myriad of other postfeminist chick flick heroines, Georgia is placed to exert a softening and humanizing impact on the brutalities of the New Economy and her (true) work as a chef is in keeping with the care roles of a large number of similarly situated cinematic waitresses, flight attendants, nannies, and others of recent years. Where *Last Holiday* might be compared in some ways to the cycle of "tourist romances" in which an American heroine discovers her identity through a European romance and expatriation, *Last Holiday* ultimately deviates from the representational habits of that form as Georgia's experiences in Europe ultimately reinforce the necessity for her to return home.[13]

Despite the film's apparent valuing of home and hometown, the New Orleans summoned by *Last Holiday* appears blank and antiseptic as the film bids for an unproblematic regionalization attached to culture and cuisine. The film's close tie-in relationship to the Food Network saw Latifah cooking New Orleans specialties on the channel while in the film itself she prepares a meal in tandem with a televised Emeril Lagasse and the DVD extras include recipes for Bananas Foster and Poulet Tchoupitoulas.[14] Within the diegesis, New Orleans itself feels undefined and vacant; it sustains none of the characteristic urban romance associated so often with preferred chick flick cities such as New York, Chicago, and San Francisco. Any attempt at a fuller or more precise rendering of the city is quashed here; even brief references to an ailing New Orleans have been excised from the film's final cut. One of the deleted scenes features Georgia preparing to leave for Europe and saying goodbye to Darius when she unexpectedly and dramatically exhorts him, "Promise me one more thing. Get off these streets." Within the film's context though it's utterly unclear why she would have cause to say such a thing; this is a film that is unprepared to acknowledge urban blight or the hazards a young black child might face growing up in New Orleans. *Last Holiday*'s consternation about how to conceptualize its urban setting is further illustrated in the way that it evokes a New Orleans whose cultural characteristics are most fully expressed elsewhere—either in a racialized, regionalized joie de vivre expressed by Georgia in Europe or through marketing and merchandising initiatives that are not place-bound.

Last Holiday constitutes a modest attempt to manage the ideological contours of mobility in early twenty-first-century America. Mobility is a particularly vexed subject in American life; it centers some of our deepest cultural mythologies about opportunity and success and has been subject to persistent cultural blindness in a nation where vast internal working class migrations tend to go unnoticed (and of course immigrant journeys have been selectively sentimentalized and vilified). Many of the landmark cultural traumas of American history are associated with enforced migration, whether those of Native Americans, black Americans, or rural Southerners in the 1930s Dust Bowl.

A significant structuring element in the aftermath of Hurricane Katrina, of course, was anxiety about post-Katrina black underclass mobility; in September 2005 authorities sought to strictly control that mobility through an extraordinary set of tardy and badly managed evacuation initiatives.[15] In the days and weeks following Katrina, predominantly African American New Orleans residents were compelled into a mandatory mobility, sometimes separated from family members and with no control over (or sometimes foreknowledge of) their destination. In this period it was not uncommon for public officials and high-profile figures to express indifference to the domestic and communal stability of these citizens. Most notoriously, Barbara Bush, mother of the then current president and wife of the former president, visited Katrina evacuees at the Houston Astrodome, and made remarks that were then included in a September 5, 2005, broadcast of NPR's *Marketplace*[16]:

> "Almost everyone I've talked to says, 'We're going to move to Houston... What I'm hearing, which is sort of scary, is that they all want to stay in Texas. Everyone is so overwhelmed by the hospitality. And so many of the people in the arena here, you know, were underprivileged anyway, so this—this is working very well for them."

In *Last Holiday* the mobility associated with New Orleans becomes elective rather than mandatory and the film's narrative of personal and (implicitly) urban renewal may be seen to model an ideologically conservative psychological reconstruction process.

In part due to the expectations generated by a Queen Latifah star vehicle, *Last Holiday* works ultimately to position preparedness and recovery as personal rather than structural concerns. Georgia's situation both approximates and idealizes the conditions faced by many of Katrina's displaced victims and the film responds with surprising directness to the challenge Katrina constituted with respect to national mythologies. The storm was seen by many to have "flushed out" a set of citizens who couldn't be accounted for within early twenty-first-century paradigms of acceptable/comprehensible American experience and subjectivity. In *Last Holiday* the management of resistant/unruly/insurgent populations is recast as the faux problem of the unruly woman who is conclusively stabilized through her affinity to traditionalist roles and the moral value of enterprise as mobility shifts from being traumatic to productive.

One of the film's most important links to its Katrina context, I would argue, is the precipitating event of the plot—the diagnosis of Georgia's fatal illness. It is this element that pulls the film into a consistency with what Nicole R. Fleetwood has deemed the "necropolitics" of New Orleans, both pre- and post-Katrina. From the time she is diagnosed, Georgia's position approximates that of the underclass residents of New Orleans, part of that group of citizens who, according to Fleetwood, have been given the status of the "living dead."[7] Caught up in an event that furthered a preexisting narrative of decline and death around a city that stood conspicuously apart from millennial concepts of economic vigor, these citizens were quickly transformed into the abject black bodies so associated with the storm and its aftermath. The film's fantasy structures are built around the way that Latifah's unruly energies contest her diagnosed position as one of the "living dead," and the film proceeds from the point of her dramatic refusal of the stasis and social and ultimately biological death ascribed to her.

Under threat of death through most of the film, Georgia manifests a nothing left to lose sense of euphoria and much of the film's comedy is tied to her conspicuously undisciplined body and an unfettered sense of delight associated with it. Indeed, as I have suggested, it is worth emphasizing the amount of time that *Last Holiday* devotes to contemplation of Queen Latifah's star body and her associations with the enjoyment of food, her lack of athletic prowess, and sense of pleasure in luxury consumerism mostly in the form of glamorous clothing and spa treatments. Latifah's body substitutes for the abject bodies of the urban poor associated with Hurricane Katrina and is granted an unusual license to deviate from the postfeminist healthism that celebrates middle class white female bodies as projects of personal discipline and expressive selfhood.

Healthism, as Shari L. Dworkin and Faye Linda Wachs have argued, is reliant on a continual sense of "body panic" and it functions to promote the

> idea that the individual is responsible for the health of the self and the nation—to simultaneously displace critiques of the social structure onto individual bodily failures and onto gender relations, while stigmatizing those who fail to participate and succeed in the existing system, body panic marshals resources to a morally valued but socially depoliticized subject in their continual quest for bodily perfection.[18]

An assiduous healthism has flourished in contemporary U.S. culture both as a means of fortifying assumed hierarchies of public morality and to compensate for public health failures. Georgia's jubilant exceptionalism to the strictures of healthism is all the more striking when we bear in mind that one of the cultural norms many Katrina victims were perceived to have violated was that of "taking responsibility" for their health and well-being. Caricatures of the "deficient" citizenship of New Orleans residents relied upon a healthism that "operates to displace blame for structural scenarios that leave marginalized individuals with fewer and qualitatively worse options onto their assumed-to-be less moral actions or individuals bodies."[19] The stigmatization of Katrina-impacted populations along these lines is thus consistent with *Last Holiday*'s abandonment of its initial critique of institutional and economic discrimination.

Last Holiday's uncanny relation to the events associated with Hurricane Katrina is further borne out in a distinct pattern of inversions and reversals it sustains.[20] The most important of these has to do with nature. The film's wintry central European setting vividly contrasts with the sultry climate of New Orleans but provides a narratively justified means of staging over and over again the relation to nature and the impact of precipitation as cars break down on snowy roads, Georgia attempts skiing, and so on. A strange oblique awareness of the flooded city a New Orleans resident would have left behind in 2005 permeates the film and complicates its visual attentiveness to the vast accumulation of snow in the mountains of the Czech Republic. Aric Mayer has underscored the singularity of post-Katrina New Orleans in which nature and urban development briefly merged generating an eerily unprecedented scene:

> here, instead of explosions and fire, the more usual metaphors of destruction, this was an apocalypse of water, which is a very different thing. Throughout Western history, water has been a symbol of the unconscious, of the indwelling unrecognized forces and agencies that operate beneath the surface of our conscious lives. This is a fitting metaphor, for we are still untangling and discovering the unseen political and social influences that contributed to the disaster.[21]

In *Last Holiday* water becomes snow, Georgia's exuberant relationship to nature is set free in a climate altogether different from the one she has left behind and she discovers herself, manifesting a vigorous appetite for food and life itself in an environment that is both tied to and altogether different from that of her hometown.

Last Holiday presents a world in which all sources of official/authoritative information are revealed to be highly fallible. Its doctors, civic and corporate leaders are all deceptive and self-deceiving; their decisions are callous and error-prone. By contrast, the "warmer" hospitality professions are associated with emotional vibrancy and life truths ("You and I, we know the secret of life" says Didier to Georgia). While on the one hand, the film's corroboration of the mistrust of authority produces a congruence with the corporate and governmental malfeasance and "disaster apartheid" associated with Katrina, the nature of the film's conclusion sharply curtails the possibility of subsequent systemic critique. This is in keeping with the nature of the class promotions it stages and the regional fantasies it conjures. Central to *Last Holiday* is a contrast between rigid authoritarianism and the suppleness and even sensuality of creative practitioners. As she undergoes her change of state and status Georgia is moved to a position approximating that of Richard Florida's "creative class"—that privileged category of citizens who enjoy the resources and prerogatives of wealth and (marketable) skills and can enjoy a balance of global freedom of movement with local communal ties.

Georgia's transformation from service worker into a high-status member of the creative class converts her from alienation and subjection and endows her labor with the creativity and personal expressivity fantasized to be widely available in the New Economy though in fact restricted to a fortunate few. The positioning of such a figure in New Orleans highlights the extent of *Last Holiday*'s race, class, and regional disingenuousness for in fact Florida argued in *The Rise of the Creative Class* that pre-Katrina New Orleans exemplified the kind of American city that tried to stay current by attracting members of the creative class but failed (in comparison to cities such as Austin, San Francisco, and Chapel Hill). Florida identifies New Orleans as a "slow growth" city akin to Buffalo or Grand Rapids. He argues that "The economic divide in America is reflected in a new geography of class. The United States is caught in a pattern of uneven regional development not seen since the Civil War."[22] In many ways the story of Hurricane Katrina became a story of "catching up"—with global warming, with environmental degradation, with technologies that had been underused for storm preparedness, and for catching up with the reality of the stark economic/regional divide that exists in twenty-first-century America. *Last Holiday* gives us a heroine who catches up to and makes a place for herself in the New Economy. Toward this end, it emplots New Orleans into a fantasy geography of creativity even as the film's title hints at the more sober premise that one must economically innovate or die off. The film's oblique invocation of that category of people who enjoy the highest quality of life in millennial America is in keeping with its reliance overall on the self-actualizing rhetoric of both the New Economy and postfeminist cultural texts.

Georgia's "right of return" to New Orleans is predicated on her transformation into an ideal neoliberal subject. The film's juxtaposition of Gerard Depardieu and Queen Latifah's star personae underwrites a narrative process in which an expatriate Frenchman tutors a black American woman in the commodification of ethnicity. Occupying an approved economic role at the close of the film, Georgia has learned to market her own localism through the production of upmarket soul food for an affluent clientele. In this way, the fantasy of a regenerative New Orleans remaking itself after Katrina works to displace the structural causes of pre-Katrina urban blight.

As we have seen, the social, racial, and economic disclosures of Hurricane Katrina hold the potential to force narrative crisis, even in as rote a form as the chick flick. Analysis of *Last Holiday* offers evidence of the unconvincing fit between standard film formulae and the catastrophic economic, cultural, and human losses in New Orleans. As I briefly mentioned at the start of this volume, such a fit is seemingly also attempted in *The Princess and the Frog*, the Disney animated film that centralizes a character called Princess Tiana, a young woman living in the French Quarter during the Jazz Age.

In order to suggest that characters like Georgia Byrd in *Last Holiday* and Princess Tiana in *The Princess and the Frog* are part of a larger political process in which triumphant and transcendent black femininities symbolically neutralize political and social dilemmas associated with race, I want to conclude this essay with a discussion of the latter film, a high-profile 2009 Christmas release that was widely seen by children and parents seeking seasonal "family" entertainment. Like many other forms of popular entertainment that resonate in a post-Katrina context, *The Princess and the Frog* was almost always assessed without reference to the events of 2005, a phenomenon that in this instance may have been heightened by the ongoing cultural assumption that children's entertainment is apolitical.[23]

A comparison of *Last Holiday* with *The Princess and the Frog* highlights the way in which these popular entertainment forms place the culinary entrepreneurialism and redemptive decency of a black female as "blocks" against any acknowledgment of race, class, and gender inequities. Both films visualize local urban sociality through the repeated image of the St. Charles streetcar and stress a New Orleans characterized by "spirit" and "spice" (although in *Last Holiday* this is more rhetorical than actual given the film's bleak early depiction of the city). *The Princess and the Frog*'s Tiana is an exemplar of rectitude, virtue, and resolve who soberly attests that "The only way to get what you want in this world is hard work." The film manifests a certain amount of consternation about Tiana's ambition (though it is clearly the driving force of her character) and seeks to counterbalance it by paying lip service to a vaguely articulated notion of "what's really important" (when Tiana misinterprets one of voodoo priestess Mama Odie's pronouncements as reinforcement of her need to be resolute in her quest to open a restaurant, we are meant to be disappointed in her and Tiana soon appreciates that the attainment of "true love" is her imperative). Like *Last Holiday*'s Georgia, Tiana needs an opportunity to loosen up ("You do not know how to have fun," she is told by the suavely amphibian Prince Naveen) and this is orchestrated in an adventure plot where in the course of their efforts to find Mama Odie the downtrodden waitress and visiting royal fall in love over a meal of "swamp gumbo" Tiana has prepared.[24]

Like her counterpart in *Last Holiday*, Tiana has a culinary gift, one that carries socially unifying benefits. Early on in the film, Tiana's father, a source of inspiration to her and a character whose own aspirations were never gratified, tells Tiana "you can do anything you set your mind to" and speaks of the social power of good food to bring people together. The restaurant Tiana aspires to open, Tiana's Place, "will be the crown jewel of the Crescent City" and will require the renovation of a dilapidated old sugar mill. Although Tiana is working several jobs and saving all she can, the realtors who have sold her the mill tell her that they have received a better offer and unless she can top it she'll lose out to the other buyer. The film's conclusion disguises how financing is achieved emphasizing instead a totalizing transcendence achieved by the heroine upon her marriage to Naveen and acquisition of princesshood. The film's strenuous efforts to inoffensively fantasize upward mobility are one of the elements that rendered it safe and dull for some critics.[25]

Another element the two films hold in common is their mutual formulation of female access to power, commerce, and self-gratification in the discursive terms of royalty. Queen Latifah's royal status is self-proclaimed and transparently fictionalized. *The Princess and the Frog* disingenuously positions Tiana's princesshood as incidental but it is in fact the project of the film for her to become the bride of Prince Naveen.[26] Her qualifications for this role (just as are Latifah's for her queenly status) are moral; both films are invested in a mingling of populism and royalty, establishing that these female "royals" are deserving subjects who see their dreams fulfilled because of their decency and humility.[27] Their elevation to positions of power and elite realms is justified because from those positions they will gently and modestly assert a moral politics. Latifah's Georgia Byrd does this through her rehabilitation of the corporate tycoons she mingles with in the Czech Republic while Tiana does so through her commitment to "remember what's really important" as well as her redemptive influence upon Prince Naveen, a shallow and extravagant playboy at the start of the film who comes to appreciate deeper values by falling in love with Tiana. At the same time, these female protagonists' "royal" status also serves to emphasize that they are one-time exceptions to a status quo in which (minority) female ambition remains culturally problematic.

The Princess and the Frog's Tiana graduates into an elite class of privilege, while Georgia has a sanctioned short-term experience of life in such a class. Both films' stagings of triumphant closure resonate within a contemporary dynamic sketched by Kimberly Springer in which "popular media reveal the attempted erasure of black collectivity in favor of black individualism with nods toward 'giving back to the community' as the black contribution to the redistributive reconfiguration of civil rights into a diluted post-racialism."[28] While it lies beyond my scope to fully assess here, I would also tentatively assert that fictions of this kind fit into what Rebecca Wanzo has identified as a protocol of "sentimental political storytelling" that carefully emphasizes and suppresses aspects of black women's experience, often concealing structural and state injuries as personal and private.[29] Springer's work helps to delineate how a shift in media coverage to disproportionate emphasis on a high-profile elite black class conceptually reinforces "a new blackness as individual striving"[30] that may be coming to be a hallmark feature of the post-Katrina representational era.

Last Holiday and *The Princess and the Frog*, I have argued, operate as narratives of black female transcendence positioned to displace the actual social outcomes of Katrina. *Last Holiday*, as we have seen, undertakes an emphatically individualized revitalization project—relieved of her death sentence, the heroine is spectacularly rejuvenated, rewarded with romance and enterprise.[31] Yet one reason why the film's revitalization project feels so narrow and unconvincing is that Georgia has not so much reintegrated into her community as she has repositioned herself for a New Economy in which the provision and performance of cultural authenticity underwrites what Clyde Woods has referred to as the "low wage tourism development model."[32] Narratives such as *Last Holiday* and *The Princess and the Frog* strikingly rewrite the realities of showplace restauranting and culinary tourism in a post-Katrina New Orleans in many ways recommitted to such a model while fantasy figures such as Georgia and Tiana work to elide the conspicuous lack of business opportunity and capital faced by the majority of African Americans in New Orleans.[33]

The films I have discussed here romantically render a world in which "the values of the market and the ruthless workings of finance capital become the template for organizing the rest of society" and where "responsible citizens are replaced by an assemblage of entrepreneurial subjects."[34] Fictions of this kind exhibit a consistent tendency to be historically, economically, and racially evasive even while they are steeped in the tenets of neoliberal global capitalism. Setting such fictions against one another and in context offers the best means currently available to map the prospects and limits of the post-Katrina filmic unconscious.

Notes

1. "Learning from New Orleans: The Social Warrant of Hostile Privatism and Competitive Consumer Citizenship," p. 455.
2. "Divas, Evil Black Bitches and Bitter Black Women: African American Women in Postfeminist and Post-Civil-Rights Popular Culture," p. 272.
3. "*Glamour*'s Portrayal of Queen Latifah: Another Unreal Ideal," p. 85.
4. Shari L. Dworkin and Faye Linda Wachs, *Body Panic: Gender, Health and the Selling of Fitness*, p. 11.
5. For pertinent discussions of the fetishization of Lopez and Kardashian, see Mary C. Beltran, "The Hollywood Latina Body as Site of Social Struggle: Media Constructions of Stardom and Jennifer Lopez's 'Cross-Over' Butt"; and Candice Haddad, "Keeping Up with the Rump Rage: E's Commodification of Kim Kardashian's Assets."
6. "*Glamour*'s Portrayal of Queen Latifah: Another Unreal Ideal," p. 85.
7. Ibid., p. 87.
8. "The Mourning After: Languages of Loss and Grief in Post-Katrina New Orleans."
9. "Queen Latifah, Unruly Women and the Bodies of Romantic Comedy."
10. Latifah's populist persona was strikingly in evidence in her prominent placement at the funeral of Michael Jackson on July 7, 2009. The first non-religiously affiliated speaker at the event, she placed a strong emphasis on Jackson's "ordinary" fans announcing, " I'm here representing millions of fans around the world who grew up listening to Michael, being inspired and loving Michael from a distance (and with a gesture indicating the audience) like all of you."
11. If Latifah's persona had already been considerably sanitized by the time she appeared in *Last Holiday*, it is worth noting that her association through the film to a post-Katrina New Orleans was part of a much broader "celebritization" phenomenon in which the storm and its aftermath served as opportunities for celebrities (from Celine Dion to Brad Pitt to Sean Penn) to reinforce the ideological contours of their personae and for others to build a significant new level of public awareness (Anderson Cooper). I should add that I don't mean to fault the probably well-intentioned behavior of these celebrities, particularly Pitt, whose efforts to speak candidly about the environmental and industrial causes of the levee failures and to play a role in re-building the city seem both sincere and praiseworthy. Brenda Weber also discusses "celebritization" in her essay for this volume. See p. 190.

12. "Diasporic Noise: History, Hip Hop, and the Postcolonial Politics of Sound," p. 180.
13. My sense is that the reason for this deviation is linked to the centering of a black woman in the narrative. The "tourist romance" is typically anxious about its heroine's whiteness and seeks a way to enliven her by connecting her to ethnicity. *Last Holiday* lacks this obligation/interest.
14. Celebrity chef Lagasse voices alligator character Marlon in *The Princess and the Frog*, a film to which I compare *Last Holiday* near the close of this essay. Lagasse's presence furthers an emphasis on culinary localism in both films as he is well known for his promotion of New Orleans-style cuisine (with a particular emphasis on "spice" and "heat") and maintains a persona sourced in New Orleans regionalism (despite being born in Massachusetts).
15. This anxiety played comedically throughout the sixth season of the satirical HBO series *Curb Your Enthusiasm* in which Larry and Cheryl David take in an African American family, "The Blacks," who are displaced after Hurricane "Edna."
16. Similar reasoning was expressed by Italian prime minister Silvio Berlusconi after an earthquake devastated the Italian city of L'Aquila in April 2009. The prime minister counseled homeless residents living in tents that they should think of themselves "as being on a camping weekend." See John Hooper, "Berlusconi: Italy Earthquake Victims Should View Experience as Camping Weekend."
17. See Fleetwood's essay "Failing Narratives, Initiating Technologies: Hurricane Katrina and the Production of a Weather Media Event."
18. *Body Panic: Gender, Health and the Selling of Fitness*, p. 104.
19. Ibid., p. 165.
20. I thank Alan Nadel for suggesting this point in a discussion at the Society for Cinema and Media Studies meeting in 2008.
21. "Aesthetics of Catastrophe."
22. *The Flight of the Creative Class*, p. 188.
23. *Entertainment Weekly* film reviewer Lisa Schwarzbaum was unusual in making mention of Katrina in her review of the film. Schwarzbaum wrote, "The story also happens to be set in an idealized New Orleans of an earlier time, a city whose historic beauty and cultural importance will forever be filtered by contemporary adults through grimmer awareness of the natural and man-made disaster of Hurricane Katrina." "The Princess and the Frog," p. 75.
24. In the course of the film's development "Tiana" was changed from "Maddie," a name that was judged too plebian-sounding and according to some critics too much like "Mammy," while the character's work as a maid was revised to waitressing.

25. Arguably, *The Princess and the Frog* is one of a growing number of chick flick narratives that employ cookie cutter romance plots to give cover to the heroine's commercial and creative interests. Writing of the implausible romance between Tiana and Naveen, Wesley Morris notes "The fairy tale here is ultimately a business transaction. She doesn't love his money but it is nice to have, no?" "The Princess and the Frog: Different Princess, Same Dilemma."
26. And of course *The Princess and the Frog* is committed to expanding (notably in racial terms) a pantheon of Disney princesses that encompasses among others Cinderella (*Cinderella*, 1950), Princess Aurora (*Sleeping Beauty*, 1959), Ariel (*The Little Mermaid*, 1989), and Princess Giselle (*Enchanted*, 2007), a representational tradition the studio enshrines in its Disney Princesses website (http://disney.go.com/princess). However the film participates more broadly in "princessing" as a bona fide cultural and representational phenomenon of at least a decade's duration. I discuss this multifaceted and hyper-commodified phenomenon in *What a Girl Wants?: Fantasizing the Reclamation of Self in Postfeminism*, pp. 48–49.
27. In the case of *The Princess and the Frog* Tiana is also tipped as royalty through her exhibition of a standard repertoire of traits handed down from the Disney tradition of representing "princesses." As Elizabeth Bell writes, "Royal lineage and bearing are personified in the erect, ceremonial carriage of ballet" and "the heroines' graceful solitude and poised interactions with others." "Somatexts at the Disney Shop: Constructing the Pentimentos of Women's Animated Bodies," p. 111.
28. "Hate the Game, Not the Playa: Unmasking Neoliberal Articulations Amongst the Black Power Elite."
29. See her book *The Suffering Will Not Be Televised: African American Women and Sentimental Political Storytelling*.
30. "Hate the Game, Not the Playa: Unmasking Neoliberal Articulations Amongst the Black Power Elite."
31. The effects of the film's revitalization project are surely heightened and intensified by Queen Latifah's status as an icon of early twenty-first-century American blackness. Latifah, it should be noted, is herself a highly enterprising figure who has attached her celebrity to a wide range of corporeally themed brands including Jenny Craig weight loss products and her signature "Queen Collection" of makeup for Cover Girl.
32. "Katrina's World: Blues, Bourbon, and the Return to the Source," p. 447.
33. For a recent example of the positioning of New Orleans as a "foodie" destination of choice, see "The Allure of New Orleans," an account of Adam Pitluk's New Orleans visit that appeared in the widely

distributed airline seatback magazine *American Way*. Pitluk asserts that "The Crescent City is back, and in a serious way. Ironically, my birthday trip coincided with the fourth anniversary of Hurricane Katrina... These days I go down there for food and music... On the plane ride home, I was full and happy."

34. Henry Giroux, *Stormy Weather: Katrina and the Politics of Disposability*, pp. 83–84.

CHAPTER 8

MEDIA ARTISTS, LOCAL ACTIVISTS, AND OUTSIDER ARCHIVISTS: THE CASE OF HELEN HILL

Dan Streible

The traumatic events wrought by Katrina floodwaters in 2005 exposed painful aspects of the social fabric of New Orleans and the nation generally. Class- and race-based inequities were laid bare. The failure of the government at every level became obvious. Yet the post-Katrina spotlight also inadvertently illuminated a small but significant community of independent media artists working devotedly in old and new media forms. Some are amateurs, in the purest sense. Others are working professionals making small films as an avocation. Still others cobble together piecework and part-time projects that allow them to pursue their creative talents—getting grants, work-for-hire, teaching gigs, and freelance projects. Neither dilettantes nor careerists, they integrate homemade media into their everyday lives, often affiliating their practice with local social and political activism. The filmmaker Helen Hill, we now understand, is a radiant emblem of this community.

Still coping with the ripples of devastation that followed the "federal floods" of 2005, the New Orleans alternative media community was staggered by the unexpected death of Hill, an artist-activist-*animatrice* killed in her home on January 4, 2007, by an armed intruder. Linked to Katrina's aftermath and the traumatic violence associated with it, Hill's murder also shone a national spotlight on the alternative media culture of which she was an integral part. That community continued to produce old and new media, even in those worst of times in and after 2005.

Alternative media practitioners in New Orleans are linked via ad hoc means to accordant ones elsewhere. There exists, in fact, an under-examined but extensive, discrete community of North American media artists who work in the mode of Helen Hill. Our knowledge of their presence is muted by its localism and its disinterest in distribution and profit. With its accessible styles and DIY practices this populist vanguard of filmmakers differentiates itself from the "difficult" works of the better-known avant gardes of New York, San Francisco, Toronto, and other capitals of culture. The funky otherness of New Orleans, which has famously produced so much music and literature of influence, has also been fertile ground for an unseen cinema.

How does this nearly-off-the-grid creative culture sustain itself? How in particular did and does twenty-first-century New Orleans cultivate it, pre- and post-Katrina? During and after Helen? The answers to these questions lead to a reassessment of the contemporary environment for alternative media production and experimental film. In this context the case of "NewOrleansHelen" (to use her e-mail handle) illuminates three insights about recent media history and practices. First, this unassuming activist web of media artists not only exists, it has had a tangible, salutary impact on the world beyond the arts sector. Second, this decentralized network of DIY filmmakers has forged a relationship with a new generation of like-minded moving image archivists, who share a devotion to the materiality of film, small-screen projection of small-gauge celluloid, and its noncommercial applications. Third, neither media historiography nor critical theory have adequately accounted for the utopian cinema of which Helen Hill is an exemplar.

When she died at age thirty-six, Helen was not a famous filmmaker. However, media coverage of her death brought belated but entirely merited recognition of her artistic accomplishments, culminating in 2009 with the Librarian of Congress naming her film *Scratch and Crow* (1995) to the National Film Registry of culturally significant works. Helen integrated her creative work into a Goldmanesque life of sweet humanitarian anarchism and her legacy continues to impact independent media arts in New Orleans and elsewhere. In the past few years, memorialization of her life and work and perpetuation of her creative practices have occurred via film restorations, screenings, tributes, benefits, musical performances, workshops, DVD distribution, web-based media, broadcast coverage, published writing (poetic, scholarly, and journalistic), philanthropy, educational programs, festival awards, and other means.

Helen Hill's Life and Work

Helen Wingard Hill was born and raised in Columbia, South Carolina, a university town and a capital city, but not one known for filmmaking. Yet here she was exposed to film, via the kinds of alternative means most accounts of media history and culture ignore. Inspired by a classroom visit from documentary filmmaker Stan Woodward in 1981, Helen made two Super 8mm films that year. When she was ten years old, the first was produced as part of a visual literacy program organized in public schools by the South Carolina Arts Commission. *Quacks*, a comic sketch about a giant duck's encounter with kids at a school bus stop, included her name alongside five of her fifth-grade classmates. At age eleven, she also made a tabletop stop-motion film at home, *The House of Sweet Magic*, showing a pixilated gingerbread construction eaten by a dragon. Although it would be a decade before she made another movie, these juvenilia resemble, in style and theme, the work she produced as an adult.

Attending Harvard from 1988 to 1992, Helen pursued creative writing and participated in a variety of artistic endeavors. On her application she had noted "I would like to learn more about the techniques and opportunities in the film medium, especially animation," adding that she saw this as a way "to help society recognize its faults and see solutions."[1] In 1990 she made the hand-drawn, three-minute piece *Rain Dance* in an animation course taught by Suzann Pitt. Like much of her later work it had a musical center, illustrating a song cowritten by her then-boyfriend Elijah Aron and her later-husband Paul Gailiunas, with the latter singing it. *Vessel* (1992) took a similar form, but was based on her poem and added extensive cut-out figures in the style of Lotte Reiniger.

After graduation, Helen and Gailiunas went to New Orleans for the summer and stayed a year. They soon became a couple, and married in Columbia two years later. Helen left her mark in the Crescent City, publishing an article on experimental animation and her poem "Vessel," both in the local literary journal, the *New Laurel Review*. After their Louisiana stint, both Paul and Helen headed off to professional schools. He studied medicine in Nova Scotia, becoming an MD in 1997. She accelerated through a program in experimental animation at the California Institute of the Arts, earning an MFA in 1995. At CalArts, Helen enlisted friends and classmates to shoot *The World's Smallest Fair* (1995), a pixilated live-action film. Ostensibly a fantasy about monsters attacking fairground-goers, the film features an out-of-control cotton-candy machine as its comic center. Her thesis film *Scratch and Crow* (1995) demonstrated a more accomplished hand and contemplative soul at work. In rich colors and poetic text she creates a spiritual homage to her favorite animal, the chicken. Nicknamed Chicken from childhood, Helen made the bird a recurring motif in nearly all of her work.

For the next five years, Helen and Paul lived in Halifax, where she joined the Atlantic Filmmakers Cooperative (AFCOOP), teaching animation workshops there and courses at Nova Scotia College of Art and Design. In 1995, she helped found a women's film festival, Reel Vision. Notes for a Winnipeg retrospective of her work in 2009 offered that, on a list of those "who made a significant impact on the Halifax film community," the "name that stands out strongest is the late animator Helen Hill. Nobody who worked with or encountered Hill in Halifax has ever forgotten her."[2]

Through AFCOOP Helen was able to make *Tunnel of Love* (1996). With its carnival setting and narrative about best friends falling in love, the film can be read as autobiographical allusion to the couple's experiences of the Crescent City in 1992. A more specific reference to both Halifax and New Orleans appears in Paul's song and Helen's film *Bohemian Town* (2004), which is quite simply a love letter from the new New Orleaneans to their Haligonian friends in the bohemian North End. Helen draws the town as a utopia in motion, where skateboarding punk-rockers join with gray-hairs in spray-painting "No War" graffiti, cars cruise by the Food Not Bombs stand, kids and animals dance in the street, and friends bicycle, all living "la vie bohème."

The time in Canada was productive for Helen Hill the filmmaker and educator. Having married a Canadian, she became a citizen herself. Canada was, she said, "a great place to get grants." This she did, making her two most lauded works, *Mouseholes* (1999) and *Madame Winger Makes a Film* (2001). She was also able to freelance, doing animation for CBC-TV's educational series *StreetCents* (1997–1998) and storyboarding for National Film Board projects.

Additionally, Helen found a niche making silent films that she processed, tinted, and doctored by hand. For the rest of her life she conducted "film bees," opening her home to amateurs and neophytes, teaching them to shoot, develop, and project Super 8 and 16mm movies in a day. At the 2000 Splice This! Super 8 Film Festival in Toronto, she curated *The Halifax Ladies Film Bee*, a compilation of these homemade movies. Otherwise, she conducted community film bees solely as generous acts of social and aesthetic pleasure. The many artisanal films made in this context seldom got projected outside of domestic or community settings. Yet small groups of viewers got to engage with this work, usually over tea, in the intimacy of an unpretentious salon.

Helen's own such films continued her animalier devotions. *I Love Nola* (1998) was a portrait of her pet cat, whose naming presaged the return to New Orleans. During a residency at Phil Hoffman's Film Farm in Ontario, she made the hand-tinted *Your New Pig is Down the Road* (1999) as a surprise announcement to her husband that, in fact, his new Vietnamese pot-bellied piglet was awaiting him. The whimsical *Film for Rosie* (2000) was her portrait of said pig and its blood relatives.

Mouseholes and *Madame Winger* were more elaborate projects, crafted over longer periods of time. Each mixed cel, cut-out, and cameraless animation techniques with live action, pixilation, found footage, home movies, voice-over narration, and soundtracks. Although made mostly in Canada, both dealt with the American South. *Mouseholes* became her signature film, an autobiographical remembrance of her maternal grandfather's life and death in Columbia. Speaking from a child's perspective, Helen narrates the story in her own quiet, breathy voice. We also hear homemade audio recordings of Helen talking with the dying "Pop." Expressions of intimacy and grief here infuse a transcendent work with the magical thinking of animation, transforming the human figure into a mouse, who silently, innocently, negotiates material and spiritual realms.

Mouseholes is the most praised Helen Hill work, but *Madame Winger Makes a Film* may be her most popular. With Helen's whiskey-voiced godmother providing narration in a genteel Southern accent, the ten-minute movie is couched as an instructional film. She explains the fundamentals of film stocks, gauges, processing, and cameras, extolling the fun to be had in making one's own films. We see Helen's hands drawing and scratching on unexposed strips of celluloid, and the outcome of such animation. When Hill family movies of 1970s South Carolina appear, Madame tells us they document her youth as "a true Southern belle." Subtitled *A Survival Guide for the 21st Century*, the film acknowledges that celluloid is a shrinking presence in the age of digital video.

In a coda, Helen appears on camera, unfurling a spiral-bound publication, *Recipes for Disaster: A Handcrafted Film Cookbooklet*. The closing title card instructs that copies of the book can be ordered by e-mailing NewOrleansHelen. In 1999 and 2000 Helen traveled to workshops in Vancouver, Calgary, and Toronto, collecting notes and technical tips from artists making handcrafted cinema and following up with postcards seeking more. Completed for the 2001 SpliceThis! festival, the self-published anthology continues to circulate among media artists and university production courses. Thirty-seven filmmakers contributed texts and drawings to the *Recipes* sourcebook. Helen distributed copies by mail order, asking only for the photocopying and postage. She added updates in 2004, and a final one on November 16, 2005:

> Since moving to New Orleans five years ago, my husband Paul and I had become part of a fun, progressive, and artistic community. I never expected that it could all disappear so quickly. When Hurricane Katrina hit, our friends scattered everywhere. It has been a strange, surreal time. But people are already coming together in surprising ways to help out and rebuild. This new edition of *Recipes for Disaster* is a case in point.

Writing from Columbia, in temporary exile, she reported that all of the originals and copies of *Recipes*—along with 90 percent of their household possessions—had been destroyed by the flood. Her filmmaking friend in San Francisco, Alfonso Alvarez, "wanted to publish a special post hurricane edition."

> When I first made this book, the whole point was to bring together the scattered community of artists making handmade films. These folks are creative powers, inventing their own recipes and methods. Hundreds more have written me for their own copy of *Recipes for Disaster*, and so this community quietly grows. Now this DIY film community is coming to the rescue. This is a great help and gets this information out there while I figure out what to do next.

Since that time, photocopies of photocopies continue to circulate and find their way into university courses and libraries. A digitized version posted online after Helen's death multiplied the number of users.[3]

Driven by a love for the city and wanting to work where they were most needed, Helen and Paul moved to Mid-City New Orleans in late December 2000. The predominantly African American neighborhood was among the city's poorest. "Dr. Paul" set up Little Doctors Neighborhood Clinic, providing low-cost medical care for the poor, and together the couple established a chapter of the vegetarian antiwar group Food Not Bombs. Helen soon made a positive impact on the alternative media scene, although she realized that relocation to Louisiana was not a careerist's move. "Some people wouldn't live here as a filmmaker," she said in a 2003 interview, "but I don't mind being out of the loop, because I'm making my little films, and I can always send them out to the world." Helen became active in production, exhibition, curating, and teaching, joining in the work of the New Orleans Video Access Center, the Zeitgeist Multi-disciplinary Arts Center, and schools including the New Orleans Center for the Creative Arts (NOCCA).

In 2002, Helen cofounded the New Orleans Film Collective with Wise Wolfe and Dean Pascal. They wanted to "provide a place where people can learn to make films at very low costs and where they can rent gear at a low cost," she said in an interview for *Timecode: NOLA*, a local cable television program. "Hopefully with our workshops—and class shows after the workshops—we'll build up a filmmaking community."[4] This they did, with Helen offering her handmade movie classes. To process the celluloid, the film collective borrowed the darkroom of the nearby housing collective, Nowe Miasto (Polish for New City). Though she jokingly called it a "punk rock warehouse," the three-story structure was renovated in 1999 as communal housing, with a library, art and performance space, and meeting rooms for activist groups. After Katrina, Nowe Miasto reorganized in utopian but pragmatic ways. The democratic "limited equity housing cooperative" aspires to generate "safe, affordable, sustainable, and self-determined communities" that are "racially and economically just," and supportive of "art, music, and activism."[5] Helen's later Film Collective workshops also convened at Fair Grinds Coffeehouse, another Mid-City public space supporting local arts and community activism.[6]

The list of creative work Helen did in New Orleans speaks to the unmapped history of filmmaking and media practices under consideration here. Although she created dozens of pieces, a traditional filmography might mislead one to think that Helen Hill produced no films of her own in these six years. *Bohemian Town* and *Madame Winger* began in Halifax, but were completed in New Orleans. Her 2001 film *5 Spells* survived only on a low-quality VHS assemblage. Two original films were incorporated into local puppet theater productions, Haley Lou Haden's *By Bread Alone* and *One Life, Magic Cone* (*ca.* 2003). In the former, the Queen of Breadland puppet learns her duties by watching an instructional film, credited to "the National Film Board of Breadland." Moreover, two completed works were done in tandem with NOCCA colleague Courtney Egan. In homage to experimental cineaste Stan Brakhage and his 1963 film *Mothlight*, they made the abstract animation *Termite Light* (2003), sticking the locally indigenous detritivores to 16mm film stock. And, in a high note of her career, Helen received a Rockefeller Foundation Media Arts Fellowship in 2004. With it she began production of a longer-form animation about a local artisan, Florestine Kinchen, whose dressmaking she hoped to save from obscurity.

Yet another creative achievement from the New Orleans years is the series of short online movies Helen and Paul completed each October. For the collective public art project Gothtober, thirty-one media artists each contribute a Flash animation for "Gothtoberfest." The Halloween-themed website, produced by Juliana Parr, is formatted like an Advent calendar. For their window, Helen annually illustrated an original song that Paul sang and recorded. The first, *Rosie Wonders What to Wear* (2003), featured drawings and photographs of the family pet pig dressed in Halloween costumes. It includes a sadly ironic end-title: "Ms. Hill also runs Films for Funerals, a company which assists people as they direct short personal films, made to be screened at their own funerals." Birth and love, however, were the themes of *Gothtober Baby* (2004). Posted shortly before the birth of son Francis Pop on October 15, 2004, the dark comedy of the song and drawings advise, in Helen's poetry: "A perfect chick is what she'd like but you can never tell / until it exits, what it's like from toe to fontanelle / But every mom should love a child distorted or obscene / and don't forget to dress it up every Halloween."

The following year, barely more than a month after Katrina, Helen and Paul persisted with their Gothtober contribution *Halloween in New Orleans* (2005). Its on-screen dedication was to "all the neighborhood kids who filled our porch last Halloween... Hurricane Katrina emptied our neighborhood and scattered all of them to unknown places." As drawings and photographs of the couple's flooded home parade by, the dark lyrics laugh in the face of death and chuckle at catastrophe.

> Now the city streets are empty 'neath the pale white moon
> Instead of little children there is only gloom
> The houses are all haunted, that is just assumed
> Down in New Orleans

Now you can see the ghost of the Zulu King
And you can see the ghost of the Voodoo Queen
You can see the ghost of just about anything
'Cause everyday is Hallowe'en down in New Orleans.

The use of self-made media to inspire continued with *A Monster in New Orleans* (2006) in which The Creeps (Paul Gailiunas, with Keith Rogers and Christian Repaal) perform the eponymous rockabilly song. A green cut-out monster interacts with Helen's black-and-white photographs, taken "in early October, over a year since the hurricane," we are told. "With the burnt out houses, doors left wide open, gigantic trash piles and overgrown yards, New Orleans is a perfect hideout for monsters."[7] As modest as these productions are, they are part of an alternative media community's efforts to rebuild and fortify itself. Against all expectations, they confront the monsters of despair that threatened the returning diaspora and resound with the genuine cheer and optimism of a New Orleans that plays on while national media dwell on the desolation. The life-affirming power of homemade media is even further demonstrated in the Gothtober entry *Francis Pop's Hallowe'en Parade* (2007). The backyard Super 8 film "by Francis Pop and Paul Gailiunas," made "With Love for Helen," shows the couple's three-year-old son modeling costumes.

More remarkable is *Cleveland Street Gap* (2006), a second Hill/Egan production. A cinematic elegy, it merges distressed fragments from Helen's pre-Katrina home movies (shot in summer 2003) with Egan's post-Katrina video documenting the same locations in June 2006. Soft-focus black-and-white images of Paul joyfully playing with children on Cleveland Avenue match-dissolve to sharp color video of their abandoned shotgun house. Helen's graffiti on the wall of the front porch reads "We are all okay, cats, baby Pop, even Rosie the pig!!! We miss y'all! {heart}, Helen & Paul." The film-video collaboration was done with Helen still in South Carolina, trying to "figure out what to do next."

Cleveland Street Gap was a brave creative response to disaster and grievous loss. Its emotional power and personal resonances represent the type of work that DIY media artists and amateurs can achieve, and which commercial film and television cannot match. Most well-intentioned independent documentary features also fall short of such empowering work. For example, *The Axe in the Attic* (2007) documents Ed Pincus and Lucia Small's response to watching the television news coverage of New Orleans drowning. Living in New York, they drive south, admitting stereotypical trepidations about Dixie. The impotent feelings of rage, fear, and grief they hoped to counter by going to Louisiana are instead reiterated. They find their role as social documentarians dismissed by the magnitude of destruction and the despair of Katrina evacuees. Within the film itself, the most powerful footage is amateur home video shot by Linda Dumas, a working-class African American woman, who narrates the flood destruction in real time. "What you're looking at," she tell us as we see a street with automobiles under water, "is the first floor apartment in the St. Bernard Housing Development, where I happen to live." She turns her camera on herself, creating a tight close-up, and yells "And all my shit is gone!" Based on what we see of Dumas's footage in *The Axe in the Attic*, her brave, defiant, and raw video is as communicative and expressive as any professional reworking of it could be.[8]

Moments such as this are exceptional, but not unique. Historians and archivists increasingly value noncommercial video documentation, taking particular interest after the events of 2005. The University of New Orleans has partnered with George Mason University's Center for History and New Media to create an ambitious project, the Hurricane Digital Memory Bank (HDMB). In "The Post-Katrina Documentary Impulse and New Media" (2007), historian Michael Mizell-Nelson describes how the initiative valorizes both raw amateur video and edited pieces.[9] Examples of the latter include the curated, online New Orleans Video Access Center Short Documentary Series, done in the mode of community-made activist production. In its mission to "collect, preserve, and present" digital documents related to the experiences of hurricanes Katrina and Rita, the HDMB includes user-submitted video. Under the heading "St. Bernard Parish, Louisiana after Katrina on Video," an exemplary item is catalogued simply as "Katrina.wmv." Videographer Benjamin Chappetta shoots a long traveling shot from a moving vehicle driving down a desolate street, past dozens of utterly wrecked buildings. Simple in execution and powerful in revelation, it arguably surpasses the more calculated opening traveling shot in Jean-Luc Godard's *Weekend*.[10]

Similarly powerful are Helen Hill's twenty-first-century home movies, particularly those she shot in New Orleans. The fact that she created more than eighty reels of Super 8 footage simply to document her everyday life and community would, in other circumstances, go unmentioned when discussing her work as a filmmaker. But with the erasure of the old New Orleans, these films take on greater documentary value. Helen shot backyard scenes, pets, and family outings, of course. But she also recorded parades, protests, gay pride events, performances, their own local "International Flag Burning Day," social gatherings of the city's creative class, and funky underrepresented parts of daily life.

The Hill-Gailiunas "home movies" are not typical of the genre. As a film purist, Helen chose not to take up the more convenient video camera, the home recording device of choice for a generation. As an artist, she was cognizant of how spontaneous shooting was part of her aesthetic. In her first post-Katrina experimental film, she melded the home movie and her painterly style. The untitled five-minute collage, completed early in 2006, consists of fragments of flood-damaged Super 8 films Helen shot in New Orleans. After hand-cleaning the tiny strands, she had them optically printed to 16 mm. Many showed her son, who was not yet a year old when Katrina struck. With emulsion scarred and swirled, the distressed film resuscitates its original subjects while also evoking ephemerality and mortality. It also resonates with New Orleans's aesthetic "atmosphere of decay" that Tennessee Williams described in *A Streetcar Named Desire* and that functions as a point of civic pride.[11]

As New Orleans exiles in 2005–2006, Helen and Paul lived with their son in Columbia for a full year. In another brave response to Katrina, Helen and Paul made home movies of their brief return to the flooded house in October 2005. Pantomiming for the camera in respirator masks and latex gloves, they document how high the water climbed. Far from mourning the loss of material possessions, they marvel at how much jetsam is heaped on the curb. Helen inserts close-ups of recovered photographs and keepsakes, damaged but also beautiful after stewing in the toxic muck. Barely two weeks later, she was already making new work: recirculating the November 2005 edition of *Recipes for Disaster,* collaborating with Courtney Egan, and making the 16mm collage.

Serendipitously in Columbia during March 2006, Helen showed her new collage at the University of South Carolina's fifth Orphan Film Symposium. There she met preservation experts who aided her reclamation project. Early in 2006, I received a typewritten note from Helen. She told me of her interest in attending the Orphan Film Symposium in March, noting the serendipity of landing in her hometown at the time the event was taking place at the University of South Carolina. Hearing about the loss of her films and her new collage, I invited her to present at the symposium, which she did on the closing night. Later I discovered she had met several symposiasts who were advising her on how to salvage the seemingly unsalvageable prints. Introducing her screening, Helen reported that the first film laboratory she contacted told her that the films could not be saved. She also presented to fellow filmmaker Bill Morrison, who was also screening new work that evening, a Katrina artifact: a mud-caked VHS copy she had found of Morrison's *Decasia* (his 2002 experimental work about film decomposition and mortality). In the ensuing months, Helen collaborated with the orphan film archivists she met in Columbia.

By August 2006, Helen persuaded her husband to move back to New Orleans, where they were needed. They rented a small house in the Marigny neighborhood and Paul resumed his medical practice at a nearby clinic. She continued making films and teaching at NOCCA. It had been an eventful couple of years for Helen Hill: finishing *Bohemian Town*, becoming a Rockefeller Media Arts fellow, giving birth, fleeing a hurricane, losing her possessions to the flood, living as an "exile" in her childhood home, salvaging films, making new work, reissuing *Recipes for Disaster*, showing at festivals, moving back to Louisiana, curating programs, teaching. But through the fall of 2006 life returned to its pre-Katrina rhythms, albeit in a less vibrant, less populated New Orleans. As late as New Year's Day 2007 Helen was shooting more movies. So it was an extreme sense of tragedy that met the news of her death.

The murder of Helen Hill became a rallying point for local protests about the lack of police protection for Katrina-ravaged communities. Press coverage coupled her life as a spirited community builder in the arts with that of Dinerral Shavers, a twenty-five-year-old musician and teacher murdered that same week—along with seven other citizens of New Orleans. Shavers had already become associated with the plight of New Orleans, a resident of the Lower Ninth Ward interviewed in Spike Lee's HBO documentary *When the Levees Broke* (2006). Both Shavers (African American, working-class) and Hill (white, middle-class) received traditional jazz funeral processions, further linking them as public figures who transcended a stark racial and class divide. Journalist Noah Adams said "their stories were entwined with the New Orleans struggle." Television networks devoted prime-time programs to the cases. CBS News' *48 Hours Mystery* called their murders "symbolic of the breakdown" in social order while CBC News offered that the shooting of Helen and Paul "became a symbol of all that's wrong with New Orleans."[12] More important than these traditional media reports, Internet postings and productions became central to the sharing of information and personal expressions of loss. Myspace.com hosts a Dinerral Shavers Official Memorial Page. Friends set up HelenHill.org, which continues to present news, letters of remembrance, photos, videos, and audio recordings related to her life and work.

The narrative of Helen Hill's life and work did not end with memorialization. Instead, a confluence of forces has extended the reach of her creative work at a time when "new media" has supposedly displaced celluloid-specific production and projection. After her passing, more people saw her work than ever saw it in her lifetime. Old media (film prints, television broadcasts) and new media (digital reproduction and display) worked in tandem.

Outsider Archivists, Anarchivists, and *Orphanistas*

The "little films" that Helen was "sending out to the world" included not just her own, but also the modest works of many who discovered that they too could make a film for fifteen dollars. She cultivated local film culture by setting up screenings and performances. In August 2006 she worked with an ad hoc group of archivists to program the first Home Movie Day in New Orleans. The nonprofit Center for Home Movies, which began local home movie screenings in 2002 in a spirit of preservation-mindedness, wanted to give special attention to the city the year after Katrina. Helen's participation in archiving and preservation was a consequential step into another kind of vanguard, one populated by self-described "outsider archivists," "orphanistas," and "anarchivists" who have been challenging archival orthodoxy since the 1990s. Because she advocated for little films, orphan films, and home movies, a group of allies in that cause came together after her passing and preserved her body of work. In a rare outcome for such a radically independent film artist, within two months ten Helen Hill films had been preserved and two sets of new 16mm prints were circulating via the Harvard Film Archive. The 2007 Ann Arbor Film Festival (which was dedicated to her) initiated the screenings of the restored films.

The orphan film movement of the past decade has brought a new kind of valorization to content and artifacts formerly neglected but now deemed worthy of study and preservation. Amateur films, home video, fragments, industrial films, experiments, found footage, and other works with no perceived commercial value (sometimes abandoned by their owners) have received new life among archivists, artists, and academics. By 2001, three playful neologisms informally entered the argot of preservationists and their allies: *orphanista, anarchivist,* and *outsider archivist.* The first term took hold among passionate advocates for neglected and orphaned films.[13] The second stemmed from "The Anarchivists' Manifesto," an anonymous prankster's document circulated among moving image archivists. It urged a "fight against authoritarian and hierarchical tendencies" in institutions, provision of "maximum public access to all collections," and confrontation of "the gatekeepers and powerbrokers who control political power and major funding sources."[14] In reality, many of those who side with this battle against bureaucratic lethargy work for archival institutions, which are anything but anarchical. Their activism is extramural.

Helen shared this sensibility, but it was the destruction of her possessions that brought her into contact with like-minded archivists. In particular she worked with Kara Van Malssen, a New York University graduate student who was writing a thesis titled *Disaster Planning and Recovery: Post-Katrina Lessons for Mixed Media Collections,* in the Moving Image Archiving and Preservation program (MIAP). Helen's disaster became a case study, alongside the Louisiana State Museum, the Hogan Jazz Archive at Tulane University, and New Orleans community radio station WWOZ-FM.[15]

After the Orphan Film Symposium, Helen corresponded with Dwight Swanson of the Center for Home Movies. By May 2006, they were planning the special New Orleans edition of Home Movie Day. Swanson asked her to assemble a screening at the Zeitgeist Multi-Disciplinary Arts Center featuring home movies and personal films "by the New Orleans filmmaking community," adding this idea was "almost entirely the result of seeing your films at Orphans."[16]

The Zeitgeist screening on August 11 made an impact. One of the NOLA media makers Helen invited was George Ingmire, who screened his late grandfather's 16mm home movie with an accompanying narration on audiotape. *Think of Me First as a Person* was Dwight Core Sr.'s edited compilation of scenes he filmed of his growing son between 1960 and 1975. This portrait of Dwight Jr., narrated by his father, is also a love letter to a child born with Down syndrome. Finding it the most stunning home movie he'd ever seen, Swanson screened it for the National Film Preservation Board at the Library of Congress.[17] In December 2006, the Librarian of Congress named *Think of Me First as a Person* to the National Film Registry—a rapid transformation from partially completed home movie to canonized exemplar of the amateur film!

Working with Helen throughout summer and fall 2006, the Center for Home Movies applied for grants to preserve some of her home movies of pre-Katrina New Orleans. Shortly after her death, the Women's Film Preservation Fund awarded the first one. The Maxine Greene Foundation then funded three more films to be preserved for the 2008 Orphan Film Symposium. Swanson and Van Malssen's inventory of her collection revealed a great diversity of material in the "home movie" collection: camera tests for other films, sequences made for *The Florestine Collection*, the Queen of Breadland instructional movie, animated promos for the New Orleans Film Collective, *Madame Winger* outtakes, a found film entitled *New Orleans Voodoo and the Past* (undated), and unidentified reels.

This gallimaufry of material was what had to be assessed upon Helen's passing. How to make the finished works available? What should become of the collection? New Orleans was no longer deemed a viable place to keep the films safe and the family agreed that the Harvard Film Archive was the best fit. Three of her films were produced at Harvard. Helen, her brother, stepfather, husband, and many friends and collaborators were alumni. The archive has a cinematheque that regularly shows experimental and independent work, an active preservation strategy, and a staff experienced in handling small-gauge films and artists' work.

After a year of memorial screenings, a more celebratory tribute opened the 2008 Orphan Film Symposium. It brought together not only the outsider archivists, but also notable insiders who shared an admiration for Helen's work. Entitled "Anywhere...A Tribute to Artist-Activist Helen Hill," the event alluded to *Mouseholes*, in which she asks her dying grandfather if he knows where he is, and he replies "Anywhere." The Academy Award-winning animator and film historian John Canemaker delivered an appreciation of her work and a life filled with "angelic sensuality, sensitivity, and fun." *Mouseholes*, "her masterpiece" he offered, "is quintessential personal-statement cinema: rough-edged, heartfelt, intelligent, daring." As an experimenter, Helen was part of a community that produces a "refreshing alternative and antidote to committee-constructed, soulless, special effects-driven commercial cinema."

The program conveyed the artist-activist's anticommercial values and her New Orleans joie de vivre. The newly preserved home movies shown were shot by Helen in her Marigny neighborhood on the Fourth of July, 2003. Through the distressed emulsion we see, in addition to the festivities of International Flag-Burning Day, Thomas Little, a friend she filmed masquerading as Jacqueline Kennedy. (He subsequently learned filmmaking at Helen's workshops and now carries on her practices, making hand-processed and animated films.)

Helen and her *Recipes for Disaster* cohorts represent perhaps the last moving-image makers choosing to shoot, edit, and project exclusively on film. As the industrial mode of movie production and exhibition has gone digital, the love of film qua film continues in the artisanal mode. Madame Winger tells us if Kodak ever stops manufacturing Super 8mm film, "don't fret, it still will be made" by small companies. However, *Madame Winger* also imagines a near future in which individuals may have to make and process their own motion-picture film in bomb shelters. (Uncannily, Helen's film released in summer 2001 asks "fellow filmmakers" "what will you do" in the event of "gigantic terrorist attacks?" And her accompanying *Recipes* drawing envisages "a worldwide recession.")

"Anywhere...A Tribute to Artist-Activist Helen Hill" included one other film as its surprise finale. Unbeknownst to nearly everyone, Becky Lewis found the Super 8mm print of *The House of Sweet Magic* only days before the New York screening. She conspired with Colorlab to unveil the rediscovery, which revealed a perfect continuity between the eleven-year-old's use of film and the hand visible in her mature body of work: an animatrix with a childlike sense of joy and fun, a maker and pixilator of handmade objects, an *animalier* whose creatures could be monstrous as well as endearing.

The Legacy of Utopian Cinema in the Twenty-First Century

To a large degree, the reception of Helen's films has emphasized their sweetness, levity, and life-affirming celebrations of love. In 2008, for example, the Robert Flaherty Film Seminar posthumously honored Helen with its Charles Samu Award, given to animators whose work conveys "a universal message illuminating our sense of world community." Certainly, her art affirms that. The flag of world-{heart}-nation she drew for "Where Will You Be in the Next Century?" (see

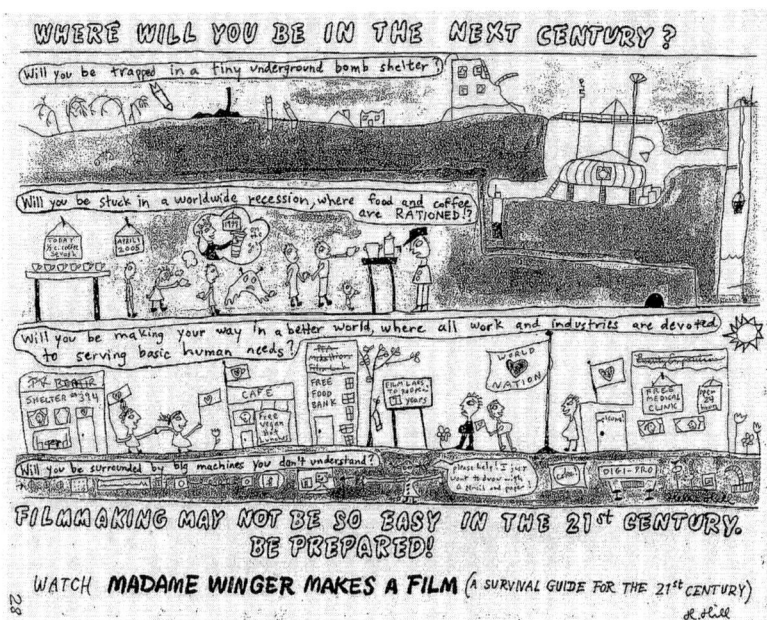

Figure 8.1 Helen Hill drawing in *Recipes for Disaster: A Handcrafted Film Cookbooklet*. The bomb shelter (upper right) appears in *Madame Winger Makes a Film*, as voiceover asks "fellow filmmakers" and "future filmmakers": "What Will You Do if there is a Nuclear War? Or gigantic Terrorist Attack? When your film lab is reduced to rubble, how are you going to keep making films?" Reproduced with permission.

figure 8.1) epitomizes the utopian vision that threads through all of her work.

However, the work is also political, not simple or naïve, as some facile descriptions put it. Although Helen's creative output accentuates optimism, love, and uplift, it also sees these as correctives to an inequitable social order. Her films take as a given that a world dominated by money, militarism, and belligerent nationalism must be made better by people doing things to serve basic human needs. She lived the life of a utopian anarchist, a citizen of the world, residing in the creolized port of New Orleans, the bohemian town of Halifax, the cosmopolitan world of Los Angeles, and the creative community of Cambridge, while also remaining a creature of Carolina. The loaded word *anarchist* may not be the first that comes to mind after viewing *Mouseholes* or *Madame Winger Makes a Film*, but anarchism is a key concept for understanding the extended group of DIY media makers of which Helen and Paul were a part.

Anarchy here does not refer to the common conception of lawless chaos and nihilistic destruction, but rather its opposite. The anarchism of the New Orleans Film Collective, Food Not Bombs, or Nowe Miasto is a belief in autonomous individuals participating in the building and sustaining of local communities. The domination of social hierarchies and nation-states is to be countered by humanitarian actions and direct democracy. "Helen believed deeply, at the core of her being, in the equality and dignity of all people," her husband wrote in an open letter to the people of New Orleans after her death. "She took part in Eracism meetings, the progressive Gillespie Community Breakfasts, and political rallies to help bring back New Orleans in the most fair and inclusive way." Or, to refer again to Helen's *Recipes for Disaster* cartoon panel, this philosophy is about the making of "a better world, where all work and industries are devoted to serving basic human needs," a world in which everyone has enough to eat. Although she did not label herself with an ism, her cookbooklet slyly alludes to *The Anarchist Cookbook* (1971).[18]

This political inflection is also part of the twenty-first-century DIY phenomenon. In the 1950s and 1960s, the marketing of Do It Yourself books to middle-class home owners extended into dozens of how-to manuals for amateur filmmaking.[19] However, contemporary DIY culture is rooted in an anti-corporate grassroots practice, as profiled in Faythe Levine's 2008 book and 2009 documentary *Handmade Nation*.[20] Writing about the New Orleans Craft Mafia's screening of the movie, a local reviewer likened its DIY subjects to a revolutionary guerilla movement, in which "do-it-yourself toilers in the craft movement exude a similar rebellious spirit."[21]

Among all of Helen's handmade work, the film that best encapsulates this connection between her art and activism is the one uncompleted at the time of her death. Her Rockefeller fellowship had kickstarted production of *The Florestine Collection*. Conceived as a hybrid of animation and live-action documentary, it would tell the story of a bunch of distinctive handcrafted dresses Helen found on a trash heap in 2001, on her way to a Mardi Gras parade. After saving some one hundred dresses, she identified their creator. Florestine Kinchen was an unheralded African American seamstress in New Orleans when she died at age ninety. Helen recorded interviews with her family and fellow churchgoers. She storyboarded *The Florestine Collection* with cut-out figures to be animated. Her planned narration would highlight issues of race and class disparities in the city. Comparing the life of two New Orleans women who made handcrafted work, it would be her most in-depth film. The materials were powerful enough to mount a museum exhibition featuring many of Kinchen's dresses alongside objects from the pre-production of the film.[22]

However, *The Florestine Collection* did not remain unfinished. "A film by Helen Hill completed by Paul Gailiunas" reads the opening title on the thirty-minute 16mm production (scheduled to preview at the 2010 Orphan Film Symposium in New York and to premiere in her hometown). Columbia's nonprofit repertory film center, The Nickelodeon Theatre, also confers a Helen Hill Memorial Award at its annual Indie Grits Film Festival, given to "the best work by a female filmmaker in honor of Columbia native and celebrated animator, filmmaker and teacher Helen Hill." The Nick also continues a long tradition of animation workshops for children. In 2009, it programmed a DIY Animation Celebration showing Helen's films. Susan Courtney, a cofounder of the Orphan Film Symposium, offered an inspirational anecdote about the impact of this legacy on her own daughter. "Chloe, a huge *Madame Winger* fan, is very keen about all this. After I told her the idea for the new center at the Nick she said, 'Does that mean we could watch *Madame Winger* in the theater and then go right next door and make a film?!'"[23]

That pedagogical legacy is even more pronounced at the New Orleans Center for the Creative Arts, where Helen taught. Her cameraless animation workshops have continued, Courtney Egan writes, "part of how we continue Helen's legacy here." In 2007, the community's annual twenty-four hour Draw-a-thon included screenings of her work.[24] Such is the impact of this, that now a young artist can be found describing her first 16mm hand-painted film as "inspired by Stan Brakhage, Helen Hill, and other avant-garde/experimental filmmakers."[25]

However, there is also a gulf between the influential "essential cinema" of Brakhage's cohort and the world of Helen Hill. The humor, love, whimsy, sweetness, and accessibility (even to children) of Helen's films differentiate them from the experimental films usually taken as emblematic of the post–World War II American avant garde. The latter is generally represented by the work of structuralists, contrarians, and male individualists—Brakhage, Hollis Frampton, Jonas Mekas, Ken Jacobs, Kenneth Anger, et al. This artists' film culture has historically been characterized as filled with conflict, internecine grudges, denunciation, and darkness. As the New American Cinema Group famously expressed in its 1961 manifesto: "we don't want rosy films—we want them the color of blood."[26] Helen wanted—and made—rosy films, figuratively and literally. Flowers were a motif in her work. Throbbing red Valentine hearts were another. (And of course her pet pigs were Rosie and Daisy). Hers was, as Egan puts it, a cinema of optimism. Even when it dealt with death, resurrection followed. *Scratch and Crow* concludes with the written, biblical-sounding evocation "If I knew, / I would assure you we are all / Finally good chickens / And will rise together, / A noisy flock of round, / Dusty angels."

Certainly Helen's work shares traits with the canonical avant garde. Like the Group, she preferred films "rough, unpolished, but alive." She knew that Mekas, Brakhage, Jerome Hill (no relation), and other cineastes had long valorized the art of amateur cinema. Helen also taught her students the history of experimental animation, showing work by Lotte Reiniger, Len Lye, Norman McLaren, and other artists who influenced her. These two schools came together briefly when Anthology Film Archives, epicenter of avant garde cinema, hosted a retrospective, *The Life and Films of Helen Hill*, in October 2007.

Yet the newer, parallel cinema of utopia remains fundamentally different in principle and practice. It is a collective that shares its tricks of the trade, comprised of people whose films are made for an audience of family, friends, and lovers as often as for festival exhibition. Helen never offered her films for distribution, not even through cooperatives. She showed at festivals, but more often in small nontheatrical venues, backyards, and homes. Hers was an interpersonal cinema experience. She never commercially released on video, television, or (save for the three Gothtober pieces) the Internet. When her family released a posthumous DVD compilation, *The House of Sweet Magic* (2008, distributed by Peripheral Produce), they did so with some reluctance, knowing that she projected her films as films—and that she did not sell or rent them. Three years after her death, no one has put a Helen Hill film on YouTube, although friends have uploaded home videos in which she appears.

Thus the "old media" of an artist eulogized as a "visionary Luddite pixilator" continues its life in the "new media" era, confounding the boundaries between the two categories.[27] Certainly Helen was an exceptional person who modestly made her mark on the world through her films and social actions. The tragic circumstances of her death brought viewers in numbers that DIY filmmakers seldom get. But Helen's handiwork also represents a category of media production practiced by many artists, artisans, collectives, and amateurs who do not seek commercial success or professional advancement. With so many producing so much material, scholarship must better account for the millions of moving-image works that exist outside of the mass media. They originate in hundreds of places. In this, the kind of DIY film practice Helen represents is even distinct from the microcinema movement of the past decade. Many microcinemas retain the art house sensibility, in which programmers select films (or more likely videos) to attract connoisseurs. Others emerged with the advent of affordable digital video, seeking to produce independent work and to develop international networks of distribution.[28]

In-person exchanges and backyard or living room viewings remain primary means of circulating the samizdat of small films. However, curated screenings also help sustain DIY media. Becka Barker, who made *Film Farm Dance* (2001), in which Helen appears, assembled the exhibition *Working on a Plan: Films Inspired by Helen Hill* for South Korea's 2008 Experimental Film and Video Festival in Seoul. Courtney Egan wrote that her "personal response to cultivating local work after the storm" was to curate locally made videos about the flood, including three annual programs for the New Orleans International Human Rights Film Festival (2006–2008).[29] Many other screenings related to Katrina's impact have been assembled, often placing the amateur video alongside professional documentaries and art pieces. These not only memorialize, they also build preservation consciousness. The Helen Hill film project has been joined by large-scale institutional efforts, such as the Hurricane Digital Memory Bank, and individual ones. Blaine Dunlap, a veteran documentary filmmaker and a video artist in New Orleans, knew Helen well. Encouraged by her frequent little "bring a movie" events, he resumed shooting—though not until the Katrina evacuation and aftermath. Responding to the enormous losses, he formed Preservista, a full-time venture devoted to "identifying and preserving the work of independent videomakers."[30]

Conclusion

Saying that Helen Hill represents a large but largely ignored community of alternative media artists does not diminish the exceptional personal impact she had on many people, both in and out of the film world. Her legacy should be celebrated, as Snowden Becker of the Center for Home Movies puts it, for "the great big little thing" it is. Her handprints are visible in many places, but especially in New Orleans. Media coverage and personal accounts reiterate that identity. "Helen was emblematic of New Orleans—a radiant bundle of energy, creativity, and good cheer," David Koen said in a national radio commentary. In his departing open letter to residents of the city, Paul Gailiunas wrote:

> Helen loved New Orleans with a great passion. She was content only when she was in New Orleans, walking among the old shotgun houses, admiring the morning glories and magnolia trees and Spanish moss, listening to WWOZ, straining to catch a Zulu coconut, marching her pot-bellied pig in the Krewe du Vieux, bringing visitors to the Mother-in-Law Lounge, and cooking vegetarian versions of famous Creole dishes.[31]

Add to this list of Helen's NOLA loves, making home movies, filming parts of the city that escaped touristic views, and teaching her Louisiana neighbors and NOCCA students how to make their own films. Her open house nurtured a creative culture. "I certainly met a lot of the participants of the DIY network," Courtney Egan confirms, "in Helen's backyard!" Profiles of Helen and Paul invariably include admiring descriptions of an inspirational couple, such as Jason Berry writing "Gailiunas and Hill were radical humanitarians with a contagious joie de vivre."[32] Talking with those who knew her, one hears beatific depictions and stories that begin "She changed my life for the better," and conclude "although I only met her that one time." I would think these reports of a New Orleans saint were idealized because of her passing—but for the fact that people spoke of her in this way during her lifetime.[33]

The narrative of Helen's life and the power of her work have become interwoven with Katrina's. That New Orleans' media artists have persevered in exile and upon return speaks to the creative and political force DIY filmmakers can wield. Despite the floods that took much of her work and the incalculable tragedy of her early death, Helen Hill's legacy continues to inspire good works, anywhere.

Notes

To the many colleagues and friends of Helen Hill who shared and informed this essay, thank you. My deepest gratitude goes to Paul Gailiunas, Becky Lewis, and Kevin Lewis, for their generosity and grace.

1. Jason Berry, "Helen Hill: An Unfinished Story," pp. 68–73.
2. Dave Barber, "House of Sweet Magic: The Animated Films of Helen Hill."
3. Philip Hood, "Helen Hill's Recipes for Disaster PDF."
4. *Timecode: NOLA Helen Hill Interview* (August 2003), posted February 10, 2008, youtube.com/watch?v=07ReG3l_9fM.
5. Nowe Miasto Housing Cooperative, http://nowemiastonola.org.
6. "Killings Bring the City to Its Bloodied Knees," *Times-Picayune*, January 5, 2007.
7. See the web pages Gothtober.com/archive and Hurricanearchive.org/object/12304.
8. TheAxeintheAttic.com website includes a trailer that begins with the Linda Dumas moment. The film's credits include the attribution "Home Movies: Linda Dumas."
9. Michael Mizell-Nelson, "Not Since the Great Depression: The Post Katrina Documentary Impulse and New Media." He refers to Courtney Egan as "a real force in video production in New Orleans."
10. Benjamin Chappetta, "Katrina.wmv."
11. Bruce Weber, "Storm and Crisis."
12. The media linking of the cases of Helen Hill and Dinerral Shavers was immediate, beginning with the front page of the local newspaper: "Killings Bring the City to Its Bloodied Knees." Also significant were activist-attorney Billy Sothern's *New York Times* op-ed, "Taken by the Tide," January 10, 2007 (reprinted in *International Herald Tribune*); Jacqueline Bishop, "Art and Death in New Orleans," *News and Notes,* National Public Radio (NPR), January 9, 2007; and Lisa Haviland, "Don't Stop the Music: A Look at How Two Murders Moved a Community," *Antigravity* [New Orleans], February 2007, 10–11. National long-form coverage included: "One Year Later, New Orleans Grieves for Artists," twenty-minute feature by Noah Adams, *All Things Considered,* NPR, December 25, 2007; "Storm of Murder," *48 Hours Mystery*, CBS News, October 13, 2007, updated August 14, 2008 (cbsnews.com/stories/2007/10/09/48hours/main3348928.shtml); "After the Storm," *The 5th Estate*, CBC News, October 29, 2008 (cbc.ca/fifth/discussion/2008/10); "Unknown Helen Hill Killer," *America's Most Wanted*, Fox Television, September 15, 2007, updated January 12, 2008, and February 14, 2009 (amw.com/fugitives/case.cfm?id=42393); and Karen Dalton-Benina, "Free at Last," *Huffington Post*, February 21, 2008, huffingtonpost.com/karen-daltonbeninato/free-at-last-second-liner_b_87912.html. See

also Billy Sothern, *Down in New Orleans: Reflections from a Drowned City*, pp. 307–308. The Hill-Shavers linkage was also immediate in parts of the scholarly community. At the University of California Santa Barbara, Prof. Janet Walker's graduate seminar "History, Memory, and Media," began with a January 6 screening of *When the Levees Broke*. When PhD student Regina Longo pointed out the January 4 murder, Walker had her present on the subject the following week. Longo had seen Helen's presentation at the 2006 Orphan Film Symposium. "I just spent two hours presenting on Helen and her work," she wrote. "I played the audio recording of Helen from the Orphans 5 website, as we talked about the notion of testimony and 'listening to silence.' The main thrust of this class is traumatic memory and its cinematographic representation and I chose to recognize the silence as the absence of imagery (her films) at that moment, rather than the absence of her voice." Regina Longo, e-mail, January 13, 2007. Other excellent accounts of Helen's life and its impact on New Orleans include Phil Nugent, "An American City: New Orleans, Helen Hill and Me," *The High Hat* 8 (Winter 2007), thehighhat.com/misc/008/nugent_helen.html; John Clark, "Remembering Helen Hill," *Fifth Estate* 42 (Spring 2007): 42–45, republished in the international libertarian journal *Divergences*, May 14, 2007, http://divergences.be; an epic-length biographical poem by activist-artist (and member of The Fugs) Edward Sanders, "Ode to Helen Hill," *Woodstock Journal* (2007), woodstockjournal.com/pdf/helenhill.pdf; and the documentary *Helen Hill: Celebrating a Life in Film* (South Carolina ETV, 2007).

13. Emily Cohen, "The Ophanista Manifesto: Orphan Films and the Politics of Representation."
14. "The Anarchivists' Manifesto," 2000, Alaska Moving Image Preservation Association, AMIPA.org/images/manifesto.pdf.
15. Kara Van Malssen, *Disaster Planning and Recovery: Post-Katrina Lessons for Mixed Media Collections*, master's thesis, New York University, 2006. See also Kara Van Malssen, "Preserving the Legacy of Experimental Filmmaker Helen Hill," *SOIMA in Practice* (2008), http://soima.iccrom.org.
16. Dwight Swanson, e-mail to Helen Hill, May 20, 2006.
17. Dwight Swanson, e-mail, August 15, 2006.
18. Paul Gailiunas, "For My Poor, Sweet Wife, Fix New Orleans," January 26, 2007. He submitted the letter to the *Times-Picayune*, but it appeared only online and circulated freely on the Internet. Confusingly, the anarchist collective known as Crimethinc, reworked William Powell's infamous *The Anarchist Cookbook* (New York: L. Stuart, 1971) as *Recipes for Disaster: An Anarchist Cookbook, A Moveable Feast* (Olympia, WA: Crimethinc, Workers' Collective), but not until 2004, three years after the Helen Hill *Recipes for Disaster* cookbook-

let. Other Crimethinc members issued DIY 'zines, such as *D.I.Y. Guide II* (Atlanta, 2002). Some people knew Helen as an activist rather than a filmmaker. Howard Besser e-mailed me on January 23, 2007: "In Seattle I ducked into the local Anarchist collective bookstore... I overhead a bit of conversation between two of the workers." One worker, Besser reported, said "We really have to send some money for Helen Hill." They knew Helen from her work with "Food Not Bombs."

19. Focal Cinebooks issued more than a dozen books for amateur filmmakers, ranging from *How to Direct as an Amateur* (1949) to *How to Animate Cut-Outs for Amateur Films* (1966).

20. Faythe Levine and Cortney Heimerl, *Handmade Nation: The Rise of DIY Art, Craft and Design*. Levine's companion documentary is described on the website HandmadeNationMovie.com. See also the Do It Yourself: Democracy and Design issue of *Journal of Design History* 19, no. 1 (Spring 2006).

21. Will Coviello, "Handmade Nation." The DIY moniker has also been applied to a separate cinematic phenomenon, the "wave of microbudget filmmaking" sometimes called "mumblecore." Narrative features, such productions are from the lineage of John Cassavetes or Jean-Luc Godard, rather than the avant garde or amateur realms. See Matt Zoller Seitz, "Three Relationships Seen through a D.I.Y. Lens."

22. *The Dresses of Florestine Kinchen: A Tribute to Helen Hill,* exhibition, McKissick Museum, University of South Carolina, Columbia SC, May–August 2007.

23. Dan Streible, "Another Moment of Joy," February 5, 2009, the *Orphan Film Symposium* blog, http://orphanfilmsymposium.blogspot.com.

24. Courtney Egan, e-mail, October 5, 2009.

25. Photographer and filmmaker Suzie Q. (www.suziq.nu) describing the online version of *No. 1* (2007), www.vimeo.com/1007724.

26. "The First Statement of the New American Cinema Group," *Film Culture* 22–23 (Summer 1961): 131–133.

27. Kevin Lewis eulogized his step-daughter as a visionary Luddite pixilator.

28. Kyle Conway, "Small Media, Global Media: Kino and the Microcinema Movement." See also, Bryan Frye, "Microcinema in 10 Easy Steps."

29. Egan's programs *Back and Forth* and *Below Sea Level Stories* were also combined to create the exhibition *New Orleans Parallax*, which combined videos made "before and after the 'Federal Flood' from the vantage point of activists, cultural workers, youth media makers, and citizen journalists." John Massier, "Prolonged Hacking and Gnawing," blog for Hallwalls Contemporary Arts Center, Buffalo, New York, August 24, 2007. http: //jmassier.blogspot.com. Also see Egan's web page, courtneyegan.net/curating.html.

30. Blaine Dunlap, aka "NolaCam," e-mail, November 7, 2009.
31. Snowden Becker, e-mail, September 29, 2009; David Koen, "A Murder Shakes Confidence in New Orleans," *Morning Edition*, NPR, January 11, 2007; Gailiunas, "Fix New Orleans."
32. "Helen Hill: An Unfinished Story."
33. Courtney Egan, e-mail, September 29, 2009; Berry, "Helen Hill: An Unfinished Story."

CHAPTER 9

IN DESPERATE NEED (OF A MAKEOVER): THE NEOLIBERAL PROJECT, THE DESIGN EXPERT, AND THE POST-KATRINA SOCIAL BODY IN DISTRESS

Brenda R. Weber

The care of human lives and happiness and not their destruction is the first and only object of good government.

—*Thomas Jefferson, as read by Brad Pitt, e2*

In its emphasis on reduced state obligations, the logic of the marketplace, entrepreneurship, and the destruction of social safety nets, neoliberalism provides not only a significant content element of makeover practices, but it also enhances the ideological values connected to transformation and care of the self where "wellness" and image function as critical commodities. Nowhere is this more evident than in those episodes of makeover television that sweep in where disaster has struck. Admittedly, makeover TV's sense of what constitutes catastrophe conflates the quotidian (aging, bodily dissatisfaction) with the seemingly pathological (hypertension, style ignorance, clutter obsession) and the exceptional (disfigurement, divorce, disaster) so that it might label any number of situations from "letting oneself go," to living in disarray, to surviving cancer as the requisite terms that mandate a makeover. Television's fascination with hyperbolic tales of woe is, of course, nothing new, yet, the proliferation of makeover-themed programming in the early

2000s marks this mode of representation as different both in scope and impact.[1]

Even in the midst of such disaster management through style renovations, Hurricane Katrina has given a new urgency to the television makeover mandate through an amalgamation of transformation-themed programs that I call Katrina TV. *Extreme Makeover: Home Edition, Assembly Required, Clean House, Deserving Design, Dog Whisperer,* and *How Do I Look?* are just a sampling of the reality TV makeover shows that have each visited the post-Katrina Gulf area and New Orleans, bringing their version of salvation-through-style-transformation to individual Before-bodies collectively marking the Gulf area as a social body in distress. Other reality television shows such as *Be Real, Storm Stories, Dirty Jobs,* and *Full Force Nature* contribute to the mediated discursive construction of New Orleans as a typically racialized body in need of a makeover, often by deploying generic visual-televisual tropes that reinforce what we might think of as a makeover text. In each of these cases, the makeover's help supersedes other forms of state interventions and subsidies, thus positioning the entertainment industry as a more sympathetic and competent, if sporadic and idiosyncratic, provider of social welfare than the state.[2] Such representation, in turn, heightens a neoliberal logic by emphasizing the superiority of privatization and free market exchange while discrediting systemic issues of poverty, racism, and tardy, even sometimes completely absent, government assistance.[3]

It's important to note in this context that since the damage wrought by Hurricane Katrina in 2005, New Orleans has been specifically targeted as the worst and most toxic element of a larger diseased social body, and NOLA's abject condition has been considered a poor reflection on the health and management capacities of the larger polity.[4] The language of Katrina TV continually speaks through hyperbole, referencing "complete and utter destruction," "desperation," and "total fragility." Such language serves to corporealize and pathologize (and in many ways feminize) both the city itself and a similarly damaged Gulf region, thus metaphorically conflating those things "below the water line" with an ontology of excess, infection, and decay. Much like a leg infected with gangrene, the urgency of these texts demands that restoration through renovation take place so as not to contaminate the larger social body. Significantly, the logic of mediation does not limit itself to post-Katrina destruction but includes the entirety of pre-Katrina New Orleans in its assessment of the diseased Before-body, for indeed, as I will show in this essay, much of the destruction and many of the problems that stemmed from Katrina are situated as the result of the "ramshackle" construction and poor design that to some gave New Orleans its character and to others marked poorer quarters of the city as places of urban blight.

Style Network's *How Do I Look?*, a makeover text geared primarily toward women, offers a telling example of the logics embedded in Katrina TV. *How Do I Look?* marked itself as an instrument of social care when it brought "new life," "fabulous style," and free product giveaways to three African American female teachers who needed instruction in how to go from "survival to revival" since "Katrina had robbed [the subjects] of their style." Each of the three women were depicted in "before" segments as downtrodden and depressed; each received the gift of self-through-style, since, as subject Barbara reports, "My clothes say who I am." Given that the makeover ideologically ties one's semiotic codes to subject status, it clearly indicates in this episode that Katrina also robbed Barbara, Kimberly, and Carla of their experiences as selves. It is the makeover's job (as aided by companies such as Pantene, Skecher, and 3M) to restore that self so subjects can continue in gorgeous confidence, each overjoyed with the gift of their "revitalized new me," a me now "jazzy" and "sassy" and fully committed to helping the rest of New Orleans in its urban revitalizing makeover. This newly energized selfhood is depicted as a critical economic tool that can make Barbara, Kimberly, and Carla not only happy as persons but viable as entrepreneurs, who are now able to deploy the raw materials of the self in a competitive marketplace. Importantly, the marketplace is here designated as a place of wellness that the pathologized victims of Katrina seek to enter.

Perhaps given the physical devastation inflicted by Katrina and the degree to which the crisis of the hurricane exposed weaknesses in the web of social and political relations necessary to stem disaster, it is not surprising that makeover TV might step in to put things aright. After all, makeover TV constitutes a rich genre of programming designed to identify, humiliate, resuscitate, and "save" the decrepit Before-body, marked by age, disadvantage, or neglect. Post-Katrina New Orleans and the surrounding Gulf area, in this regard, comprise the perfect desperate body needing the restorative powers the makeover offers. As in other television makeover texts, a rigid narratological formula establishes the terms that enable the magic of transformation. In brief, these include surveillance of the ravaged "body," testimonials of subjects in need, adulation of intercessionary aid workers, dependence on visiting style gurus, engineers, architects, and designers, and celebration of renovations in elaborate reveal ceremonies. All of these elements of makeover TV also manifest through Katrina TV.

It is the racialized power dynamic depicted between two key aspects of the makeover that I want to focus on in this essay: the distressed body in need and the energized expert itching to intervene. These positions of abject (black) body in distress and empowered (white) agent of salvation are even more attenuated in the mediated representation of post-Katrina New Orleans than they are on makeover TV, since I have yet to view footage of the city's urban renewal that has not also lingered gratuitously on images of houses torn asunder, muddy garbage-filled brown water choking the streets, or desperate primarily African American citizens clinging to rooftops in hopes of rescue by primarily white heroic figures. Indeed, even if rescuers code as people of color, the larger visual logic of these texts coheres to situate black bodies as needy and white bodies as agents of salvation. Just like the makeover text, footage of New Orleans must now offer these obligatory before and after images, the hope of renewal forever wed to the memory of destruction. As Joy Fuqua rather tellingly noted, the coverage of Katrina suddenly revealed the "existence of the poor, the sick, and poor sick black and white people in the U.S." to an "oftentimes conveniently disbelieving country."[5] Fuqua likened this representation to "an *Extreme Makeover: Home Edition* 'reveal' moment that shows not the results of 'renovation' or 'remodeling' but, rather, the *destruction, devastation*, and continued *displacement* of thousands of people," those people disproportionately African American.[6]

In this essay I will detail how such mediated representations of post-Katrina New Orleans affirm a racialized neoliberal logic by situating a geographical area as a body in distress that can only be effectively "healed" through the design ministrations offered by the experts who populate makeover television. These mediated restorations operate through narratives that naturalize the uneven economic relationship between the needy makeover subject and the powerful makeover expert, in this case represented through an exaggerated relationship between the helpless residents of New Orleans (a helplessness projected onto certain parts of the city itself) and the helpful designers, engineers, and even style consultants who rush in as aid volunteers. Although I have no doubt that altruism is a part of these salvation moments, on-screen narratives tell a more complicated tale of neoliberal entrenchment, where a logic of seemingly neutral market competition in the context of state absolution prevails. Because the bad design that led to disaster and the good design (and designers) needed to salvage the crisis situation are so critical to the neoliberal narratives espoused by these transformation texts, I move my consideration beyond those television formats that self-consciously identify themselves as makeover shows, looking more closely at adjacent design-centered series such as *e2* (pronounced e-squared), *Holmes in New Orleans*, and *Architecture School*, arguing that they deploy the uneven neoliberal power relations of the makeover to further validate their transformation narratives.

Of the three shows that I place at the heart of my analysis, only one, *Holmes in New Orleans*, might automatically be generically grouped within the confines of makeover TV, since this particular series is bracketed within the larger home-renovation show *Holmes on Homes*, a Canadian fix-it program airing in the United States on HGTV. I have more fully addressed elsewhere the difficulties of precisely defining what constitutes the genre of the makeover. But in the particular context of the case study texts I have selected here, a key question is not only whether these Katrina TV programs fit within makeover TV but also whether they count as reality TV? Both *e2* (which aired on PBS) and *Architecture School* (which aired on The Sundance Channel) might more easily be identified as documentary in nature, since they purport to offer a nonfiction mode of address in regard to pressing social ills. Indeed, given the higher cultural capital afforded to documentary in relation to what Michael Hirschorn has typified as the "visual Hamburger Helper" that is often associated with reality TV, I am sure the producers of *e2* and *Architecture School* as well as the networks that aired them would vastly disdain my grouping of these shows together as reality makeover shows working through the logic of Katrina TV. Yet, as I hope to demonstrate, the narrative logic deployed in these design-centered shows fully sutures their narratives to the larger neoliberal devices of makeover TV, in turn naturalizing transformation-themed television in a way that allows its ideological and structural form to extend across a wide spectrum of television contents.

"24-Hour Design People": Reality TV's Neoliberal Design-Utopia

Before I address *e2*, *Holmes in New Orleans*, and *Architecture School* specifically, I want to establish the broader context in which these programs are airing. For anyone who has spent much time charting trends in reality TV, it is evident that designers are everywhere. Indeed, I would argue we are the midst of a veritable fetishization of the designer and a fascination with all that he or she is capable of doing for us. From the hip and edgy fledgling fashion stars who populate *Project Runway* to the science geeks of *Smash Lab*, reality TV is awash in problems that can best be solved by a new breed of reality TV superheroes—what I call 24-Hour Design People—who stand at the ready, prepared to intervene upon a dystopic nation of overweight, cluttery, inefficient, uninteresting, and dysfunctional people. These television design shows, couched as they are in recommendations for lifestyle-oriented consumerism, offer a rich panoply of solutions for living, which as Lynn Spigel notes, conflate "high-tech products with related ideals of 'good taste' and 'class privilege.'"[7]

There are roughly fifty design/makeover reality shows presently airing on expanded U.S. cable that specifically enunciate the word "design"—such shows as *Divine Design, Design Inc, Design Star, Deserving Design, Sheila Holmes: Designer Living, Design Remix, Designer Finals, Design U, Designed to Sell, 24 Hour Design, Design Rivals, Surprise by Design, Designers, Fashions & Runways,* and my personal favorite, *What's Your Sign Design*. Even those shows that we would not normally consider to be about design—such as weight loss programs or child-rearing shows—take advantage of the rhetorical cachet attached to the words design and designer. So, for instance, my local newspaper listing described a not-to-be-missed episode of *Supernanny*, saying: "Jojo tries to bring some order to a family of nine...while helping the lonely and angry mother design a plan to reconnect with her estranged father."[8] It is not surprising, then, that when Hurricane Katrina gave the nation a Before-body on a colossal scale, the schematic for salvation would require, as *e2* phrases it, that "architects, designers, and engineers all over the world" would use their technological expertise "to create a smarter, greener, and more sustainable future." Significantly, this design innovation is presented as metonymic, New Orleans here standing in for a larger national body.

I have argued elsewhere that makeovers more specifically and television more broadly appear to be invested in normalizing the subject around a series of affective identity locations coded as white, heterosexual, and middle class, and that the people who intervene on behalf of the design-challenged tend to occupy "discredited," or at least non-hegemonic, social locations. So, for instance, there is Vern Yip, the Asian and seemingly gay host and designer of *Deserving Design*; we have

What Not to Wear's fashion stylists Stacy London, who with her Yiddish exclamations plays to urban Jewish stereotypes, and her perfect foil, the patrician and seemingly gay Clinton Kelly; there is Bob Harper and Jillian Michaels, the chiseled and über-muscled fitness coaches of *The Biggest Loser*, neither of whom are overtly labeled in terms of their sexuality, but both of whom are considered gay on fan sites and Internet message boards. And, of course, there is the veritable queer utopia of *Project Runway*, a rainbow coalition of tattooed, countercultural, and mestiza identities and sexualities (though even in the domain of high fashion, the lesbian designer has yet to be featured).

Of particular concern, it seems to me, is the way in which stereotypes attached to certain identity locations, specifically those coded through gay male sexuality, are naturalized, and thus neutralized, through the designer profile. It's not by accident, for example, that *Queer Eye for the Straight Guy* plays according to a superhero motif, whereby five gay men throw on hip clothes and dark glasses and get into their black SUV on "Gay Street," immediately rushing over to "Straight Street" to dispense fashion, interior decorating, grooming, culinary, and cultural advice so that "all things will only get better." Indeed, such representations reinforce the idea that designers are somehow "not like us," and that, much like the superhero, who lives apart from the culture s/he must save, the designer's extraordinary powers are what sustains the normal operations of everyday life.[9] Such reinforcement and naturalizing of the ordinary through the labors of the extraordinary are characteristic even of such shows as *Toolbelt Diva*, *Carson Can*, or *Take Home Handyman*, where designers are coded as highly heterosexual.

But here I want to suggest why such glorification of designers as exceptional to the point of being like superheroes furthers a neoliberal logic. A first link shows itself in the examples I've cited earlier, for in the guise of the hero, identity locations marked by race, class, and gender become unimportant both in the body of the superhero and in a governing logic of neoliberalism. This is not to say that we do not perceive the superhero as being raced, classed, or gendered in some way (almost always white, rich, and male), but that any social, cultural, or embodied factor that might accrue to a superhero's identity is not considered to be relevant to his/her powers. Superheroes, even if in the guise of reality TV style gurus and designers, make intelligible the fantasy of a selfhood free of, because transcendent to, identity politics. In this respect, the fantasy of operating outside of systemic prejudice and discrimination seems feasible, although the exceptionalism of the superhero literally makes him or her a singular being, the only person who might experience such social freedom. Still, the attributive logic suggests that if one person can transcend social impediments so as to exist on a level field of achievement, all people can.

Tropes of the superhero do not, in themselves, produce a neoliberal mindset. A second link to neoliberalism evident on both makeover TV and Katrina TV appears in the situation of need that the superhero occasions. Put simply, when the protections and services of municipalities and governments are working effectively, superheroes are not needed. Across the rich intermedial cannon of superhero fiction comprised of comic books, movies, television, and lore, it is when Gotham City faces a nemesis that the chief of police cannot handle or when Metropolis is flummoxed by the evil machinations of a despotic criminal that Batman or Superman are called to the rescue. An important distinction between these more classic deployments of superheroes and those we see activated on reality TV has very much to do with whether government is impotent or simply unwilling to act. As we shall see further in this essay, many of the narratives that attach themselves to the renewal of a post-Katrina New Orleans make much of the absence and incompetence of government. Neoliberalism as a political and economic reality stands for the idea that people should take care of themselves so that the state won't have to. It is not, however, an extraordinary leap to move from government's unwillingness to care for its citizens to its inability to do so. As depicted on both makeover and Katrina TV, the absence/neglect/incompetence of the state necessitates intervention from nongovernmental sources. So here we see that the heroic design expert delivers a set of democratizing premises that quell recognition of structural inequalities.

In combination with reduced state intervention, neoliberalism also stands for increased privatization, entrepreneurialism, and free markets. Even in the context of a global economic crisis that has mandated that many right- and left-leaning governments offer bail-out money to keep large financial institutions from collapse (the government as makeover superhero?), a larger neoliberal philosophy prevails. This is undoubtedly due to the fact that neoliberalism finds sustaining value in principles of American meritocratic achievement, which suggest that all men [sic] are created equal and all citizens within the democracy are fettered only by the limitations of their will and effort. This philosophy permeates the reality and makeover TV ethos. If some subjects require the television makeover's helping hand, the indication is that this is a one-time, significant boost that will prevent the subject from ever needing such assistance again. Significantly, then, across a broader set of makeover TV texts, the nose job, the pimped out car, or the stylish wardrobe a subject receives through the makeover equips that subject to transcend the need that made him or her eligible for the makeover in the first place. A similar logic sustains those programs that I have been calling Katrina TV. As Tom Darden, the executive director of Brad Pitt's Make it Right Foundation, explains on *e2*, "Brad designs the program as a hand up not a hand out," the movie star here getting discursive props as a designer as well as a social engineer, rather than a wealthy philanthropist, offering a privatized social welfare net (figure 9.1).[10]

Figure 9.1   Through his "Make It Right" Foundation Brad Pitt has maintained a high profile in celebrity efforts to make over post-Katrina New Orleans.

In terms of reality TV's fascination with designers, not only does design matter, but the more insistent refrain makes decisively clear that bad design can be disastrous. On one episode of *Holmes on Homes* set in Toronto, for instance, the host Mike Holmes comes to the rescue of Jean, who hired a female interior decorator to do the work of a contractor. Not only did the decorator make poor, time-consuming, and costly design choices, her decision to turn a gas fireplace into a wood-burning fireplace, her failure to file for permits, and her authorization to cut into three load-bearing joists compromised the entire stability of the home. Holmes takes the camera on a survey of the property and is aghast at the poor workmanship, narrating as he goes. "What does it show?" he asks looking at the mess in Jean's basement. "It shows everybody on that job did not know what they were doing. No common sense. None whatsoever on this job. As a matter of fact, I'm surprised the house did not fall down." The chagrined homeowner reinforces that she was taken for a ride by the (female) interior decorator pretending to be a contractor: "I didn't realize what had happened until Mike pointed it out to me. I'm not a builder." Later she says, "I do have faith in *Holmes on Homes*. They're going to make it right." In this respect the designer's ethos is heightened through mediation—whether he accepts the label of hero or not, Holmes lives up to his hype to make the world right because the accountability built into the televised aspect of the show itself can allow for no other outcome.

So, regardless of how the design theme manifests on these shows, each program offers messages that TV designers (of buildings, rooms, bodies, clothing, lives, and lifestyles) are distinctly different from other design professionals. They not only possess the necessary skills, services, and solutions that will alleviate the complicated experience of living in an increasingly messy and globalized world, but they are held accountable for competence through their mass mediation. A similar logic holds true on Katrina TV, where aid workers speak directly into cameras with pledges that the residents of New Orleans will no longer be the victims of bad design. Or rather that good design will save them from "bad luck" (coded language for generational poverty). These references to bad luck or hard times work in a covert way to reinforce media scholar John McMurria's reading of reality TV shows, such as *Extreme Makeover: Home Edition*, that position poverty and economic hardship as matters of "individual inadequacy" rather than systemic abuse.[11]

The logic of design-centered television texts further reinforces the idea that we need these shows because we do not have government resources to draw on and the pace of modern living is exhausting. Without the assistance designers provide, viewers are tacitly informed, we will surely capsize in a sea of mis-directed busy-ness. As *Time Makeover* asks as a prelude to the time-management regime it aims to impose: "Ever feel like every day is a race against the clock? You're always trying to fit one more thing into your daily agenda? Five minutes to spare means five minutes you could have been doing something that gets you closer to the finish line?" Reality subjects on this show, Cathy and DC, surely do. In fact, when asked to describe their life together in five words, they say: "It's like a circus—everyday." Help comes for Cathy and DC in the form of a time management expert, who assesses their activities, their calendars, and their cupboards, and itemizes a list of three issues and four solutions that will simplify their lives. This is a theme we see repeated across design-oriented shows: the problems of living have solutions, and designers possess the skills we need to make sense of our lives.

Given this, I would argue there are three interlocking components that are critical to the rise of design-themed shows, each of these components bearing a distinct neoliberal quality and holding relation to Katrina TV. First, we must be inundated with a sheer mass of details that are both confusing and difficult to negotiate. Indeed, the labyrinthine nature of these design dilemmas must increase the risk that we will either be taken in by charlatans or that, if we decide to go it alone, we will make big mistakes. In either case, without assistance we are at risk of making poor investments of our time, energy, and capital, and since market logics rule in a neoliberal economy and there is no welfare safety net, it is critical that every person make sound choices.[12] Designers thus provide a critical service in that they reduce the risk of costly error. Second, in order to need designers in the first place, we must have sufficient resources of time and money that allow us to turn away from subsistence concerns, so it is not racism, poverty, or malnutrition that worry us but the inundation of material surplus as manifested through the over-filled spaces of bodies and homes. The redesign of New Orleans, as I will soon demonstrate, both reinforces and obscures this point, since the "solutions for living" that designers offer on Katrina TV are very often tied to the transcendence of subsistence concerns so that makeover renovations might provide shelter with high-end design features. And third, we must feel some fear that a failure to manage the excesses of our everyday lives will result in not just a "dangerous problem of living" but in the indisputable evidence of decay at our moral centers. So, New Orleans, just like the ubiquitous Before-body of makeover TV, provides a site of broader recognition, suggesting that a failure to make good choices and to regulate the physical/social body will result in catastrophe and collapse. Both New Orleans' decayed infrastructure pre-Katrina and the endless bureaucratic delays post-Katrina attenuate an overall sense of NOLA's desperate need.

My characterization of a mediated cultural moment in which Reality TV responds to the problems of living through design solutions may sound a little hyperbolic, but then you hear a soothing "clutter engineer" on the Fine Living Channel's *Simplify Your Life*, say reassuringly, "Sometimes messiness isn't a character flaw, it's a design flaw." His statement is both comforting and alarming (I would argue deliberately so), offering participants and at-home viewers a solution to a problem that they scarcely knew existed. Clutter has a long historical provenance, particularly in the United States, of being a site of shameful excess, of exposing a lack of discipline, and of indicating that an insufficiently regulated domestic sphere gives rise to a diseased individual body that, through an osmotic theory of disarray, jeopardizes the health and well-being of the social body. There is perhaps no better example of civic clutter than that represented by post-Katrina New Orleans.

The designer's intervention on both makeover and Katrina TV indicates that what we might have otherwise understood as either the flotsam and jetsam of daily existence, the indisputable signs of poverty, or evidence of poor sanitary standards are, sometimes, merely design issues. So, the problem is not that we have too much stuff, we eat too much food, we have an ineffective or uncaring government, or even that we are too poor, the problem is we have insufficiently designed mechanisms to deal with our needs. Yet, the reversibility of this clutter engineer's statement is also ominous, for if sometimes clutter isn't a character flaw but a design flaw, then equally, sometimes messiness is not about design but about character. And it's not just clutter that designers ask us to worry about in the name of our character. It's other forms of excess that must be managed, such as fat or debt or a closet stuffed with unwearable clothes. It's other markers of insufficient self-scrutiny, such as an inability to see one's kids, one's body, one's dog, one's behavior, or one's home the way others do. It is deviation in adhering to appropriate and normative codes, ways of looking, ways of acting, ways of thinking that seem too "out there," "eccentric," or "over the top." Designers are thus critical in helping us achieve utopias where—if we pay close attention and obey the rules—we will be confident, happy, and energized. But since the ideal is by definition unattainable, design solutions ultimately lead not to confidence and well-being but to anxiety and despair, an inevitability equally espoused through the mediated discourses of Katrina TV.

e2: Making it Right

Though not announcing itself as a typical makeover show, *e2* follows the conventions of design-iphilia mapped across the reality TV mediascape.[13] Its double "e"s stand for environment and economy, thus underscoring the symbiotic connection that mandates green living as a standard bearer for future market success. In its episode specifically taking up the need for new design after Katrina called "New Orleans: The Water Line," *e2* glorifies the all-white visiting crew of designers and architects who will work with the (seemingly) all-black indigenous residents of the Holy Cross and Lower Ninth Ward of New Orleans to build affordable and sustainable housing. The episode is narrated with extraordinary gravitas by Brad Pitt, who, due to being "appalled and embarrassed" by the bureaucratic nightmare of government emergency readiness and his consequent stewardship of the Make it Right Foundation, is called in to voice the more philosophical elements of the episode.[14] These philosophical guideposts include the quote from Thomas Jefferson that functions as epigraph to this article. At first, "New Orleans: The Water Line" appears to be a critique of neoliberalism, since Pitt poignantly informs the viewer of the interrelation between commerce, living, and industry. "Suburbs in Los Angeles affect the melting ice caps of Antarctica; deforestation in the Congo affects the typhoons of Japan."[15] His remarks constitute a pointed reminder that a global marketplace operates within a planetary ecosystem. Tellingly, those in a position of greater cultural power (namely Los Angelinos) must be cognizant not only of how to increase their competitive edge in the marketplace but also of how their fiscal desires have global ramifications. Enlightened self-interest demands that market imperatives cannot always prevail.

This critique of the neoliberal mandate is furthered in *e2* by the frequent reminders of how significantly both local and federal government agencies failed in disaster preparedness and emergency management. Says Bob Berkebile, a founding principal with BNIM Architects, "The government failed the community at almost every level. At the city level, at the state level, at the federal level." Ted Horne, a former Metro editor for the *The Times Picayune*, speaks of Lower Ninth residents as "yearning for direction, for cohesive leadership, which was not available." Pitt's voice reinforces such failures of leadership, noting, "[A]ll over New Orleans, derelict houses and vacant lots bear mute witness to the city's exodus and to government's absence."

Yet, here is where the critique of neoliberalism loses its sustaining momentum, since the text uses the absence of government to suggest an emergence of opportunities for entrepreneurship as led by "visionary" designers. Lack of government leadership compelled the residents of lower New Orleans to turn to the only institution they can trust, Pitt tells us. That institution being the community. Berkebile reinforces this claim, "[I]n that hostile environment, this community, particularly Holy Cross and the Lower Ninth Ward, came together and decided that they would form their own government." Similarly, Pamela Dashiell, president of the Lower Ninth Ward Center for Sustainable Engagement and Development (CSED), affirms that community-based urban renewal has given residents the possibility of agency and ownership that they would not otherwise have had. The people, she claims, have developed a new attitude: "They're not going to take this. We're going to reclaim it." The government's absence thus created a "nexus for change," says Dashiell, an "unprecedented opportunity" to renew and restore a place with an old culture through the aid and protection of the "wonderful planners," the architects and engineers, who have come to their rescue.

As I've mentioned earlier, my point here is not really to suggest that there is no altruism in these urban renewal projects or that nonprofit organizations such as Pitt's Make it Right Foundation don't do good work. More significant, I think, is the degree to which, within the relentlessly optimistic larger narrative of televisual transformations, it becomes practically impossible for *e2*, or any design-related program, to reference positive outcomes outside of the language and logic of the marketplace. Laurie Ouellette has noted about what she terms "Do Good TV": "TV has fused charity work with the rationality of the market, so that there's no distinction between public service and cultural product."[16] As seen on Katrina TV, misery and neglect function as the necessary change-agents that bring new life and new opportunities, new possibilities of being healthy and productive citizen-workers who can contribute (happily) to the global supply chain. Importantly, disaster and remediation are represented as community-cohering events that invite the makeover and lead to better lives where economic opportunities are plentiful. In this respect, "community" functions as an incredibly plastic term that often obscures neoliberal economic maneuvers.

A moment in *e2*'s "New Orleans: The Water Line" inadvertently makes this connection between destitution and transformation clear. Throughout the program, multiple experts speak of the edifying effect New Orleans can have on the rest of the nation, indeed on the rest of the world, since NOLA's devastation allows it to be a model for sustainable building practices that are environmentally responsive. These practices include using recycled, repurposed, and salvaged materials. Houses, in turn, are designed to withstand high winds, endure flooding, and to operate with reduced gas and electric needs. All well and good. Even commendable. Yet, here's what makes me uncomfortable. Expert after expert praises the capacity of New Orleans' poorest residents to practice sustainable measures. Berkebile reflects, "My experience is, for the most part, they really understand sustainability. They know how to be resourceful." The camera immediately cuts from Berkebile in direct-address to an image of a group of black children and teenagers, clustered around a kneeling white man, who seems to be lecturing them (one presumes, not on sustainability practices, since they already know these so well). The "natural" connection between economically disadvantaged people and ecological prudence is accentuated when Dashiell speaks for the black community,

> We've always had a lot of environmental awareness, partly, again, because of our location at the confluence of three bodies of water, and partly because it's just something that's a part of our nature, I guess. Simple living. Re-use. It's just what grandma and grandpa used to tell us. You do the best you can with what you have.

What people on the screen pointedly do not comment on is that such affinity for sustainable practices has been driven by generations of economic disenfranchisement. Through a rhetorical alchemy, it is only when hand-me-downs are called salvage materials, when living close to the land becomes a "natural systems approach," when low-income housing is replaced by high-concept design that the Before-body of the pre-Katrina Lower Ninth can become the After-body of post-storm New Orleans.

The irony here is rich, since design will save the day, and yet it is design that lulled residents of the Lower Ninth into a sense that all was well with the world. Horne notes, for instance, that many of the people who lost their homes when the levees broke, owned those residences

> free and clear. Which is why, for lack of mortgaging they had often dropped out of the federal flood insurance program because the faith and good credit of the federal government often isn't necessary because you figure, after all, didn't they build us this wonderful levee system here. Well the levee system turned out to be not so wonderful. And the people whose homes were in that Niagara of water that came out of the industrial canal in the Lower Ninth ward had lost everything they owned.

People living in the Lower Ninth Ward had thought themselves protected by a government-certified levee, designed, built, and inspected by the Army Corps of Engineers. Its failure, as well as the incompetence of the Federal Emergency Management System, the Louisiana National Guard, and the Department of Homeland Security, gave poignant testimony to the neoliberal maxim that industry can be trusted more than governments.

Tellingly, as depicted on Katrina TV, however, those nongovernmental safety nets often carry celebrity currency, so that it is not just an anonymous volunteer but the likes of *Dog Whisperer* Cesar Milan, movie stars Sean Penn and Brad Pitt, or most of the makeover shows on TLC, Discovery, and Style that bring new style, life, and hope to New Orleans (VH1 made its contribution in June 2009, when it sent the girls of its female discipline-themed reality franchise *Charm School* to witness the destruction of Katrina and then volunteer in the city). As the image that appears earlier in this essay demonstrates, Brad Pitt's celebrity both authorizes and publicizes the neoliberal makeover underway in New Orleans. As the world's most famous movie star stands in front of one his high-end green homes, his Fedora hat jauntily askew, Pitt's good looks and charismatic profile function as the epitome of can-do volunteerism. The sleek design, of both the renovated home and of the image itself, function in stark relief to the desolation out of which the makeover arises.

The logic of the makeover as seen on Katrina TV thus suggests that, just as in the broader genre of makeover TV, trauma is a critical form of currency that will purchase mediation and rescue, creating what Anna McCarthy has termed a "neoliberal theater of suffering."[17] As long as you have a horribly sad story to tell and designers can solve the problem you present, you've got a valuable commodity worthy of air time. The exchange principle expressed here mirrors the neoliberal values Amy Hasinoff has detected in the racialized discourse of a different reality TV favorite, *America's Next Top Model*. Hasinoff contends, and I believe rightly so, that the seemingly post-race domain of *ANTM* is actually rife with neoliberal racism, since the text makes a marketable commodity out of contestants' feminine racialization and suggests that hardship and discrimination can be overcome through hard work. On Katrina TV, where residents of the Lower Ninth are perpetually referenced as "victims," race is an implied impediment that can be overcome through improved design.

Holmes to the Rescue

In this fetishization of design and the designer, which relies on both disaster scenarios and a glorification of those who will save the downtrodden from calamity, there can be no more perfect a savior than Mike Holmes. Described by HGTV Canada's website as "280 pounds of muscle and determination," the burly and hypermasculine host of *Holmes on Homes* might tell viewers, "I'm not a hero. I just make things right," but both the logic of the show and its surrounding iconography on websites and commercials suggest that Mike Holmes is an exalted man's (super)man, who has homeowners' interests and well-being in mind. As episode after episode relentlessly demonstrates, Holmes will engage in "profiles of innovation" to "make it right," a rather vague phrase that seemingly means Holmes will verify the safety and aesthetic appeal of the structures he remodels. Since Holmes can only make right what has previously been made wrong, his is an authority grounded in (somebody else's) error. Holmes, named Canada's most-trusted contractor, travels across the expanse of the nation (mostly represented by Toronto but now expanding into other provinces and the United States), putting right the mistakes and mishaps inflicted on innocent homeowners by bad, irresponsible, and otherwise incompetent contractors (though we would imagine these designers making "piece of crap" housing do not have their own TV shows).

Like Brad Pitt with whom he shares the "make it right" slogan, Holmes also has a nonprofit foundation, his called the Holmes Foundation, that uses the pithy catch phrase, "Lien on Me" and is grounded in the principles we've seen rehearsed in the neoliberal terrain of makeover and Katrina TV. The goals of his foundation are twofold, Holmes says: (1) to address serious construction malfeasance, since his activism is predicated not on "the little bathroom rip-off or the tiny little job, or the poor work of a small job, but for the big, for the financially distressed, that is changing lives forever" and (2) to train young people through "apprenticeships [and] scholarships" that will help the "young to become the next generation of pros out there" (www.makeitright.ca). These two goals, one for financial justice, the other for a competent workforce, are brought together to compose a neoliberal platform in which a television makeover host and his nonprofit foundation, rather than the federal government, will oversee the regulation of building codes and the certification and training of laborers.

In 2008, Holmes traveled to New Orleans for a six-part special that aired in both Canada and the United States in 2009[18]. The special, called Holmes in New Orleans, begins as do most makeovers, with establishing need as the camera follows the overall-clad Mike through the streets of the city as he surveys and documents the "crap construction" that awaits his remedial touch. As so depicted, New Orleans' Before-body is a composite of both pre-Katrina shoddy construction and post-Katrina destruction, all collapsed into a chaotic field of urban blight. As one blogger at Reality TV Suite 101 rather bluntly put it, "The Lower Ninth Ward is nothing more than a graveyard of broken down houses, shattered trees, garbage, and mud when Holmes arrives in the summer of 2008. There's no grocery store, no playground, and no businesses nearby. It's as if the Hurricane just hit"[19]. Such visual information reinforces a notion that residents of New Orleans have done little to improve their own desolate situation. In these series of episodes, Holmes teams with Pitt to create a low-cost green home for Gloria Guy, a sixty-eight-year-old "feisty" grandmother of fifteen, who waits with her grandchildren in Atlanta while the make-it-right teams construct her home. The camera frequently comes back to images of Guy's neighbor, Mrs. LeBlanc, who watches from her porch as the house goes up. "When you're good, goodness follows you," she says to no one in particular, the makeover here posing as divine payment for goodness rather than as material response to need.

Proving the validity of the Canadian HGTV website's claim that "there was nothing easy about the Big Easy," the heart of the dramatic tension arises when "hero contractor Mike Holmes and his dedicated crew" endure "intense rainstorms and sweltering heat" in order to rebuild Guy's home. Conforming to another principle of makeover TV in the truncated time allocated for transformations, Mike and his team are arbitrarily allowed only ten weeks, rather than the twenty they need, in order to construct the new house and meet a deadline for a handover of the keys of August 29, 2008, thus marking Hurricane Katrina's third anniversary (all well and good, but why couldn't they have started the project ten weeks sooner?). The challenges of heat and schedules both underscore, in this case, the constructed nature of "reality" TV, which must make narrative hay while the literal sun shines. But the speed of the rebuild project also underscores the heroics and efficacy of the makeover stylist, since even in adversity Holmes can triumph where government agencies fail.

While we might consider these scenes where a movie star and a makeover host struggle to direct the hard labor of home construction for New Orleans' post-Katrina homeless as positive, what we also see unfolding before our eyes is a complex narrative about race in America. Stephen Steinberg notes, for instance, that "the essence of racial oppression" in the United States is what he calls a "grand apartheid," which he takes to mean "a racial division of labor, a system of occupational segregation that relegates most blacks to work in the least desirable job sectors or that excludes them from job markets altogether."[20] In *Holmes in New Orleans* there is both a reversal of this grand apartheid and a substantiation of its meaning, for while it is white designers, foundation heads, and contractors who direct white workers as black residents sit by and watch (or live in an entirely different place), the show so glorifies the innovation and labor it depicts on the screen that a racial separation remains constant. That the narratives play unproblematically as "salvation stories" where everyone gets along and rejoices in the products and aspirations of the white design team suggests not only a neoliberal sensibility in which race and class are figured as irrelevant (because transcended) but a mediated color blindness. Herman Gray calls such inclinations for represented universal harmony on television an "assimilationist discourse of invisibility," since the refusal of difference creates a world where race factors as an individual experience rather than as a collective identity or form of oppression. This, in turn, Gray argues, favors a "subject position...necessarily that of the white middle class" where "whiteness is the privileged yet unnamed place from which to see and make sense of the world."[21]

Architecture School: "What an ego massage!"

I want to conclude this discussion of how makeover and Katrina TV fetishize the role of designers through neoliberal tropes that accentuate a racialized power imbalance by turning finally to *Architecture School*. Airing as a six-part series on the Sundance Channel, *Architecture School* chronicles the efforts of a group of architecture students at New Orleans's Tulane University, who work to design and build a new home in Central City, an area of New Orleans between the toney Garden District and the destitute Ninth Ward that was hard hit by Hurricane Katrina. Although appearing on a network renowned for cutting-edge independent films and fronted by the high-minded tag-line "stakes + students = humanity," *Architecture School* is, in fact, a form of reality TV replete with neoliberal messages about racial relations and free markets.[22]

Architecture School deploys many of the visual and aural devices that mark reality TV's design competition shows, including behind-the-scenes images of participants waking up or in their underwear, harsh critiques from judges (in the guise of "badgering" professors), and some of the same rap music scratching sound effects that splice together a series such as *Project Runway* or *America's Next Top Model*. As in most design-centered television programming, students are pitted against one another in a contest of innovation as they seek to create a winning design that will actually be built. Apparently, this tangible aspect of designing is what excites students the most, for the post-Katrina need for housing in New Orleans means that student-workers can direct their labor toward a clear and necessary goal. For this reason the students are depicted as fascinated with the teleology of material production rather than bored by the abstractions of academic learning. This, I would argue, bespeaks a neoliberal investment in both creativity and intellectualism that works in the service of commodification, particularly since the winning design will not only be built into an actual home but will be featured in a television show. As one of the student designers exclaims, "What an ego massage!" Much like *e2*, *Architecture School* gives some space to altruism, with one white female student noting off camera, "You have privileges, you have an obligation to give back. I think you should be out there, involved and engaged and trying to make the world a better place, because otherwise, why would you be here?" Her rhetorical question is soon answered by a surfeit of images and dialogue crowding the screen. One white male student laughs to another, "I just can't imagine people saying, 'So what did you do for studio last year?' I built a house."

Because *Architecture School* is set in a post-Katrina New Orleans and footage makes much of what it describes as "a devastated New Orleans area," we have another moment where the hurricane is depicted as a tipping point for necessary and salutary social change. As Professor Byron Mouton reflects to the camera, however, the visually arresting conditions that startled so many people about the city existed far before the storm hit. When driving people through New Orleans to witness its appearance, Mouton says, they often remark, "Wow, I can't believe the storm did this." Yet, Mouton acknowledges, much of the destruction is not due to the storm. "This type of condition has existed in this city for decades now. Really, it's been a problem for thirty years. Katrina has given us in some ways the opportunity to repair or fix pre-Katrina problems." Reed Kroloff, the cofounder of Urban Build, is a bit less upbeat. "This city is a place that hides true decay under a thin veneer of charm," he says bluntly. For all of their direct talk, neither man addresses the root causes of the city's "degradation" in racism, poverty, crime, or neglect.

Indeed, if you follow the logic of *Architecture School*, the reasons for the mass of unsafe and crumbling shotgun shacks packed into New Orleans's poorer neighborhoods and occupied by primarily African American residents seems to be a commitment to outmoded design traditions. So, for instance, those residents who live in the areas where new designs are being erected and who resist the unusual structures imposed by "innovative architects" are depicted as unable to appreciate the forward thinking represented by avant-garde design, making the tension between black residents and white designers a conflict expressing cultural capital. Lakica Watkins, who is otherwise supportive of *Architecture School*'s efforts, describes one architect-designed house as "look[ing] like it's from outer space." Big Jack, a resident of a neighborhood where previous Tulane-inspired houses have been built, flatly admits, "I think they're ugly. Put it back like it was!" It doesn't seem to matter that many highly educated and culturally refined designers, scholars, and artists outside of the confines of *Architecture School*'s narrative share Big Jack's opinion about the incongruity of the newly designed structures. Within the episode, Big Jack's moment of resistance is an opportunity for intra-diegetic repetition, as the show both ends and begins segments with his declarations. It does not, however, repeat his more serious critique that suggests the degree to which racial power systems are at work: "You're back in the black neighborhood experimenting on shit," Big Jack intones. "If you want to experiment, experiment on St. Charles Street."

These narrative mechanisms whereby certain statements and phrases are repeated and others are glossed over serve to manage potential resistance. They thus fit firmly within the tropes of makeover TV, which often uses subjects' initial recalcitrance to reinforce the values of transformation.[23] The harder subjects resist at the beginning of the intervention, the firmer they believe by the big reveal. In a similar way, video-cinematic conventions within *Architecture School* neutralize potential concerns that designers are forcefully overwriting the needs of New Orleans residents. As one student Amarit (who self-identifies as Asian) puts it:

> Hopefully, all of us that are designing are taking in mind the scale of the neighborhood, but you're always trying to push the envelope a little bit and come up with things that are more exciting... recreating something or trying to mimic something that was built a hundred years ago or fifty years ago, I don't think that's an homage to something that's built a long time ago. I think that's just about a bastardization of something that was built a long time ago.

Clearly, design is king, and if people who have to live in that design do not like it, the sentiment here maintains that those residents are not sufficiently educated as to its value.

Much as with the whitening universalism inculcated within a neoliberal mandate that all laborers compete on a level playing field, the design training premises of *Architecture School* foreclose scenarios where potential residents will not appreciate good design. This is true even in a case when a professor critiques Amarit's concept for a house centered around a rectangular core: "Why as a user do I give a damn about your core?" Though Amarit dismisses the review by saying "I fucking got raped in there," the implication is clear: good designers make their designs matter to consumers. Since *Architecture School* makes clear that an architect's skill is as much about presentation as inspiration, Amarit's failure is not one of design development but of persuasion. Says student Carter before his pitch to defend his design, "I'm definitely in the mindset of being a salesman and not an architecture student." Here we see demonstrated that a designer must strategize in terms of market(ing) appeal as well as artistic merit, and the true mark of a great designer is not solely artistic vision but business savvy. As such, *Architecture School* turns the devices of innovative design to serve the values of a larger marketplace, thus reinforcing a neoliberal universalism that finds validation in the workings of a "free" market economy. In all, *Architecture School* suggests a complex formula where creativity commodified + competition × mediated makeovers ÷ by neoliberalism = Katrina TV.

After the Storm

Given makeover TV's primary directive that transformation is the gateway to selfhood, *e2*, *Holmes in New Orleans*, and *Architecture School* equally suggest that without designers, the messiness of life and urban blight represents not only a character flaw but a dangerous schism in identity. In the case of Katrina, that schism is writ large across the sections of New Orleans lying below the water line, and the abject primarily African American residents of these wards are coded as bodies in desperate need of salvation. Although much is made of indigenous community empowerment, the neoliberal televised agency voiced by residents of New Orleans' worst-hit areas is claimed only as a consequence of Katrina TV's interventions, never as a precondition of its involvement. Remembering the episode of *How Do I Look?* that I alluded to in the introduction to this essay, it is when the show gives Barbara, Kimberley, and Carla the transformative experience of style that they emerge as empowered selves. Just as with Pitt's "hand up not a hand out," makeover gifts are conditional and one-time only and the presence of the makeover's designers and style professionals is short-term. This is not *Pygmalion* where the designer falls in love with the designed, it is makeover TV where a mad world of mess demands that experts get in, do their work, and leave. As one blogger writing to the Sundance Channel in response to *Architecture School* commented:

> When it comes to rebuilding or revitalizing a community, especially New Orleans, its [*sic*] always the same story. A bunch of people not from the area, never been to that area, trying to put their footprint on it. That's the problem with architecture in general. If there were diversity in the education and diversity in the students, maybe the show wouldn't be a student version of extreme makeover.

This posting, tellingly titled "Not about race, but it's about race," puts its discursive finger squarely on the power differentials at stake in urban renewal projects, where design is implemented by ostensibly well-meaning but largely outsider white, middle-class designers.[24] When those renewal projects happen through the mediated domains of television, the problems of living are both exacerbated and seemingly neutralized.

If we all end up living in the same 150 types of pre-fabricated but sustainable houses, well such is the nature of things in this homogenized design-utopia, where sameness assures that one is not deviating, that one has not committed a moral infraction through excesses of devastation, clutter, or fat. But here we should not be misled into thinking that design-related shows only and always produce identical outcomes.[25] Indeed, the point of these shows is rarely that everyone should look alike, act alike, or be alike. Rather our critical quality of sameness should manifest through the degree to which we all need and appreciate professional and mediated assistance in managing our worlds.

In the design shows of makeover and Katrina TV, good taste and design solutions are represented as plural. Pathology arises not from heterogeneity but from the absence of trusted and competent mediated design professionals, who host television shows and offer solutions to what is represented as the terror of everyday living, a chaos Katrina made evident in a startlingly graphic form. So, in this regard, TV designers help produce utopias, whereas those lives not augmented by television's design superheroes—or worse yet, contaminated by bad or unmediated design—represent a dystopic disaster zone from which the design show is determined to save us. But since salvation in this context can only be conceptualized as a series of neoliberal bromides that turn crisis into opportunities for engaged entrepreneurism and systemic disenfranchisement into details to be overcome, Katrina TV's emergency aid ultimately reifies the power inequities that mark New Orleans as a social body in distress.

Notes

1. For more on the proliferation of makeover-themed texts, see in particular Rachel Moseley's "Makeover Takeover on British Television."
2. It remains to be seen how and if neoliberalism will hold such ideological prominence in the context of global financial instability and new measures being put forth by Barack Obama's administration beginning in January 2009. Since Katrina and neoliberalism are so strongly linked to George W. Bush's administration, and since the programming I analyze was made and largely aired while Bush was

president, references to "government" in this essay are both specifically about a U.S. government led by Bush and a more abstract (and not exclusively U.S.) form of governmentality where neoliberal principles have largely dominated decision-making processes for the last twenty years.

3. For more on the intricate interrelation of neoliberalism and television, see Laurie Ouellette and James Hay, *Better Living Through Reality TV: Television and Post-Welfare Citizenship*; Janice Peck, *The Age of Oprah: Cultural Icon for the Neoliberal Era*; Gareth Palmer, ed., *Exposing Lifestyle Television: The Big Reveal*; Toby Miller, *Cultural Citizenship: Cosmopolitanism, Consumerism, and Television in a Neoliberal Age*; and Nick Couldry, *Media Consumption and Public Engagement: Beyond the Presumption of Attention*.
4. It's significant that Katrina occurred when Americans were at a particular height of financial investment in their homes, a subject discussed in Alyssa Katz's *Our Lot: How Real Estate Came to Own Us*. Historian Richard Bushman might well argue that the American investment in household structures is not new at all but a marker of the American project since the country began. See Bushman's *The Refinement of America: Persons, Houses, Cities*.
5. "Home is Where the Tarp Is: Katrina, Commercialism, and Class in *Extreme Home Makeover: Home Edition*," p. 2.
6. Ibid., emphasis added.
7. *TV by Design: Modern Art and the Rise of Network Television*, p. 2.
8. "Best Bets on TV," p. E2.
9. In 2009, Tim Gunn, one of the design experts on *Project Runway*, was actually folded into a four-issue series of Marvel Comic's *Model's Inc*, where he dons the high-tech red and gold battle armor of superhero Iron Man.
10. See Jo Littler's engaging article that analyzes how the "public display of support for 'the afflicted' can be a way for celebrities to appear to raise their profile above the zone of the crudely commercial into the sanctified, quasi-religious realm of altruism and charity, whilst revealing or constructing an added dimension of personality: of compassion and caring" (p. 237). "'I feel your pain': Cosmopolitan Charity and the Public Fashioning of the Celebrity Soul."
11. See "Desperate Citizens and Good Samaritans: Neoliberalism and Makeover Reality TV."
12. In his landmark work on culture and neoliberalism, Nikolas Rose comments on the imperative that citizen-subjects be wise consumers: "The enhancement of the powers of the client as customer—consumer of health services, of education, of training, of transport—specifies the subjects of rule in a new way: as active individuals seeking to 'enterprise themselves,' to maximize their quality of life through acts of choice, according life a meaning and

value to the extent that it can be rationalized as the outcome of choices made or choices to be made" (p. 57). "Governing 'Advanced' Liberal Democracies."
13. *e2* is produced by Kontentreal (content real) Productions, a company that is making a name for itself as a producer of environmentally aware programming.
14. "Brad's Fight for New Orleans," p. 73.
15. As featured in a public service announcement, Kevin Bacon is also intent on communicating the message that economics affect ecosystems through his foundation, Six Degrees. One PSA features him sitting in a window sill as he speaks seriously to the camera, "For most people God is a very important thing, in all kinds of religions. And the idea that hurricanes, floods, drought, could actually be a result of man's hand as opposed to God's hand is a difficult thing for people to get their head around. And something that we have an obligation to fix." For more, go to http://www.sixdegrees.org/
16. "Do Good TV?"
17. In a cogent essay, McCarthy adeptly shows how the neoliberal theater of suffering made salient on reality TV is both "utterly banal" and "pregnant with [dangerous] possibility" (p. 34). The scope of this affective range, McCarthy contends, is fueled by narratives of shame and trauma that foster a hope for the possibility of neoliberal salvation and a willingness to subject oneself to its disciplinary demands.
18. you can friend the show on Facebook at http://www.facebook.com/album.php?aid=113065&id=75991030794
19. Holmes Make it Right
20. "Occupational Apartheid in America: Race, Labor Market Segmentation, and Affirmative Action," p. 216.
21. *Watching Race: Television and the Struggle for Blackness*, p. 86.
22. The sources of *Architecture School's* artistic provenance reveal themselves in the production credits, particularly since one of its creators as well as its director and writer, Michael Selditch, has producing, writing, and directing credits for such shows as *Plastic Surgery: Before & After*, *Queer Eye for the Straight Guy*, *The EcoZone Project*, and *Project Jay*, a TV documentary about the first winner of *Project Runway*.
23. There exist rare exceptions to this rule of resistance and conquest, but even exceptions tend to reinforce a larger sense that resistance to the "benevolent" transformations wrought by the makeover is futile. For an illuminating discussion, see Martin Roberts' "The Fashion Police: Governing the Self in *What Not to Wear*."
24. As Larry Bennett and Adolph Reed, Jr. note about attempts to remake Cabrini Green in Chicago, stereotypes about race and "concentrated poverty" often incline urban planners to disrupt community and "neighborhood viability" in the service of a radically rebuilt environment. "The New Face of Urban Renewal: The Near North

Redevelopment Initiative and the Cabrini-Green Neighborhood," p. 181.

25. One way to see how these shows fetishize multiple design options rather than homogenous outcomes is to look at those programs featuring numerous designers. Design competition shows such as *Project Runway, Top Chef, Design Rivals, Trading Spaces, Moving Up, How Do I Look?*, and *Mail Order Makeover* suggest that taste is not a monologic top-down indoctrination from high to low but a survival of the fittest (or the hippest) that pits one set of aesthetic judgments against another. Significantly, these contests to prove and hone superior skills do not happen in a democratizing medium where everyone can participate, but in the rarified domains of already-established expertise, where designers are placed outside of the dowdy commonplace that announces itself through a run-down appearance, boring rooms, "crazy" choices, and schizophrenic styles.

CHAPTER 10

FROM MR. PREGNANT TO MR. PRESIDENT: PREPOSITIONING KATRINA ONLINE

Jeff Scheible

A Klee painting named "Angelus Novus" shows an angel looking as though he is about to move away from something he is fixedly contemplating. His eyes are staring, his mouth is open, his wings are spread. This is how one pictures the angel of history. His face is turned toward the past. Where we perceive a chain of events, he sees one single catastrophe which keeps piling wreckage upon wreckage and hurls it in front of his feet. The angel would like to stay, awaken the dead, and make whole what has been smashed. But a storm is blowing from Paradise; it has got caught in his wings with such violence that the angel can no longer close them. This storm irresistibly propels him into the future to which his back is turned, while the pile of debris before him goes skyward.

—Walter Benjamin, "Theses on the Philosophy of History"

Of justice where it is not yet, not yet there, *where it is no longer, let us understand where it is no longer* present, *and where it will never be, no more than the law, reducible to laws or rights. It is necessary to speak* of the *ghost, indeed* to the *ghost and with it, from the moment that no ethics, no politics, whether revolutionary or not, seems possible...*

—Jacques Derrida, Specters of Marx *(emphases in the original)*

It's all about the present. Presentness. Presenty qua qua.

—Mr. Pregnant, "Where Is Santa Claus"

On August 30, 2005, Yahoo! News published two photographs online—one by Dave Martin for the Associated Press, and another by Chris Graythen for AFP/Getty

Images. Both images depict people chest-deep, surrounded by water with no land in the frame, looking ahead and off to the side. Martin's image is of an African American, with a box of soda cans halfway-submerged underwater under one shoulder and with what looks like a trash bag floating along the water in his other hand. The first sentence of this photograph's caption reads, "A young man walks through chest deep flood water after looting a grocery store in New Orleans on Tuesday, Aug. 30, 2005." Meanwhile, Graythen's image is of two people—white, both wearing backpacks, with the woman in the front dragging a bag through the water.[1] The caption running with this began, "Two residents wade through chest-deep water after finding bread and soda from a local grocery store after Hurricane Katrina came through the area in New Orleans, Louisiana."

A user on Flickr, dustin3000, then set the two captioned photographs side by side. Bloggers and critics were quick to pick up on the problematic difference in the word choice accompanying these two very similar photographs. The skin color of the people depicted is the major difference between the two images, with the captions identifying the darker-skinned person as "looting" and the lighter-skinned persons as "finding." This troubling juxtaposition, which some have termed the "Two-Photo Controversy," led many people to scrutinize the depictions media outlets were using to represent different people's actions during Katrina and its aftermath. Scholar and public intellectual Michael Eric Dyson writes, for example,

> The looting of New Orleans, though largely overplayed in the media, and often narrowly, and unfairly, viewed as the rioting of thugs and not largely the survival activity of folk abandoned by their government, raised once again the specter, splashed across national television, of blacks out of control.[2]

Responding to the outcry, Yahoo! News pulled the photos at the request of Agence France-Presse (AFP), and General Manager Neil Budde issued an apology. He explained that they "present the photos and their captions as written, edited and distributed by the news services with no additional editing" and that "Yahoo! News regrets that these photos and captions, viewed together, may have suggested a racial bias on our part."[3] In a statement about the "looting" caption, AFP's multimedia director Olivier Calas offered, "This was a consequence of a series of negligences, not ill intent." It seems worth noting that Calas's apology for word choice strangely echoes broader discourses around Katrina itself, particularly the ways in which the U.S. Army Corps of Engineers was characterized as neglecting proper levee engineering and maintenance, leading to New Orleans's flooding.

At issue here are the divergent connotations of the words looting and finding. People wanted to know how these words were selected by the photographers. *Boston Globe* correspondent Christina Pazzanese asked, "Were interviews conducted as they swam by?"[4] Representatives at both agencies responsible for the photographs expressed that there was in fact some degree of care put into the choice of wording based on what each photographer actually witnessed. In an interview with *Salon*, Santiago Lyon, an AP photography director, justified Martin's caption, "When we see people go into businesses and come out with goods, we call it 'looting.' When we just see them carrying things down the road, we call it 'carrying items.'" Regarding Graythen's choice of wording, a *New York Times* article on the controversy explained that Graythen "described seeing the couple near a corner store from an elevated expressway. The door to the shop was open, and things floated out to the street. He was not able to talk to the couple, 'so I had to draw my own conclusions,' he said."[5]

This controversy illustrates that the precise words we and the media use to frame events carry significant weight, in no small part in this case because of the enormous cultural anxieties attached to what Katrina revealed about the status of race and class in the United States. Moreover, it demonstrates the impact of the kinds of juxtapositions the Internet as a specific medium facilitates, and the critical knowledge, perspective, and discussions that images, texts, and such juxtapositions can generate.

In what follows, I propose that, as if italicizing prepositions like Derrida in the epigraph from *Specters of Marx*, we use a series of tiny, unassuming words—"against," "before," "post," "in," "as," and "without"—even more inconspicuous than the verbs "loot" and "find"—to categorically navigate our way through a series of online media texts and narratives, and their relationships to Katrina. Derrida's interest in locating justice where it is "not" is elaborated by trying out different prepositional relationships with "the ghost," speaking "*of*," "*to*," and "*with*" this spectral presence. These different discursive strategies, he proposes, are "necessary" when facing what seems politically and ethically impossible. This is a claim that compels us to "speak," and by extension, think, research, explore, and write in multidirectional paths to do "justice" to one's object of study and elucidate challenging political and ethical terrains such as Katrina.

Prepositioning, focusing on connections, directions, and shades of relationships, can help us think with more specificity about Katrina, but also about what it is that media texts and objects do. The small words I am signaling, while not all strictly prepositions, nevertheless like prepositions, are used to make connections between bigger words with more transparent meanings, and nevertheless charge our thought, and the words and ideas that come after, in specific directions.[6] Attending to these words and directions forces us to consider how we position, and how we *can* position, Katrina in historical representation, in scholarship, and online. Taken together, these prepositional words also suggest salient and varying ways of specifying, orienting, and problematizing the time and space we associate with Katrina, so that it becomes less a tragic exception in a teleological narrative of progress (a narrative and discourse that with the Obama administration seems to have, understandably, struck a chord) and more like Walter Benjamin's angel of history, for whom historical wreckage exists never only in the past but in a continual *present*, another word to which I shall return.

A search for "Katrina" on Google returns over thirty-nine million results. The first is the Wikipedia entry on the hurricane, then comes katrina.com—a website devoted to the hurricane—followed by a link to CNN articles about the event. These are followed by images of Hong Kong-born Bollywood actress Katrina Kaif in a variety of seductive poses, alongside YouTube and Google videos related to the hurricane, blogs by people named Katrina, a website on which you can buy "Katrina Activewear" (completely unrelated to the hurricane), and one with resources for the design and construction of "Katrina Cottages" (completely related to the hurricane).

Google searches routinely bring information and media we seek into contact with information and media that we don't intend to seek, and we navigate differences between the two to engage in meaning-making processes. As media scholars, moreover, while we might want to be critical of the motivations behind the ways such sources are seamlessly presented to Internet users, we might also methodologically learn a lesson from search sites. Uniting disparate media sites together by a common thread can in fact generate a provocative, informative, and often insightful visual mapping of the thread being researched and can also, in turn, become tools for criticism and analysis, helping provide sharp focus and original perspectives on the individual mediated sites retrieved by the search.

This essay takes as its assumption, and as its organizing logic, that the Internet is particularly conducive to opening up the productive opportunity to consider what I shall refer to as "Katrina *as...*" With this open-ended phrase, I mean to suggest the different kinds of roles that the hurricane has played *in* narrations of the event, our imaginations and discussions *of* its significance, as well as what media studies can do *with* Katrina—the role that it can play as an analytical framework. Moreover, it helps us consider the uncertainty and inevitability of the *post*: what comes *after* Katrina, and the media and comments we *post* about it, after it, in its context. I will explore a variety of "posts" online, mostly on YouTube, and categorically but flexibly consider different narrative configurations "Katrina" takes in relation to them. I aim to demonstrate an analytical logic similar to a Google search that is able to bring together an unexpected collection of media works, which promises to shed focused light on the individual posts and that at the same time speaks to and suggests the broad reach of a post-"Katrina" context.

I use scare quotes because I want to emphasize that these are not "Katrina" narratives per se; I think it is misguided to accept without critical pause the hurricane as the title for the events that surrounded it and for the troubling conditions it exposed. Referring to all of these events and circumstances in terms of a natural disaster (with a woman's name attached to it) undoubtedly frames how narratives might proceed from and about the events. At the same time, it is important to acknowledge that news media have framed the events in such a way that the hurricane *is* the starting point, so it is also important to work with these existing frames to be better able to think critically about them and to branch out of them to understand Katrina *as* other things as well. These concerns are tied up with narrative and strategies for telling, reading, and analyzing narratives in specific contexts.

Artist Paul Chan in November 2007 too saw Katrina *as: in* a narrative that long predates Katrina itself. He staged an outdoor performance of Samuel Beckett's *Waiting for Godot* (entitled *Waiting for Godot in New Orleans*) in front of a barren home in the devastated landscape of New Orleans' Lower Ninth Ward, over two years after the levee failures flooded the city. In his artist statement, Chan explains, "there was a terrible symmetry between the reality of New Orleans post-Katrina and the essence of this play, which expresses in stark eloquence the cruel and funny things people do while they wait: for help, for food for hope. It was uncanny."[7] Chan's re-appropriation of this emblematic, absurdist story about waiting opens up some questions about stories and their relationship to historical events. How do we understand and characterize the "symmetries" between the factual and the fictional? How do we, how should we, emplot narratives about what happened, what is happening, what did not happen, and what continues to not happen in New Orleans? How might we—as spectators, readers, and performers of narratives—see or read a "Katrina" story into a narrative where Katrina does not explicitly present itself?

One of the goals of this chapter is to continue the project of opening up the site of Katrina, to see it where it is less obvious and more pervasive. George Lipsitz, for example, has attributed the waiting, disenfranchisement, and neglect that many people across the globe were surprised to see in New Orleans to a pervasive attitude in the contemporary moment, a "social warrant of competitive consumer citizenship."[8] In his view, (and as Diane Negra has noted earlier in this volume) what makes the types of neglect and discrimination that Katrina exposed possible is the "ideological legitimation they receive from cultural practices, stories, images, and ideas deeply rooted in the quotidian activities of life in the United States."[9] To open up Katrina, we must be mindful of the messages found in stories (and practices, images, and ideas) that circulate not only before it—shaping the conditions of possibility in which the event happens—but also in the stories we tell about it and after it, which then perpetuate the ideological legitimation to which Lipsitz refers.

Katrina *as* Meteorological Event

To embark on our comparative narratography, let's consider an official story that will be a helpful point of reference from which we can understand the significance of other types of Katrina narratives. As we have observed, the first hit that the Google search for Katrina returns, indexing relevance and popularity, is Wikipedia's entry on the subject. The entry itself features both a lock and a star icon in the upper right corner of its page. The lock indicates that there has been controversy in revisions of the entry and that it is no longer open to revision. The star indicates that it is featured by Wikipedia's editors as one of the site's best articles—a mark to which, according to the site, only 1 in 1,140 articles lays claim.[10]

The page's contents begin with what the writers refer to as "storm history." The storm history is a completely meteorological narrative, detailing when the hurricane formed and how. The entry starts, "Hurricane Katrina formed as Tropical Depression Twelve over the southeastern Bahamas on August 23, 2005 as the result of an interaction of a tropical wave and the remains of Tropical Dimension Ten. The system was upgraded to tropical storm status." The discussion then details how and when (to the minute) the storm moved through the region, and it gives all sorts of measurements and speeds. As such, it provides in the most basic sense a narrative of the storm as a sequence of causes and effects over time. It begins in the Bahamas on August 23, 2005, and it ends with a "resulting extratropical storm" that "moved rapidly to the northeast and affected eastern Canada." Wikipedia's storm narrative features a clear narrative climax in the middle, which occurs after the hurricane "enter[s] the Gulf":

> An eyewall replacement cycle disrupted the intensification, but caused the storm to nearly double in size. Katrina again rapidly intensified, attaining Category 5 status on the morning of August 28 and reached its peak strength at 1:00 p.m. CDT that day, with maximum sustained winds of 175 mph (280 km/h) and a minimum central pressure of 902 mbar.

A simple space-time diagram of the narrative's beginning, middle, and end that this history posits would look like this:

> Bahamas, August 23 —> Gulf of Mexico, August 28 —> Canada, August 31.

Katrina's second and third landfalls in Louisiana and Mississippi on August 29 as a Category 3 storm occur after the narrative's climax and end right before Wikipedia describes it as "finally losing hurricane strength."

This narrative of the storm history is only the first section in the site's broader overview of the hurricane and, as such, might be seen as a micro-/framing narrative. Following this "history" portion of the entry, as clearly outlined at the entry's beginning, are sections titled "Preparations," "Impact," and "Aftermath." Each of these sections begins its own narrative centered around the storm's beginning ("preparations"), middle ("impact"), and end ("aftermath"), and each of these sections identifies the storm as the causal agent in the narrative that follows. "Preparations" begins with a section titled "Federal government," yet still begins with the storm: "On the morning of August 26, at 10 a.m. CDT (15000 UTC), Katrina had strengthened to a Category 3 storm in the Gulf of Mexico." (If one wishes to discuss the federal government's preparations, wouldn't it seem intuitive to begin one's narration with the federal government?) The "impact" section then begins, "On August 29, Katrina's storm surge caused 53 different levee breaches in greater New Orleans submerging eighty percent of the city."

As the entry begins with a meteorological storm history, perhaps it is to be expected that Hurricane Katrina's preparations, impact, and aftermath all also begin with meteorological causal factors. Addressing the significance of beginnings upon social narratives, Patrick Colm Hogan writes,

> The assumption of an absolute and singular origin is widely taken to imply a particular moral evaluation. Specifically, in the case of destructive events, the initiating action is commonly taken to define who is morally culpable *for all subsequent events*. Thus it assumes a sort of absolute moral culpability. This idea is strange...It presupposes that the situation prior to the initiating act was just or at least normal (i.e., a form of moral ordinariness undisturbed by large injustices). We form our sense of *moral normalcy* in the same way that we form our sense of causal or any other sort of normalcy.[11]

Hogan's comments suggest the importance of attending to and calling into question the beginning points of narratives about destructive events, and they resonate with the way in which Wikipedia begins its narrative and thereby positions natural, meteorological agents as the initiating actions of Katrina. In Wikipedia's overview of the event, these natural agents become normalized, and the tone set at the beginning shapes a set of expectations for the discourse that follows, which make the event seem predominantly scientific and minimally social. This narrative origin could also be challenged in its own scientific terms, if the entry took other scientific and environmental factors that contributed to the event's disaster, such as global warming, into account.

Criticism of Wikipedia's scientificity, a reader might want to suggest, should be tempered. This is, after all, an entry about a hurricane, a meteorological phenomenon, and what the entry provides is meteorological discourse and narrative. However, I would argue, to align my own views with many others who have written about the event, that Hurricane Katrina has become more than meteorological and is most importantly relevant as a social phenomenon.[12] Part of any responsible informational resource about, or encyclopedic narration of, the hurricane's history, and its causes and effects, should provide a frame that accommodates the event's social significance alongside its more mathematical significance.

Equally worthy of critical attention is the simple narrative diagram I have made of Wikipedia's charting of the storm's meteorological history—beginning in foreign island territory, violently climaxing in a body of water named for another foreign nation it touches (Mexico, the same nation that in spring 2009 was the focus of U.S. media's panicked discussion of the origins of the "Swine Flu"), and ending with after-effects felt in yet a third foreign nation. Framed in this way, Katrina's presence on U.S. land becomes surprisingly incidental to the narrative of the storm's history. In a way, this narrative makes Katrina a non-U.S., foreign phenomenon—beginning and ending on non-U.S. land, and climaxing in water named after Mexico. As such, this story's structure would seem to expunge the storm's significance even more from American social life. Nevertheless, at the same time, the very elision of the United States here might also actually expose the ironic unevenness regarding the event's history: the fact that this storm did begin, climax, and end outside the United States, and did *not* most violently strike U.S. land; yet it undoubtedly had its most insidious consequences on U.S. territory.

One might in the context of this discussion revisit Hayden White's remarks about historical narrative. He writes, "As a symbolic structure the historical narrative does not *reproduce* the events it describes; it tells us in what direction to think about the events and charges our thought about the events..."[13] Wikipedia certainly seems to be telling its reader to "think about" Hurricane Katrina in the "direction" of a meteorological event, and, more specifically, its narrative structure and content seem to direct our thoughts away from American social life.

A Counter-Narrative: Katrina as Social Experience

In his YouTube video "The Truth about Hurricane Katrina," Eric Arceneaux very deliberately articulates the direction *against* which he frames his narrative testimony of experiencing Katrina firsthand. Arceneaux's video is divided into three parts—the first lasts eight-and-a-half minutes, the second is seven minutes long, and the third is five-and-half—totaling twenty-two minutes. "The Truth about Hurricane Katrina" is formally simple and rhetorically powerful. Arceneaux directly addresses his home camera, and he narrates, very compellingly, his personal experience of Katrina.

He begins,

> I'd like to start off by saying that there were many of us that went through a lot, and unfortunately, when the media would go with people to tell the story, they would single out those who were least capable of expressing themselves verbally in a clear way, and least capable of articulating the events that happened. I believe that this was done on purpose. However, I am quite capable of expressing myself. I have a strong command of the English language. And I intend to use it to paint as vivid a picture as possible of my experiences during this time. I feel burdened by the truth and burdened by the fact that it has yet to be fully expressed, and hopefully by doing this little testimony, I can alleviate this burden.

Arceneaux spends the first two minutes explaining that he is seeking to counter "the story" that media have normalized. While he suggests that he wants to counter the relatively inarticulate stories fellow witnesses and survivors have told, the broader significance of his commentary is, by inference, that it also attempts to direct our thoughts away from more official narratives of the kind represented by Wikipedia's entry. Wikipedia's narrative directs our thoughts away from the racial politics the storm exposed, and this exposure is precisely the dramatic focus of Arceneux's testimony. The personal experience that he narrates dismisses the official history of Katrina as being about a disastrous storm. He explains toward the beginning of his narration,

> When Hurricane Katrina hit, everything was fine. It was noisy, but aside from one broken window, there was no problems at all. When

the hurricane was over, and daylight broke, everything looked OK. And in fact, we all went to sleep. Cause we stayed up all night worrying. And it almost felt like we worried for nothing. I remember our biggest concern was that we'd have to redo the carpets, and my mom was talking about how she might get a chance to redo the kitchen since there was a little bit of damage from some mud and water that had flown in through the cracked window. However I woke up to hear my mom yelling that I had to move my car because water was rising up. It was so confusing because there was no rain coming down and yet water was continuing to rise up. And uh it was just really weird. And at the time we had no knowledge of the levees breaking or anything like that. It was just, um, it seemed very random. And very surreal.

Arceneaux's testimony then vividly details how his family stayed in their attic for several days, and how, when they were finally rescued, they were brought to a makeshift aid station, where the unbearable heat, stench, and squalor made for even worse conditions than those in their attic. He makes central to his narration, which he emphasizes by stating, "and I want everyone to hear this," how deeply racist military officials stationed there were, how in their eyes, he was a "nigger," and how they forced the people waiting to behave like animals and to turn on each other, despite the deep bonds they felt with one another. He ends by restating the point he made at the beginning, "I'd like to think that perhaps I've just given voice to some of the feelings and concerns of those who might not have had the words to express it... I have exaggerated nothing. This is just the truth."

If Wikipedia's entry on the storm's history represents an official narrative, this represents a counter-narrative, an account that directly responds, and is a corrective, to the official narrative and its ideological framing of the storm's history. Rather than focusing on the meteorological circumstances of the storm (and its formation, climax, and conclusion outside U.S. boundaries), this story takes us inside an attic and to the racism encountered at a government-sponsored rescue site, centralizing a singular victim's traumatic experience. Contrasted to the objective, locked-and-starred, collectively written Wikipedia narrative, Arceneaux's is a first-person video, made accessible via YouTube. Both Internet accounts attempt to present real, informative accounts of "Hurricane Katrina," but they look nothing alike. Arceneaux's story comes from "within" the storm, and he foregrounds his truth claims "out," *to* the YouTube community. The writers of Wikipedia's entry, on the other hand, presumably were from "without" the storm, gathering information from various news sources as events unfolded, and through presentation of objective, detailed narration, make a strong, implicit truth claim on Katrina's "within."

YouTube and Katrina

Hurricane Katrina's specific temporal coincidence in 2005 with YouTube's launch and instant, widespread popularity seems to urge one to think about how major events in the American social landscape intersect with cultural forms of expression and the representational practices at play in a major new forum for media circulation. As our knowledge-gathering about and discursive engagement with historical events increasingly occurs online, it is particularly important to think through online narratives such as Wikipedia's and Arceneaux's, and the ways in which they mediate high-profile events such as Katrina.

The large impacts of Katrina and YouTube both gave momentum to popular redefinitions of the concept of "community" in their respective contexts. These redefinitions carry with them very different implications and are characterized by very different imaginings of the communal. After YouTube, *community* refers to people sharing content with each other, and this practice maps onto a space that is networked, virtual, and allegedly widely accessible. After Katrina, and its associated displacement and disenfranchisement of a community, there is a heightened desire to envision a politically productive *community*, a group of people that, together, reacts to the segregation of geographical space by class and race. The utopian possibilities found in both redefinitions of community have been stopped short by encounters with obstacles set in place by private interests that often frustrate these communities' experiences. In neighborhoods in New Orleans where homes have been damaged, rather than rebuilding and providing for displaced American citizens, the U.S. Department of Housing and Urban Development planned to demolish forty-five hundred low-income public housing units and build mixed-use housing that would contain space for commerce.[14] And when networks and corporations such as Viacom sue YouTube for copyright infringement for figures as high as one billion dollars, the access the site promises to provide quickly becomes uneven and fleeting.

Addressing YouTube's discourse of community in an essay on *Flow*, John McMurria writes that in "the utopian references to radical democracy from critics, or the paternalistic promises of the founders to not forget the 'community' that launched their fame and fortune, there was little space for the two pressing issues of community that have emerged concurrently with the rise of YouTube": "the Katrina disaster" and the "immigrant rights movement."[15] He goes on to write,

> the mythic idealizations of electronic frontiers such as YouTube also obfuscate the ways in which video culture has reproduced, or at least has failed to excite a concerted challenge to, the inequalities that persist in our American culture. Perhaps we might think about the difference between what it means to be a YouTube community and what it would take to use the YouTube video sharing technologies to help expand the movement for racial and economic justice.

Lisa Nakamura, in her important work on race and cyberspace, has suggested that this kind of work must be preceded by ideological analysis. She writes, "The ideological uses to which race is put in this medium must be examined before we can even begin to consider cyberspace's promise as a democratic and progressive medium."[16] Indeed, while I am reluctant to agree that one type of analysis must necessarily precede or follow another, in addition to imagining the possibilities for social change the site could *potentially* offer, it is important to unpack the ideological significance of the racial and economic rhetorics that *do* circulate on more popular YouTube videos and to think about the cultural work that such videos negotiate. Rather than focus exclusively on ways in which Hurricane Katrina is represented and explicitly addressed, one could also be mindful of materials on the site that do not make explicit mention of or reference to the hurricane. One would thereby look to ways in which racialist logics associated with the hurricane interact with, live on, or perhaps even more troublingly, die off, ubiquitously and residually in a range of media representations and performances, and in their popular reception. I hope this suggests the value of Katrina *as* an analytical context and, with this in mind, propose that we consider a specific case in a work by a YouTube comedian known as Mr. Pregnant.

What's Mr. Pregnant Pregnant With?: Katrina as an Analytical Context

Black comedy has... always overtly and *covertly explored the trials, tribulations, and triumphs of African American communities.*

—Bambi Haggins, Laughing Mad: The Black Comic Persona in Post-Soul America

Most historical sequences can be emplotted in a number of different ways, so as to provide different interpretations of those events and to endow them with different meanings.

—Hayden White, in Narrative Dynamics: Essays on Time, Plot, Closure, and Frames

On a VH-1 list of the forty "greatest internet superstars," Mr. Pregnant comes in at number twenty-five. The network's blurb about him reads, "Madman from New York City whose videos are offensive yet somehow hilarious." As a YouTube artist with over one million channel views and over seventeen thousand subscribers, he is the fifty-second most viewed content provider of all time on the website, and his fans' enthusiasm might be gauged by the assessment of user "HunterLAL" on Mr. Pregnant's user-page on February 23, 2008: "Mr. Pregnant for president 08."

Donning fake missing teeth, lacking a shirt (calling attention to his "manboobs" and big belly), and often not speaking at all or speaking made-up words or in unintelligible sounds and fake accents, Mr. Pregnant's skits feature him wearing panties and pots on his head, painting his face white, wearing lipstick, sucking pacifiers, indulging in body-touching and exhibitionism, and prank-calling police. Some are in the direct-address, webcam format common to amateur YouTube video-making, in some he is more clearly acting and putting on a show, and sometimes his videos straddle unevenly between the two modes.

If we set, or preposition, Mr. Pregnant's videowork against the context of Hurricane Katrina and its aftermath, this superimposition provides a critical lens to bring into focus ways in which representations of blackness in popular culture often congeal around excess and hyperbole. And there are ways in which these same logics of cultural representation have very real and insidious consequences for how the American government has responded to Katrina and how

From Mr. Pregnant to Mr. President ❊ 217

Figure 10.1   YouTube character Mr. Pregnant performs a post-Katrina racial burlesque.

media have managed representations of the event. It is these representations that we could consider alongside Lipsitz's concern about ideological legitimation in cultural practices, and these logics that Michael Eric Dyson—and hosts of bloggers—criticize when referring to news media's framing of the activities of homeless Katrina victims, as exemplified by the two-photo controversy discussed at the start of this essay.

Two days before Christmas 2007, Mr. Pregnant posted "Where Is Santa Claus" on YouTube. This seven-minute long video, after being uploaded for only two months, was viewed over 28,000 times and received over 650 comments. It opens with Mr. Pregnant looking at the camera in close-up, sitting in front of a Christmas tree. The song "Santa Baby" plays in the background. He is shirtless, but wearing a pot over his head, and his fake gapped upper teeth protrude over his lower lip. He pulls his dreadlocks out from over his ears as if trying to hear something, and he looks at his watch and looks around the room, with unblinking eyes (figure 10.1). The image dissolves to an intertitle that reads, "two hours later." We see him continuing to wait, chewing on air, accentuating his gapped teeth, looking around the room, crossing his arms over his chest, getting impatient and looking confused. Another "2 hours later" title appears, and then yet another shortly after. After a minute-and-a-half of not talking, in a moment of realization, he declares to himself, "I know. I know. Maybe Santa already came down the chimney and left my present under the tree." He looks around under the tree, and repeatedly calls out to the missing present: "Present-ness. Present-ness. It's all about the present-ness. Presenty qua qua. Pres-aah ahnt..." He goes to sit under the tree and begins wrapping himself in wrapping paper, because, he explains, "If I dress up like a present, a present will come out; present attract present."

He repeats several times, "Hey present..." But Santa still does not come. He bemoans, "Where is Santa Claus? Santa Claus been to everybody house. Santa Claus never show up at my house." Then he goes back to his seat and cries in front of the camera. The video has an interesting symmetry in the lengthy wordlessness of the beginning and ending versus the wordiness of the middle, which includes lots of nonwords, too, such as some of Mr. Pregnant's trademark neologistic phrases, "shnacker shnaw," or "shnakkady qua qua," and variations of these phrases incorporating the word "present."

It all makes for a pretty funny skit, a claim the dozens of "lol"s and smiley faces on the video's comment board would seem to corroborate. Many users' comments try to help Pregnant out, going along with the skit, by suggesting actions that he take to try to get Santa to come, such as going to sleep, leaving the room, or leaving Santa some cookies. One user, "EmpyrealX20," addressing the question posed in the video's title (which interestingly contained no question mark in its original posting), writes, "he's with OPRAH!!! LOL." "modoZaffa" writes, "According to my mum Santa does'nt come until 2008" [*sic*]. And "troyerrrr" insightfully comments, "How politically correct." This strand of commentaries seems to be picking up on the more latent significance of Mr. Pregnant's performance—as a performance of an inarticulate black man waiting for the fictional white man in charge to come and bring presents, and then crying upon realizing he's been neglected despite all his efforts. Indeed, described this way, the skit's narrative might sound strangely familiar and far less funny, resonating with Katrina's narrative of waiting and of class and race neglect.

I suggest we think about this video's narrative in contrast to Arceneaux's. As with Chan's *Waiting for Godot*, they certainly share themes of waiting and neglect, and they are certainly both deeply racially charged. And they are both in dialogue with and set themselves up against more popular narratives—the familiar narrative of Santa leaving Christmas presents under a tree, and the popular *not* telling of stories of racial and class discrimination by government officials who were supposed to be providing help to those in New Orleans after Katrina.

A point of contrast between the two videos might center upon the idea of articulateness. Recall that Arceneaux wants to speak for those who don't have the "words" to do so, and that he feels that the media have "singled out" those not capable of "expressing themselves verbally in a clear way." Mr. Pregnant's character, in his extensive silences, and then in the middle, with his outbursts "shnakkady qua qua" and "shnacka shnaw," in a sense seems to foreground, exaggerate, and mock the kind of incoherent black-speak that Arceneaux suggests has been culturally represented by the media. It seems to me that both Arceneaux and Pregnant, in diametrically opposed ways, are in dialogue with and trying to break out of these representational practices—Arceneaux by countering them with a measured coherence, and Pregnant by exploding the stereotype to its extremes. In some ways, Arceneaux's piece might come off as more dismissive, implying that the words spoken by others are somehow inadequate. Mr. Pregnant, on the other hand, seems to perhaps be more effectively challenging the entire system and logic of representation that gives rise to such racist types of discourse, revealing how ridiculous they are. This is certainly a complicated issue (especially in light of the varying comments users post about the videos), one that I do not think can be boiled down to one type of speech being more or less appropriate than the other; I simply would like to point out the different ways the two artists' stories are working with the idea of articulateness in a post-Katrina context of race and representation.

If we triangulate these two narratives with Wikipedia's Katrina narrative in these terms, it becomes clear just how diverse the range of "Katrina" narratives can be. I think that it might not be inaccurate to suggest that the narrative of Mr. Pregnant's "Where Is Santa Claus" has at least as much to teach us about the meaning of Hurricane Katrina as Wikipedia's storm history.

As "Mr. Pregnant" obviously is not carrying a child, the very name he goes by invites us to question his character's wider significance, which points us to the register of "pregnancy" that indicates an "endowment" and abundance of "meanings," to also recall the language of this section's epigraph from Hayden White about the emplotment of historical events. It takes little imaginative stretch to recognize that his character is pregnant with the burdens of race relations in contemporary America, and that the sketches he performs are endowed with cultural and historical significance.

"Where Is Santa Claus" in particular invites one to think about the pregnancy of the *present*—in three senses, not only as (1) a gift but also as (2) the "current moment" and (3) "being there." If "present attract present," and no present comes (just as no child will be born of his pregnancy), Mr. Pregnant is not (a) present. As the present is not present, neither is he, a subaltern searching for his missing presence online.

"Tomorrow Begins Today": Katrina as Political Opportunity

Continuing on this selective tour through Katrina-related Internet content, I'd like to direct us to another video—one set in yet another triangulation of YouTube, Hurricane Katrina, and Christmas. Here, post-Katrina becomes a presence, a setting—both a physical backdrop but also an overtly political scene, setting the stage for the 2008 presidential election.

This video, "Tomorrow Begins Today," was posted on YouTube by John Edwards, who, to hold onto the pregnancy metaphor, "aborted" his campaign midway through the 2008 Democratic presidential primary and even more recently sought to disprove claims in the media regarding impregnating Rielle Hunter out of wedlock. (Hunter herself is a pioneer user of YouTube for distributing and marketing political content.) In Edwards' video "Tomorrow Begins Today," he announces his plan to "announce" his candidacy. He begins by saying, "I'm John Edwards, and I'm in the upper ninth ward of New Orleans where we've been working this afternoon—me along with these kids who are working behind me—trying to restore a home that was devastated by the hurricane, and tomorrow morning from this place, I will announce that I'm a candidate for president of the United States." Edwards stands talking to the static camera, as black children work in front of the damaged home behind him, ignoring the presence of Edwards and the camera. Toward the end of the two-minute video, Edwards addresses the viewer as "you," and he asks you to forward the video to all of "your friends" because he wants "you to hear it first."

This announcement *of* an announcement to come itself indicates a heightened activity of prepositioning—removing the speaker (Edwards) doubly from the message communicated (his presidential candidacy). In this rhetorical space, Katrina figures prominently, and we ought to sort out some of the directions in which it takes Edwards' gesture. Moreover, in the broader terms of the historical narrative of the 2008 presidential campaign, this video could certainly be understood as an official "beginning," a point of entry, which, like Wikipedia's scientificity, is in need of critical attention. It begins the strand of a historical narrative that includes the Democratic primary, as Edwards was the first candidate to publicly announce his intention to run. But it also, it seems, begins a strand in what will certainly amount to a much wider-ranging narrative that introduces the centrality of the Internet in presidential politics—from the much talked-about CNN-YouTube presidential debates to the campaign's marked presence on Facebook to Barack Obama's weekly addresses on YouTube. Journalist Katherine Zaleski has suggested that these "fireside chats for the web generation" help present Obama as "Franklin Roosevelt 2.0" and now contributes to a uniquely "transparent presidency."[17] This transparency, and the invisible obscurities that undoubtedly accompany it, certainly characterize the post-millennial, post-Katrina, political generation and shape public perception of the president.

Edwards uploaded "Tomorrow Begins Today" two days after Christmas 2006, one year before Mr. Pregnant shared "Where Is Santa Claus" with the YouTube community. Edwards' video, with over 150,000 views, has been watched significantly more. With 103 comments, though, it doesn't even have one-sixth as many comments as "Where Is Santa Claus."

Edward's announcement-of-announcement ("I'm in the upper ninth ward of New Orleans...and tomorrow morning from this place, I will announce that I'm a candidate for president..."), this beginning of multiple historical narratives, was delivered in the same sentence as—and *after*—a reference to Hurricane Katrina and to his appearance amidst an effort to ameliorate the hurricane's over-one-year-old devastation of the American landscape. As with his fellow Democratic primary candidates, Edwards positioned himself as someone taking relevant actions in a contemporary political climate in which the then current administration's values and interests had allowed someone such as George W. Bush to dismissively refer to Katrina's victims as "those people from that part of the world."[18]

"Tomorrow Begins Today" should not be underestimated in terms of how it set Edwards up as a candidate. With Katrina as an unavoidable "presence" and prepositioned as a "before," he stood in New Orleans' hard-hit ninth ward, a physical acknowledgment of many people's frustration with the American government's reaction to, and failure to react to, the damage done to the city and its people by the storm. But Edwards was simultaneously positioning himself as relevant on a second axis. By announcing his candidacy on a video circulated online, he was in effect also announcing that he is in touch with and fluent in new media forms and practices; he was demonstrating that he too, like YouTube's users, can generate video content, circulate it on the website, and thereby communicate with American citizens. He repeatedly speaks to the viewer as "you" in the video, rather than using a more standard first-person "we" or third-person "American people," a distinct mode of address that emphasizes that he knows the discursive importance of YouTube as a social network—that it is about communication between "me" and "you."

And even though his video displays fewer comments than "Where Is Santa Claus," and it might lack Mr. Pregnant's fan's enthusiastic endorsement, "Mr. Pregnant for president 08," YouTube users did respond to Edwards' presence, many expressing excitement and inspiration but others criticism and concern. One viewer observes the irony of Edwards talking in front of a team of black children who were doing all the work of rebuilding the home, which is indeed a striking, troubling visual message. Is the image of "tomorrow beginning today," an image of a white politician with a southern accent speaking to a camera in front of black children, a desirable vision of national revitalization? This video might have too closely resembled "yesterday" for many Americans frustrated by the political status quo that enabled the infrastructural neglect that led to Katrina in the first place.

"Wassup 2008": Posts Post-Katrina

If Katrina was a setting *for* Edwards, and a setting *up of* the presidential campaign, the popular viral video "Wassup 2008" also uses Katrina as background, as a before, as a piece of history also within the historical narrative of the 2008 presidential campaign. "Wassup 2008" is a short promotional video for Barack Obama made by Charles Stone III, the same director of "Whassup?!," the 2000

Budweiser commercial featuring a group of friends on the phone with each other repeating "Whassup" that became a pop culture phenomenon in terms of its popularity and the parodies it inspired. "Wassup 2008" has been viewed over six million times and is, as of May 2009, the thirtieth most viewed "News & Politics" video of all time, the fifth "Top Favorited," and the eighty-sixth "Top Rated." The video gathers the cast from the original commercial to reveal how these once friendly, familiar characters have now been worn down, their lives negatively affected by the turns the preceding eight years took.

"Wassup 2008" begins with a title that reads "8 YEARS LATER," and a sound clip of senator and U.S. presidential candidate John McCain saying the "fundamentals of our economy are still strong, but these are very, very difficult times"—a remark Obama repeatedly attacked during their political rivalry. As we hear this, we see a man in a white undershirt with classifieds section in hand sigh and shake his head. His phone rings, and on the other end is a soldier on an improbable payphone in a desert in Iraq, who says "Whassup B?" He replies, "Nothing, lost my home. Looking for a job." The man tells his roommate, immobilized with bandages around his neck and left arm, to pick up the phone. He responds, "Forget the phone, I need painkillers." Eventually the three are all on the call, all struggling to say "Whassup" in their poor conditions. The friend in Iraq asks where Dookie is, and we see him in his bedroom looking at a graph representing a stock market crash on his laptop screen. Dookie picks up the phone and expels a loud, sad breath into it, adding to the chorus of sorry sounds. The telephone reunion is then completed when the bandaged roommate responds to someone buzzing to get into their apartment. We see a man apparently outside screaming to get in, in the midst of a hurricane—rain pours hard, and a heavy, violent wind blows large chunks of debris in his direction. The video then cuts rapidly between the five men sorrowfully screaming what sound like parts of the word "Whassup" into their phones—and we see Dookie unsuccessfully trying to hang himself, and the man in the storm holds on to the building attempting to keep the wind from blowing him away. After this montage settles down, the friend in Iraq says to the man watching TV in a quieter voice, "So what's up B?" He looks at the TV screen—Michelle and Barack Obama are on it—he calmly smiles, and says, "Change. That's whassup. Change." A series of three words in white text then appear over the black screen, one at a time: "TRUE"/"CHANGE"/"VOTE."

The video has its own website, wassup08.com, which explains,

> Looking back on the last 8 years since *Whassup?!* debuted, Charles [Stone III] realized how much our country has changed and seized on the opportunity to reunite the whole cast for a searing film on our current condition with the hope that it reminds people of the importance of voting and more specifically, the importance of choosing Obama, a candidate who is a clean break from the policies that got our country in this condition in the first place.[19]

Each of the five characters can be understood as being affected by a different condition—unemployment and the housing crisis, the war in Iraq, health care, the economy, and Katrina. The man outside in the hurricane gets a total of about three seconds of screen time out of the video's two minutes, but as one of the few historical references in the video, it is difficult to miss. Several messages on the video's comment board pick up on it—many comment that it's the funniest part. But it also is the example the most people draw on to criticize the video's politics and logic. Representative is "Anomoly314"'s sarcastic "Finally...A presidential candidate who can prevent natural disasters!!" or "holytoast"'s "I'm all for Obama but I don't think he can change hurricanes."

These messages on the video's comment board open up several conversations about Katrina, the government's handling of it, and New Orleans's infrastructural problems. "Texasags" writes to another user,

> What environmental disasters are you trying to blame on Bush? He can't, contrary to what some say, create and strengthen hurricanes. He also could not force the mayor of New Orleans and the Governor of Louisiana to do their jobs. They dropped the ball during Katrina. And man-made global warming is being discredited more every day.

And in a follow-post, Texasags writes,

> The problem was that the local people didn't do enough BEFORE the hurricane got there. Also, the system requires them to ask for federal assistance. The feds don't just go in and take over. Can you imagine the outcry if Bush had taken over? He would have been seizing power from a black mayor and a woman governor[.] Local authorities had plenty of opportunity to evacuate people. There were hundreds of school buses that were never used. Nagin and Blanco should be held accountable—not Bush.

"jstnorv" replies, "texas don't you think Bush could have put off the birthday celebration with McCain to help a little more after Katrina hit? Manmade global warming discredited? Are you serious?"
Or, consider another exchange:

> reset22312: you can change hurricanes not to happen? Wow didn't know Obama fixed them too.
> Askquestionslater: "No but at least he can deploy military help within hours. It took Bush 3 days to help in our own back yard…but he miraculously managed to get troops to Iraq in 24 hours. I think you get the point."

Because health care, the economy, the war in Iraq, and unemployment were all major campaign issues that the nominees were forced to address, it is not surprising that the hurricane is the one issue people who disagree with the video's message tend to use as an anchor to voice their frustration, disparaging the notion that Obama would have any ability to prevent a natural disaster. They take issue with the video's use of Katrina as an easy opportunity to be politically persuasive.

These debates hinge, with varying degrees of acknowledgment from commentators, on *Katrina as*. The official narrative of Katrina, what we learn about it from Wikipedia, does frame it as a meteorological event, something over which a president could have little control. Understanding Katrina as a social and political experience, though, as the three-second reference to it in "Whassup 2008" clearly does, makes its place perfectly clear and rhetorically effective and sensible. "Whassup 2008" should be understood as part of the 2008 presidential campaign's historical significance; the extent to which so many conversations about the elections happened online, with youth, and through user-generated media projects was certainly an unprecedented and defining quality of the campaign. "Whassup 2008" also demonstrates Katrina as a piece of recent American history, as a crucial event in an implied narrative about the decline of America that will, perhaps rather improbably, be turned around.

On Links and Doing Without

As a major historical event that coincided with the emergence of YouTube, Katrina, *as* meteorological phenomenon, traumatic experience, analytical context, political opportunity, and so on, is woven through Internet representations and conversations. Online, we gather information and watch content through links and connections. In order to give critical language to online media and activity, I hope I have suggested the helpfulness of attending to, and thinking with, prepositions, the words we use in language to make links and connections. The "from" and the "to" of my essay's title are meant to invoke a wide-ranging movement across disparate links: from Mr. Pregnant to 2008 U.S. presidential campaign videos. As we try out various prepositions in relation to Katrina—whether it is Katrina as a "before," what comes "after" Katrina, or Katrina as a setting *behind* which a different narrative takes place—the event's significant place in post-millennial American politics and representations is opened *up*.

The Internet and associated digital media technologies, as many popular viral videos on sites such as YouTube make clear, have facilitated what we might refer to as practices of recontextualization—whereby more people have more access to image files, texts, sound bites, and technologies that can generate and rearrange content. In this environment of user-generated content, file-sharing, file-looting, and media-mixing, discourse multiplies and de-centers. As the "two-photo controversy" demonstrates, practices of recontextualization can incorporate significant critical commentary, allowing a Flickr user to simply place two images and captions published by the same news source side by side, revealing the troubling, implicitly racist ideologies underlying the consumption of popular news online.

I hope this essay can be read as a continuation and extension of dustin3000's work of critically juxtaposing, or as I have proposed, prepositioning, Katrina-related Internet content. Prepositioning, focusing on and making links between, is a means of attending to ideological currents, and of putting disparate discourses into contact with one another. On one hand, this is already happening all the time online, and we might think of prepositioning as a mode of criticism that attempts to emerge out of, and respond to, this activity of media navigation. On the other hand, however, it is a mode of criticism that has the potential to generate new connections in a given context, enabling a more "networked" critical perspective of the context in question.

In this selective browsing of online content, perhaps somewhat paradoxically, I hope I have suggested the importance of doing *without* Katrina as a necessary starting point in order to better wrap our heads around its cultural significance. Rather than navigating exclusively through media artifacts from *within* the storm—survivor videos, home videos of return, and storm-chasing videos—that are often fascinating and of which there are numerous examples online, we instead have charted a more multidirectional, dispersed route, trying out various paths toward, and modes of, capturing Katrina's online presence. This is tied up with a philosophical curiosity about *without*, not unrelated to Derrida's call to speak of, to, and with the "ghost," which is worth continued exploration, even if it has only been implicit and preliminary here. What I mean to underscore is the importance of thinking through one's object of study without confining oneself to the object proper or to its assumed boundaries, to see something where it may not be apparent and to thereby better feel out its contours.[20]

Approaches to understanding Internet media and culture, and moving image media culture more generally, should not only be directed by precharted paths that map the grids in which our objects of study must be thought. We should look from an object's or issue's without, which will often be a larger and less obvious conceptual territory than its within. The without certainly includes the ubiquitous, the quotidian, and the popular, and these fields, which I have tried to give adequate attention to here by focusing on frequently trafficked YouTube videos, a major contemporary political campaign, and an "official" source of information are especially important to recontextualize and understand outside and beyond the logics that generate them.

What, then, becomes of Katrina, when approached from without, through this networked perspective? Most importantly, I think, an argument emerges not about Katrina but about the possibility of navigating Katrina, like the Internet, as space for analysis, which is particularly heightened because of its explicit and, of equal significance, its implicit ubiquity. Not only are there many narratives and perspectives that circulate about Katrina, but there are even more that deal with associated issues of political neglect and racial and class injustices, cutting *across* stories *from* the obscene *to* the presidential, *on* YouTube (Mr. Pregnant) and *through* YouTube (the presidential campaign). The significance of these, in very different ways, should not be considered without Katrina, as an event that so blatantly exposed its own deeply problematic without-ness and which through its networked presence, seeped into productions of and conversations about politics and comedy, online and beyond.

Notes

Thanks to all those who have generously helped shape ideas in this paper—Diane Negra, Janet Walker, Edward Branigan, Porter Abbott, Joshua Neves, and Nicole Starosielski.

1. I say that these two people are white, based on a survey of reports about the controversy, with some reluctance. They are definitely light-skinned, and a couple of sources identify the woman as "light-skinned," and I have read no authoritative coverage that discusses the very problem of reading their color definitively. As several scholars have pointed out in different contexts, though, racism often also corresponds to gradations of skin color amongst blacks.
2. *Come Hell or High Water: Hurricane Katrina and the Color of Disaster*, p. 114.
3. "Questions of racism in hurricane photo captions; Yahoo responds."
4. Quoted in Aaron Kinney, "'Looting' or 'Finding'?"
5. Tania Ralli, "HURRICANE KATRINA: THE PHOTOGRAPHS; Who's a Looter? In Storm's Aftermath, Pictures Kick Up a Different Kind of Tempest."
6. Dick Hebdige has, in "Staking out the Posts," conceded of "post," the only non-preposition, "To say 'post' is to say 'past.'" "Staking out the Posts," in *Hiding in the Light: On Images and Things*, p. 183.
7. "Waiting for Godot in New Orleans: An Artist Statement."
8. "Learning from New Orleans: The Social Warrant of Hostile Privatism and Competitive Consumer Citizenship," p. 455.
9. Ibid., p. 454.
10. "Wikipedia: Featured Articles," http://en.wikipedia.org/wiki/Wikipedia:Featured_articles (last accessed May 17, 2009).
11. "Stories, War, and Emotions: The Absoluteness of Narrative Beginnings," p. 47.
12. See, for example, Chester Hartman and Gregory D. Squires, eds., *There Is No Such Thing as a Natural Disaster: Race, Class, and Hurricane Katrina*; and Janet Walker, "Rights and Return: Perils and Fantasies of Situated Testimony after Katrina," in *Documentary Testimonies: Global Archives of Suffering*.
13. "The Historical Text as Literary Artifact," in *Narrative Dynamics: Essays on Time, Plot, Closure, and Frames*, p. 201.
14. Linda Young, "U.N. Criticizes U.S. For Violating Human Rights Of Internally Displaced Hurricane Katrina Victims."
15. "The YouTube Community."
16. *Cybertypes: Race, Ethnicity, and Identity on the Internet* p. xii.
17. "Obama's Transparent Presidency: Weekly YouTube Addresses."

18. Henry Jenkins, "'People from that Part of the World': The Politics of Dislocation."
19. http://www.wassup08.com/about.html.
20. For more on this see, for example, Mary Ann Doane's discussion of "contingency" in "The Object of Theory."

Bibliography

Andrejevic, Mark. "Life on Animal Planet." *FlowTV* 4(4) (April 28, 2006, and April 4, 2007). http://flowtv.org/?p=232.

Asbury, Herbert. *The French Quarter: An Informal History of the New Orleans Underworld*. New York: Pocket Books, 1955.

Aufderhide, Pat and Jessica Clark. "Public Media 2.0: Dynamic, Engaged Publics." Center for Social Media at American University. www.centerforsocialmedia.org/resources/publications/public_media_2_0_dynamic_engaged_publics/ February, 2009.

Ball, Millie. "Empty Vessels." *New Orleans Times-Picayune*, January 30, 2007. http://www.floodwall.org/press/timespic_text.html (accessed September 12, 2009).

Barber, Dave. "House of Sweet Magic: The Animated Films of Helen Hill" (December 5, 2009). winnipegfilmgroup.com/content/view.aspx?content=57af558e-3a0a-47d4-9d91-f6d77eddf931.

Barker, David Christopher. *Rushed to Judgment: Talk Radio, Persuasion, and American Political Behavior*. New York: Columbia UP, 2002.

Barsalou, Judy and Victoria Baxter. "The Urge to Remember: The Role of Memorials in Social Reconstruction and Transnational Justice." United States Institute for Peace: Stabilization and Reconstruction Series No. 5, January 2007. www.usip.org/pubs/specialreports/srs/srs5.html.

Bartelson, Jens. "We Could Remember it for you Wholesale: Myth, Monuments, and the Constitution of National Memories," in *Memory, Trauma and World Politics*, ed. Duncan Bell. Houndmills and New York: Palgrave Macmillan, 2006, 33–53.

Bell, Elizabeth. "Somatexts at the Disney Shop: Constructing the Pentimentos of Women's Animated Bodies," in *From Mouse to Mermaid: The Politics of Film, Gender and Culture*, eds. Elizabeth Bell, Lynda Haas, and Laura Sells. Bloomington: Indiana UP, 1995, 107–124.

Beltran, Mary C. "The Hollywood Latina Body as Site of Social Struggle: Media Constructions of Stardom and Jennifer Lopez's 'Cross-Over' Butt." *Quarterly Review of Film and Video* 19(1) (2002): 71–86.

Benjamin, Walter. "Theses on the Philosophy of History," in *Illuminations*, ed. Hannah Arendt, trans. Harry Zohn. New York: Schocken Books, 245–255.

Bennett, Larry and Adolph Reed, Jr. "The New Face of Urban Renewal: The Near North Redevelopment Initiative and the Cabrini-Green Neighborhood," in *Without Justice for All: The New Liberalism and Our Retreat from Racial Equality*, ed. Adolph Reed, Jr. Boulder, CO: Westview Press, 1999, 175–214.

Berry, Jason, "Helen Hill: An Unfinished Story." *New Orleans Magazine*, January 2009, 68–73.

"Best Bets on TV." *Hoosier-Times*, Sunday, May 18, 2008, E2.

Biesecker, Barbara. "Remembering World War II: The Rhetoric and Politics of National Commemoration at the Turn of the 21st Century." *Quarterly Journal of Speech* 88 (2002): 393–410.

"The Big Hurt," *Broadcasting and Cable*, September 5, 2005. http://www.broadcastingcable.com/article/CA6253849.html (accessed October 30, 2008).

Bignell, Jonathan. *Big Brother: Reality TV in the Twenty-First Century*. Houndmills: Palgrave Macmillan, 2005.

Blair, Carole. "Contemporary U.S. Memorial Sites as Exemplars of Rhetoric's Materiality," in *Rhetorical Bodies*, eds. Jack Selzer and Sharon Crowley. Madison: U of Wisconsin P, 1999, 16–57.

Blair, Carole and Neil Michel. "Reproducing Civil Rights Tactics: The Rhetorical Performances of the Civil Rights Memorial." *Rhetoric Society Quarterly* 30 (2000): 31–55.

Blair, Carole, Marsha S. Jeppeson, and Enrico Pucci, Jr. "Public Memorializing in Postmodernity: The Vietnam Veteran's Memorial as Prototype." *Quarterly Journal of Speech* 77 (1991): 263–287.

Bordo, Susan. *Unbearable Weight: Feminism, Western Culture and the Body*. Berkeley: U of California P, 1993.

Brockington, Dan. *Celebrity and the Environment: Fame, Wealth and Power in Conservation*. London: Zed Books, 2009.

Browne, S.H. "Reading Public Memory in Daniel Webster's *Plymouth Rock Oration*." *Western Journal of Communication* 57.4 (1993): 464–477.

Burgess, Jean and Joshua Green. *YouTube: Online Video and Participatory Culture*. Cambridge: Polity Press, 2008.

Bushman, Richard L. *The Refinement of America: Persons, Houses, Cities*. New York: Vintage Books, 1992.

Butler, Judith. *Precarious Life: The Powers of Mourning and Violence*. New York: Verso, 2004.

Camp, Jordan T. "'We Know This Place': Neoliberal Racial Regimes and the Katrina Circumstance." *American Quarterly* 61(3) (September 2009): 693–717.

Cavender, Gray. "In Search of Community on Reality TV: *America's Most Wanted* and *Survivor*," in *Understanding Reality Television*, eds. Su Holmes and Deborah Jermyn. London: Routledge, 2004, 154–172.

Chan, Paul. "Waiting for Godot in New Orleans: An Artist Statement" (June 2007). http://creativetime.org/programs/archive/2007/chan/artist_statement.pdf (last accessed March 16, 2008).

Chappetta, Benjamin. "Katrina.wmv," Hurricane Digital Memory Bank (January 27, 2006). Hurricanearchive.org/object/1694.
Childress, Cindy. "*Glamour*'s Portrayal of Queen Latifah: Another Unreal Ideal." *Feminist Media Studies* 5(1) (March 2005): 84–87.
Cohen, Elisia and Cynthis Willis. "One Nation under Radio: Digital and Public Memory after September 11." *New Media and Society* 6.5 (2004): 591–610.
Cohen, Emily. "The Ophanista Manifesto: Orphan Films and the Politics of Representation." *American Anthropologist* (December 2004): 719–731.
Collins, Jim, ed. *High-Pop: Making Culture into Entertainment*. Malden, MA: Blackwell Publishers, 2002.
Conway, Kyle. "Small Media, Global Media: Kino and the Microcinema Movement." *Journal of Film and Video* 60 (Fall/Winter 2008): 60–71.
Couldry, Nick. *Media Consumption and Public Engagement: Beyond the Presumption of Attention*. New York: Palgrave Macmillan, 2007.
Coviello, Will. "Handmade Nation," *Gambit Weekly* (New Orleans), September 14, 2009. http://bestofneworleans.com/gyrobase/Content?oid=oid%3A61352.
Coyer, Kate. "Community radio licensing and policy: An overview." *Global Media and Communication* 2(129) (2006). gmc.sagepub.com.
Cruz, Anne Marie and Bob Meadows. "Brad's Fight for New Orleans." *People*, September 18, 2006, 73–74.
Dark, Alice Elliot, "Senseless," in *110 Stories: New York Writes After September 11*, ed. Ulrich Baer. New York and London: New York UP, 2002, 65–67.
Dean, Mitchell. *Governmentality: Power and Rule in Modern Society*. London: Sage, 1999.
Derrida, Jacques. *Specters of Marx*, trans. Peggy Kamuf. New York: Routledge, 1994.
Dimock, Wai Chee. "World History According to Katrina." *Differences: A Journal of Feminist Cultural Studies* 19(2) (2008): 35–53.
"A Distinguished Audience." www.wqln.org/CorporateSupport/npr.asp.
Doane, Mary Ann. "The Object of Theory," in *Rites of Realism*, ed. Yvonne Marguiles. Durham, NC: Duke UP, 2005, 80–89.
Douglas, Mary. "The Idea of Home: A Kind of Space." *Social Research* 58(1) (1991): 287–307.
Draaisma, Douwe. *Metaphors of Memory: A History of Ideas about the Mind*. Cambridge: Cambridge UP, 2000.
Duggan, Lisa. *The Twilight of Equality?: Neoliberalism, Cultural Politics, and the Attack on Democracy*. Boston: Beacon Press, 1993.
Dworkin, Shari L. and Faye Linda Wachs. *Body Panic: Gender, Health and the Selling of Fitness*. New York: New York UP, 2009.
Dyson, Michael Eric. *Come Hell or High Water: Hurricane Katrina and the Color of Disaster*. New York: Basic Books, 2006.
Edmonds, Guy. "Amateur Widescreen." *Film History* 19(4) (2007): 401–413.
Ehrenreich, Barbara. *Bright-Sided: How the Relentless Promotion of Positive Thinking Has Undermined America*. New York: Metropolitan Books, 2009.

Engelman, Ralph. *Public Radio and Television in America: A Political History*. Thousand Oaks, London and New Delhi: SAGE Publications, 1996.

Engelmann, Stephen G. *Imagining Interest in Political Thought: Origins of Economic Rationality*. Durham: Duke UP, 2003.

Eugene, Nicole, Henry Armstrong, and Dorothy Griffin. "Henry Armstrong and Dorothy Griffin Remembering Katrina." *Callaloo* 29 (2006): 1512–1525.

Faludi, Susan. *The Terror Dream: Fear and Fantasy in Post-9/11 America*. New York: Picador, 2008.

"FEMA Computers Hampered During Katrina." United Press International, October 10, 2005. www.physorg.com/news7110.html.

Ferrari, Matthew. "Primal Giggles: Thoughts on Reality Television's Recent Pieties and Parodies of the 'Masculine Primitive." *FlowTV* 10(7) (September 3, 2009).

Fertel, Randy. "Katrina Five Ways." *The Kenyon Review* 28(3) (June 2006): 71–84.

Fish, Adam. "Television, Ecotourism, and the Videocamera: Performative Non-Fiction and Auto-Cinematography." *FlowTV* 5(6) (January 12, 2007, and April 7, 2007). http://flowtv.org/?p=80.

Fleetwood, Nicole R. "Failing Narratives, Initiating Technologies: Hurricane Katrina and the Production of a Weather Media Event." *American Quarterly* 58(3) (2006): 767–789.

Florida, Richard. *The Rise of the Creative Class and How It's Transforming Work, Leisure, Community and Everyday Lives*. New York: Basic Books, 2003.

——. *Cities and the Creative Class*. New York and London: Routledge, 2005.

——. *The Flight of the Creative Class: The New Global Competition for Talent*. New York: Harper Business, 2005.

Folkenflik, David. "NPR CEO Ken Stern Forced Out." www.npr.org/templates/story/story.php?storyId=87980852.

Foucault, Michel. *The Birth of Biopolitics: Lectures at the College de France, 1978–79*, trans. Graham Burchell. Basingstoke: Palgrave Macmillan, 2008.

Frye, Bryan. "Microcinema in 10 Easy Steps." *Independent: Film and Video Monthly* (July 2001): 37.

Fuqua, Joy V. "Home is Where the Tarp Is: Katrina, Commercialism, and Class in *Extreme Makeover: Home Edition*." Paper Delivered at Society for Cinema and Media Studies Conference, 2006.

Gailiunas, Paul. "For My Poor, Sweet Wife, Fix New Orleans." *New Orleans Times-Picayune*, January 26, 2007, online edition.

Gaither, Chris and Matea Gold. "Web Proves Its Capacity to Help in Time of Need." *Los Angeles Times*, September 10, 2005, 4.

Gillin-Schwartz, Megan. "Still Life in a Series of Open Drawers." *Downtown Express* 19(33) (January 12–18, 2007). Accessed August 2009.

Giroux, Henry. *Stormy Weather: Katrina and the Politics of Disposability.* Boulder: Paradigm Publishers, 2006.

———. "Beyond the Biopolitics of Disposability: Rethinking Neoliberalism in the New Gilded Age." *Social Identities* 14(5) (September 2008): 587–620.

Glynn, Kevin. *Tabloid Culture: Trash Taste, Popular Power, and the Transformation of American Television.* Durham: Duke UP, 2000.

Gray, Herman. *Watching Race: Television and the Struggle for Blackness.* Minneapolis: U of Minnesota P, 1995.

Great Britain. CRED. *Disaster Risk Reduction: 2007 Global Report.* GPO, 2007.

Grisbaum, Gretchen A. and Douglas H. Ubelaker. "An Analysis of Forensic Anthropology Cases Submitted to the Smithsonian Institution by the Federal Bureau of Investigation from 1962 to 1994." *Smithsonian Contributions to Anthropology* (45) (2001): 1–15.

Grosz, Elizabeth. *Architecture from the Outside: Essays on Virtual and Real Space.* Cambridge: MIT P, 2001.

Haddad, Candice. "Keeping Up with the Rump Rage: E's Commodification of Kim Kardashian's Assets." *FlowTV* 8(6) (August 2008).

Haggins, Bambi. *Laughing Mad: The Black Comic Persona in Post-Soul America.* New Brunswick: Rutgers UP, 2007.

Hall, Stuart. "On Postmodernism and Articulation: An Interview with Stuart Hall," ed. Lawrence Grossberg. *Journal of Communication Inquiry* 10 (2) (1986): 45–60.

Harriford, Diane and Becky Thompson, eds. *When the Center is on Fire: Passionate Social Theory for Our Times.* Austin: U of Texas P, 2008.

Hartley, John. "Radiocracy: Sounds and Citizenship." *International Journal of Cultural Studies* 3(2) (2000): 153–159.

Hartman, Chester and Gregory D. Squires, eds. *There is No Such Thing as a Natural Disaster: Race, Class, and Hurricane Katrina.* New York: Routledge, 2006.

Hartnell, Anna. "Katrina Tourism and a Tale of Two Cities: Visualizing Race and Class in New Orleans." *American Quarterly* 61(3) (September 2009): 723–747.

Hasinoff, Amy Adele. "Fashioning Race for the Free Market on *America's Next Top Model*." *Critical Studies in Media Communication* 25(3) (August 2008): 324–343.

Heath, Rebecca Piirto. "Tuning in to Talk—Popularity of Talk Programming." *American Demographics* (1998). http://findarticles.com/p/articles/mi_m4021/is_n2_v20/ai_20302979/.

Hebdige, Dick. *Hiding in the Light: On Images and Things.* London: Routledge, 1989.

Herron, Jerry. "Detroit: Disaster Deferred, Disaster in Progress." *South Atlantic Quarterly* 106(4) (Fall 2007): 663–682.

Hess, Aaron. "In Digital Remembrance: Vernacular Memory and the Rhetorical Construction of Web Memorials." *Media Culture Society* 29 (2007): 812–820. mcs.sagepub.com/cgi/content/abstract/29/5/812.

HGTV Canada website. http://www.hgtv.ca/neworleans/about.aspx (accessed July 7, 2009).

Hill, Helen. "Vessel." *New Laurel Review* 18 (1993).

———, ed. *Recipes for Disaster: A Handcrafted Film Cookbooklet*. 2001, rev. 2004, 2005.

Hilliard, Robert and Michael Keith. *The Quieted Voice: The Rise and Demise of Localism in American Radio*. Carbondale: Southern Illinois UP, 2005.

Hirschorn, Michael. "The Case for Reality TV." *The Atlantic* (May 2007). http://www.theatlantic.com/doc/200705/reality-tv.

Hobbes, Thomas and J.C.A. Gaskin. *Leviathan*. Oxford: Oxford UP, 1996.

Hogan, Patrick Colm. "Stories, War, and Emotions: The Absoluteness of Narrative Beginnings," in *Narrative Beginnings: Theories and Practices*, ed. Brian Richardson. Lincoln: U of Nebraska P, 2008, 47.

Holmes Make it Right. http://www.makeitright.ca/makeitright/Make_It_Right_Video/index.php?channelid=26&video_id=223 (accessed July 17, 2009).

Hood, Philip. "Helen Hill's Recipes for Disaster PDF," Frameworks listserv, February 20, 2007. www.hi-beam.net/fw/fw34/0632.html.

Hooper, John. "Berlusconi: Italy Earthquake Victims Should View Experience as Camping Weekend," Guardian.co.uk, April 8, 2009. http://www.guardian.co.uk/world/2009/apr/08/italy-earthquake-berlusconi.

Hoskins, Andrew. "Television and the Collapse of Memory." *Time & Society* 13(1) (2004): 109–127. http://tas.sagepub.com/cgi/content/abstract/13/1/109.

Jenkins, Henry. "'People from that Part of the World': The Politics of Dislocation," *Cultural Anthropology* 21(3) (2006): 469–486.

Jermyn, Deborah. *Crime Watching: Investigating Real Crime TV*. London: I.B. Tauris, 2007.

Jervis, Rick. "Movie and TV Crews Help Louisiana Recover." *USA Today*, July 16, 2008.

———. "43 Victims Still a Mystery." *USA Today*, January 10, 2009. http://usatoday.com/news/nation/2009-01-20-body-ie_N.htm?POE=click-refer (accessed January 23, 2009).

Johnson, Peter. "'Man vs. Wild' host Grylls lives to tell about it." *USA Today*, June 15, 2007.

Kammen, Michael. *Mystic Chords of Memory: The Transformation of Tradition in American Culture*. New York: Vintage, 1993.

Kaplan, E. Ann. *Trauma Culture: The Politics of Terror and Loss in Media and Literature*. New Brunswick: Rutgers UP, 2005.

Katz, Alyssa. *Our Lot: How Real Estate Came to Own Us*. New York: Bloomsbury, 2009.

Kemp, John. "When the painter met the Creoles." *The Boston Globe*, November 30, 1997, G3.
Kher, Unmesh, Michael D. Lemoneck, Margot Roosevelt, and Daren Fonda. "How to Seize the Initiative." *Time*, April 3, 2006.
"Killings Bring the City to Its Bloodied Knees." *New Orleans Times-Picayune*, January 5, 2007.
Kinney, Aaron. " 'Looting' or 'Finding'?" *Salon.com*. http://dir.salon.com/story/news/feature/2005/09/01/photo_controversy/index.html, September 1, 2005 (accessed May 20, 2009).
Kitch, Carolyn. "Anniversary Journalism, Collective Memory, and the Cultural Authority to Tell the Story of the American Past." *Journal of Popular Culture* 36(1) (Summer 2002): 44–67.
Klaassen, Abbey. "This is the Discovery We've Been Looking For." *Advertising Age*, October 16, 2006, 4.
Klein, Naomi. *The Shock Doctrine: The Rise of Disaster Capitalism*. New York: Penguin, 2007.
Kompare, Derek. "Reality TV." *FlowTV* 3(2) (September 23, 2005, and April 5, 2007). http://flowtv.org/?p=280.
Kracow, Gary. "Ham Radio Operators to the Rescue after Katrina." MSNBC.com, September 6, 2005. http://www.msnbc.msn.com/id/9228945/.
Lacey, Kate. "Toward a Periodization of Listening: Radio and Modern Life." *International Journal of Cultural Studies* 3(2) (2000): 279–288.
Lee, Legacy. "Trouble the Water." *Cineaste* 34 (2008): 88.
Lee, Pamela M. *Object to be Destroyed: The Work of Gordon Matta-Clark*. Cambridge: MIT P, 2001.
Lee, Susanna. " 'These are Their Stories': Trauma, Form and the Screen Phenomenon of *Law and Order*." *Discourse* 25(1 & 2) (2003): 81–97.
Leigh, E. Rich, Jack Simmons, David Adams, Scott Thorp, and Michael Mink. "The Afterbirth of the Clinic: A Foucauldian Perspective on 'House M.D.' and American Medicine in the 21st Century." *Perspectives in Biology and Medicine* 51 (2008): 220–237.
Leitl, Eugen. "Information Technology Issues during and after Katrina and Usefulness of the Internet: How We Mobilized and Utilized Digital Communications Systems." *Crit Care* 10(1) (2006): 110. Published online December 14, 2005 www.pubmedcentral.nih.gov/articlerender.fcgi?artid=1550804.
Levine, Faythe and Cortney Heimerl. *Handmade Nation: The Rise of DIY Art, Craft and Design*. New York: Princeton Architectural P, 2008.
Lewis, Peter M. "Private Passion, Public Neglect: The Cultural Status of Radio." *International Journal of Cultural Studies* 3(2) (2000): 160–167.
Lewis, Peter M. and Jerry Booth. *The Invisible Medium: Public, Commercial and Community Radio*. Washington, DC: Howard UP, 1991.

Lipsitz, George. "Diasporic Noise: History, Hip Hop, and the Postcolonial Politics of Sound," in *Popular Culture: Production and Consumption*, eds. C. Lee Harringon and Denise D. Bielby. Methuen, MA: Blackwell, 2001, 180–199.

———. "Learning from New Orleans: The Social Warrant of Hostile Privatism and Competitive Consumer Citizenship." *Cultural Anthropology* 21(3) (August 2006): 451–468.

Littler, Jo. "'I feel your pain': Cosmopolitan Charity and the Public Fashioning of the Celebrity Soul." *Social Semiotics* 18(2) (June 2008): 237–251.

Luther, Linda. "Disaster Debris Removal after Hurricane Katrina: Status and Associated Issues," Congressional Research Service Report for Congress, April 2, 2008, 4. http://www.fas.org/sgp/crs/misc/RL33477.pdf (accessed October 31, 2008).

Lyons, James. *Selling Seattle: Representing Contemporary Urban America*. London: Wallflower P, 2004.

Maliniak, David. "In Katrina's Wake, Ham Radio Triumphs." *Electronic Design*. September 19, 2005. www.elecdesign.com/Articles/Index.cfm?AD=1&AD=1&AD=1&ArticleID=11136.

Martin, Randy. *An Empire of Indifference: American War and the Financial Logic of Risk Management*. Durham: Duke UP, 2007.

Massey, Doreen. *Space, Place, and Gender*. Minneapolis: U of Minnesota P, 1994.

Massier, John. "Prolonged Hacking and Gnawing," blog for Hallwalls Contemporary Arts Center, Buffalo, New York, August 24, 2007. http://jmassier.blogspot.com.

Mayer, Aric. "Aesthetics of Catastrophe." *Public Culture: An Interdisciplinary Journal of Transational Cultural Studies* 20(2) (Spring 2008): 179.

Mbembe, Achille. "Necropolitics." Trans. Libby Meintjes. *Public Culture* 15(1) (2003): 11–40.

McCarthy, Anna. "'Stanley Milgram, Allen Funt, and Me': Postwar Social Science and the 'First Wave' of Reality TV," in *Reality TV: Remaking Television Culture*, eds. Susan Murray and Laurie Ouellette. New York: New York UP, 2004, 19–39.

———. "Reality Television: A Neoliberal Theater of Suffering." *Social Text* 25(4) (2007): 17–41.

McCauley, Michael. *NPR: The Trials and Triumphs of National Public Radio*. New York: Columbia UP, 2005.

McChesney, Robert W. *The Political Economy of Media: Enduring Issues, Emerging Dilemmas*. New York: Monthly Review Press, 2008.

McMurria, John. "The YouTube Community." *FlowTV* 5(2) (October 20, 2006), http://flowtv.org/?p=48.

———. "Desperate Citizens and Good Samaritans: Neoliberalism and Makeover Reality TV." *Television & New Media* 9(4) (July 2008): 305–332.

McPherson, Tara. *Reconstructing Dixie: Race, Gender, and Nostalgia in the Imagined South*. Durham: Duke UP, 2003.
McRobbie, Angela and Jenny Garber. "Girls and Subcultures: An Exploration," in *Resistance Through Rituals*, eds. Stuart Hall and Tony Jefferson. Birmingham: Centre for Contemporary Cultural Studies, 1976, 209–222.
Melamed, Jodi. "The Spirit of Neoliberalism: From Radical Liberalism to Neoliberal Multiculturalism." *Social Text* 24 (2006): 1–24.
Metz, Christian. "Aural Objects." Trans. Georgia Gurrieri. *Yale French Studies* 60 (1980): 24–32.
Middleton, David and Steven Brown. *The Social Psychology of Experience*. London: Sage Publications, 2005.
Miller, Toby. *Cultural Citizenship: Cosmopolitanism, Consumerism, and Television in a Neoliberal Age*. Philadelphia: Temple UP, 2007.
Miller, Toby and Alec McHoul. *Popular Culture and Everyday Life*. London, Thousand Oaks, and New Delhi: SAGE Publications, 1998.
Mindlin, Alex. "Perhaps iPods aren't Replacing Radio." *The New York Times*, October 26, 2008. www.nytimes.com/2008/10/27/technology/27drill.html?_r=4&ref=todayspaper&oref=slogin&oref=slogin&oref=slogin.
Mitchell, Jack. "Lead Us Not into Temptation: American Public Radio in a World of Infinite Possibilities," in *Radio Reader*, eds. Michelle Hilmes and Jason Loviglio. London and New York: Routledge, 2002, 405–422.
———. *Listener Supported: The Culture and History of Public Radio*. London and Westport, CT: Praeger, 2005.
Mizejewski, Linda. "Queen Latifah, Unruly Women, and the Bodies of Romantic Comedy." *Genders*, Fall 2007.
Mizell-Nelson, Michael. "Not Since the Great Depression: The Post Katrina Documentary Impulse and New Media." http://media.nmc.org/2007/11/michael-mizell-nelson.mp3.
Mjos, Ole J. *Media Globalization and the Discovery Channel Networks*. London and New York: Routledge, 2009.
Monahan, Torin. "Marketing the Beast: *Left Behind* and the Apocalypse Industry." *Media, Culture and Society* 30(6) (2008): 813–830.
Morley, David. *Home Territories: Media, Mobility and Identity*. London: Routledge, 2000.
Morris, Wesley. "The Princess and the Frog: Different Princess, Same Dilemma." *The Boston Globe*, December 11, 2009.
Moseley, Rachel. "Makeover Takeover on British Television." *Screen* 44 (2000): 299–314.
Murray, Susan. "'I Think We Need a New Name for It': The Meeting of Documentary and Reality TV," in *Reality TV: Remaking Television Culture*, eds. Susan Murray and Laurie Ouellette. New York: New York UP, 2004. 40–56.
Nakamura, Lisa. *Cybertypes: Race, Ethnicity, and Identity on the Internet*. New York: Routledge, 2002.

Nakamura, Lisa, Laurie Beth Clark, and Michael Petersen. "Vampire Politics." *FlowTV* 11(3) (2009).

Negra, Diane. "TV in the Season of Compassion Fatigue." *FlowTV* 3(4) (2005).

———. "Structural Integrity, Historical Reversion and the Post-9/11 Chick Flick." *Feminist Media Studies* 8(1) (March 2008): 51–68.

———. *What a Girl Wants?: Fantasizing the Reclamation of Self in Postfeminism.* London: Routledge, 2008.

Nelson, Rob. "Screenings: *Trouble the Water*." *Film Comment* 44 (2008): 69–70.

Newitz, Annalee. *Pretend We're Dead: Capitalist Monsters in American Pop Culture.* Durham: Duke UP, 2006.

Nichols, Bill. *Introduction to Documentary.* Bloomington: Indiana UP, 2001.

Noorani, Yaseen. "The Rhetoric of Security." *CR: The New Centennial Review* 5 (2005): 13–41.

"NPR Audience Profile." www.nprstations.org/prc/2003/profile2003pdf/npr_fact_sheets.pdf.

"NPR: Hurricane Katrina, One Year Later." www.mobilcastnetwork.com/nprhurricanekatrinaoneyearlater.

Nugent, Phil. "An American City: New Orleans, Helen Hill and Me." *The High Hat* 8 (Winter 2007). thehighhat.com/misc/008/nugent_helen.html.

Otte, Marline. "The Mourning After: Languages of Loss and Grief in Post-Katrina New Orleans." *The Journal of American History* 94(3) (December 2007): 828–836.

Ouellette, Laurie. *Viewers Like You? How Public TV Failed the People.* New York: Columbia UP, 2002.

———. "'Take Responsibility for Yourself': Judge Judy and the Neoliberal Citizen," in *Reality TV: Remaking Television Culture*, eds. Susan Murray and Laurie Ouellette. New York: New York UP, 2004, 231–250.

———. "Do Good TV?" *FlowTV* 3(12) (2007). http://flowtv.org/?p=1218.

Ouellette, Laurie and James Hay. *Better Living Through Reality TV: Television and Post-Welfare Citizenship.* Methuen: Blackwell, 2008.

"Our Networks: Discovery." *Discovery Networks*, April 21, 2008. http://tlc.discovery.com/our-networks.html.

Palmer, Gareth, ed. *Exposing Lifestyle Television: The Big Reveal.* London: Ashgate, 2008.

Peck, Janice. *The Age of Oprah: Cultural Icon for the Neoliberal Era.* New York: Paradigm, 2008.

Pine, John C. *Technology in Emergency Management.* New York: John Wiley & Sons, 2007.

Pitluk, Adam. "The Allure of New Orleans." *American Way*, December 15, 2009, 12.

Poster, Mark. *Information Please: Culture and Politics in the Age of Digital Machines.* Durham: Duke UP, 2006.

Potter, Hillary, ed. *Racing the Storm: Racial Implications and Lessons Learned from Hurricane Katrina*. Lanham, MD: Lexington Books, 2007.
"Questions of Racism in Hurricane Photo Captions; Yahoo Responds." http://rawstory.com/news/2005/Blogs_raise_questions_of_racism_in_hurricane_photo_cap_0902.html (published September 2, 2005, accessed May 20, 2009).
Ralli, Tania. "HURRICANE KATRINA: THE PHOTOGRAPHS; Who's a Looter? In Storm's Aftermath, Pictures Kick Up a Different Kind of Tempest." *The New York Times*, September 5, 2005. http://query.nytimes.com/gst/fullpage.html?res=9403EEDF1531F936A3575AC0A9639C8B63&sec=&spon=&pagewanted=all.
Raphael, Chad. "The Political Economic Origins of Reali-TV," in *Reality TV: Remaking Television Culture*, eds. Susan Murray and Laurie Ouellette. New York: New York UP, 2004, 119–136.
Rapping, Elayne. *Law and Justice as Seen on TV*. New York: New York UP, 2003.
Renov, Michael. *Theorizing Documentary*. New York: Routledge, 1993.
Roberts, Martin. "The Fashion Police: Governing the Self in *What Not to Wear*," in *Interrogating Postfeminism: Gender and the Politics of Popular Culture*, eds. Yvonne Tasker and Diane Negra. Durham: Duke UP, 2007, 227–248.
Rojecki, Andrew. "Political Culture and Disaster Response: The Great Floods of 1927 and 2005." *Media, Culture and Society* 31(6) (2009): 957–976.
Rose, Nikolas. "Governing 'Advanced' Liberal Democracies," in *Foucault and Political Reason: Liberalism, Neo-liberalism and Rationalities of Government*, eds. Andrew Barry, Thomas Osborne, and Nikolas Rose. Chicago: U of Chicago P, 1996, 37–64.
———. *Powers of Freedom: Reframing Political Thought*. Cambridge: Cambridge UP, 1999.
Ross, Andrew. *Strange Weather: Culture, Science and Technology in the Age of Limits*. New York: Verso, 1991.
Rozario, Kevin. "What Comes Down Must Go Up: Why Disasters Have Been Good for American Capitalism," in *American Disasters*, ed. Steven Biel. New York and London: New York UP, 72–102.
Ruoff, Jeffrey. "Home Movies of the Avant-Garde: Jonas Mekas and the New York Art World." *Cinema Journal* 30(3) (1991): 6–28.
Saltzman, Joe. "The Brave New World of Multimedia Convergence." *USA Today*, May 2001. http://findarticles.com/p/articles/mi_m1272/is_2672_129/ai_74572243.
Savage, Barbara. "Radio and the Political Discourse of Racial Equality," in *Radio Reader*, eds. Michelle Hilmes and Jason Loviglio. London and New York: Routledge, 2002, 231–256.
Savage, Kirk. "The Past in the Present: The Life of Memorials." *Harvard Design Magazine* (Fall 1999): 14–19.

Schwarzbaum, Lisa. "The Princess and the Frog." *Entertainment Weekly*, December 4, 2009, 74–75.
Sconce, Jeffrey. *Haunted Media: Electronic Presence from Telegraphy to Television*. Durham: Duke UP, 2000.
Seltzer, Mark. *Serial Killers: Life and Death in America's Wound Culture*. New York: Routledge, 1998.
Shapiro, Stephen. "*True Blood* and *Mad Men*'s Passive Revolution: Utopian Reaction in the Age of Obam(a)mnesia." Paper Presented at Television Cities Conference, University College Dublin, 2009.
Smith, Neil. "Gentrification Generalized: From Local Anomaly to Urban 'Regeneration' as Global Urban Strategy," in *Frontiers of Capital: Ethnographic Reflectiosn on the New Economy*, eds. Melissa S. Fisher and Greg Downey, Durham: Duke UP, 2006, 191–206.
Snauffer, Douglas. *Crime Television*. Westport: Praeger, 2006.
Sothern, Billy. *Down in New Orleans: Reflections from a Drowned City*. Berkeley: U of California P, 2008.
Souther, J. Mark. "The Disneyfication of New Orleans: The French Quarter as Façade in a Divided City." *The Journal of American History* 94(30) (December 2007): 804–811.
Spigel, Lynn. *TV by Design: Modern Art and the Rise of Network Television*. Chicago: U of Chicago P, 2006.
———. "Entertainment Wars: Television Culture after 9/11," in *American Quarterly* 56(2) (June 2004): 235–270.
Springer, Kimberly. "Divas, Evil Black Bitches and Bitter Black Women: African-American Women in Postfeminist and Post-Civil Rights Popular Culture," in *Interrogating Postfeminism: Gender and the Politics of Popular Culture*, eds. Yvonne Tasker and Diane Negra. Durham: Duke UP, 2007, 249–276.
———. "Hate the Game, Not the Playa: Unmasking Neoliberal Articulations Amongst the Black Power Elite," Sterling Brown Visiting Professor Lecture, Williams College, 2010.
Stabile, Carol. "No Shelter from the Storm." *South Atlantic Quarterly* 106(4) (Fall 2007): 684.
"The State of the News Media, 2009: An Annual Report on American Journalism." Pew Center for Excellence in Journalism Report. www.stateofthemedia.org/2009/narrative_audio_intro.php?media=10.
Steinberg, Stephen. "Occupational Apartheid in America: Race, Labor Market Segmentation, and Affirmative Action," in *Without Justice for All: The New Liberalism and Our Retreat from Racial Equality*, ed. Adolph Reed, Jr. Boulder, CO: Westview P, 1999, 215–233.
Strauss, Neil. *Emergency: This Book Will Save Your Life*. New York: IT Books, 2009.
Streible, Dan. "*In Memoriam* Helen Hill." *Film History* 19(4) (2007): 438–441.

———. "The Role of Orphan Films in the 21st Century Archive." *Cinema Journal* 46(3) (Spring 2007): 124–128.

———. "The State of Orphan Films." *The Moving Image* 9(1) (Spring 2009): 1–13.

Strombeck, Andrew. "Invest in Jesus: Neoliberalism and the *Left Behind* Novels." *Cultural Critique* 64 (2006): 161–195.

Sturken, Marita. *Tourists of History: Memory, Kitsch and Consumerism from Oklahoma City to Ground Zero.* Durham: Duke UP, 2007.

Sundance Channel. *Architecture School.* Discussions. "Not about race, but it's about race." Eastender21, August 22, 2008. http://www.sundancechannel.com/discussions/post/390367394 (accessed June 30, 2009).

Sylvester, Judith. *The Media and Hurricanes Katrina and Rita.* Houndmills and New York: Palgrave Macmillan, 2008.

"Symposium on Media Convergence." Geneva: International Labor Organization. January 1997. www.ilo.org/public/english/dialogue/sector/techmeet/smc97/smcrep.htm.

Tacchi, Jo. "The Need for Radio Theory in the Digital Age." *International Journal of Cultural Studies* 3(2) (2000): 289–298.

Thompson, Anne. "Risky Business." *Hollywood Reporter*, May 5, 2006, 15–16.

Troutt, David Dante et al., eds. *After the Storm: Black Intellectuals Explore the Meaning of Hurricane Katrina.* London and New York: The New Press, 2006.

Tuana, Nancy. "Viscous Porosity: Witnessing Katrina," in *Material Feminisms*, eds. Stacy Alaimo and Susan Hekman. Bloomington: Indiana UP, 2008, 188–213.

Van Malssen, Kara. *Disaster Planning and Recovery: Post-Katrina Lessons for Mixed Media Collections,* master's thesis, New York U, 2006.

———. "Preserving the Legacy of Experimental Filmmaker Helen Hill," *SOIMA in Practice,* online publication for the Sound and Image Collections Conservation program, initiative of the International Centre for the Study of the Preservation and Restoration of Cultural Property, 2008. http://soima.iccrom.org.

Vivian, Bradford. "Neoliberal Epideictic: Rhetorical Form and Commemorative Politics on September 11, 2002." *Quarterly Journal of Speech* 92(1) (2006): 1–26.

Walker, Janet. "Rights and Return: Perils and Fantasies of Situated Testimony after Katrina," in *Documentary Testimonies: Global Archives of Suffering,* eds. Bhaskar Sarkar and Janet Walker. New York: Routledge, 2009, 134–184.

Walker, Rob. "Tragicommerce." *New York Times Magazine,* June 25, 2006, section 6, column 1, p. 22, Lexis Nexis.

Wanzo, Rebecca. *The Suffering Will Not Be Televised: African American Women and Sentimental Political Storytelling.* Albany: State U of New York P, 2009.

Weber, Brenda R. *Makeover TV: Selfhood, Citizenship, and Celebrity*. Durham: Duke UP, 2009.

Weber, Bruce. "Storm and Crisis." *The New York Times*, October 29, 2005.

White, Hayden. "The Historical Text as Literary Artifact," in *Narrative Dynamics: Essays on Time, Plot, Closure, and Frames*, ed. Brian Richardson. Columbus: The Ohio State UP, 2002, 191–210.

"Wikipedia: Featured Articles." http://en.wikipedia.org/wiki/Wikipedia:Featured_articles (last accessed May 17, 2009).

Wilburn, Tracey E. "The Site of Memorial: Current discussions in the negotiation of memorial forms and spaces appropriate for the World Trade Center Memorial on the World Wide Web." Paper for Communication 6720, University of Utah, June 18, 2003. http:/www.hum.utah.edu/hgc/papers/wilburn.pdf.

Woods, Clyde. "Katrina's World: Blues, Bourbon, and the Return to the Source." *American Quarterly* 61(3) (September 2009): 427–453.

Yesil, Bilge. "Watching Ourselves: Video Surveillance, Urban Space and Self-Responsibilization." *Cultural Studies* 20(4) (2006): 400–416.

Young, James. "The Counter-Monument: Memory Against Itself in Germany Today." *Critical Inquiry* 18 (1992): 267–296.

Young, Linda. "U.N. Criticizes U.S. For Violating Human Rights Of Internally Displaced Hurricane Katrina Victims" (February 28, 2008). http://www.gantdaily.com/news/35/ARTICLE/13946/2008-02-28.html (accessed May 17, 2009).

Zaleski, Katherine. "Obama's Transparent Presidency: Weekly YouTube Addresses." *The Huffington Post*, November 14, 2008. http://www.huffingtonpost.com/2008/11/14/obamas-transparent-presid_n_143805.html.

Zoller Seiz, Matt. "Three Relationships Seen Through a DIY Lens." *The New York Times* August 22, 2007.

Contributors

Jane Elliott is lecturer in the Department of English and Related Literature at the University of York. She is the author of *Popular Feminist Fictions as American Allegory: Representing National Time* (Palgrave, 2008) and her essays on contemporary literature, culture, and theory have appeared in *Cultural Critique, Modern Fiction Studies*, and the *PMLA*. With Derek Attridge, she is a coeditor of the forthcoming volume *Theory After "Theory,"* to be published by Routledge in 2010.

Joy V. Fuqua is assistant professor in the Department of Media Studies at Queens College/City University of New York where she teaches in the areas of media history, television theory, queer film/video, and cultural studies of media. Her first book, *Ill Effects: Prescribing Television in the Hospital and at Home*, is under contract with Duke. Her second book, a study of disaster, home, and nation in relation to Hurricane Katrina and New Orleans, is in preparation.

Andrew Goodridge earned his MA at the School of Media Arts, University of Arizona, Tucson. He has presented television research at New Directions: Renegotiating Borders and the Southwest Popular Culture Association Meeting.

Diane Negra is professor of film studies and screen culture and head of film studies at University College Dublin. She is the author, editor, or coeditor of five books: *Off-White Hollywood: American Culture and Ethnic Female Stardom* (Routledge, 2001), *A Feminist Reader in Early Cinema* (Duke, 2002), *The Irish in Us: Irishness, Performativity and Popular Culture* (Duke, 2006), *Interrogating Postfeminism: Gender and the Politics of Popular Culture* (Duke, 2007), and *What a Girl Wants?: Fantasizing the Reclamation of Self in Postfeminism* (Routledge, 2008).

Maria Pramaggiore is professor of film studies at North Carolina State University. She has coauthored *Film: A Critical Introduction* with Tom Wallis.

Jeff Scheible is a PhD candidate in the Department of Film and Media Studies at the University of California-Santa Barbara.

Lindsay Steenberg is a lecturer in film and television studies at the University of East Anglia. She has published on violence in the art cinema, the postfeminist martial arts heroine, the gendered nature of criminal profiling, and the works of filmmaker Guillermo Del Toro. Her doctoral thesis focused on female investigators and forensic science in contemporary crime thrillers and her wider research interests include representations of gender and violence in postmodern and postfeminist media culture.

Dan Streible is associate professor of cinema studies at New York University and associate director of its Moving Image Archiving and Preservation master's program.

Brenda R. Weber is associate professor in gender studies at Indiana University. She is the author of *Makeover TV: Selfhood, Citizenship and Celebrity* (Duke, 2009).

Index

"Absolut New Orleans," 3, 4
America's Most Wanted, 6, 18, 23, 25–38
　see also Walsh, John
"Anarchivists," 161–164
Angel Heart, 2
L'Aquila Earthquake, 145
Arceneaux, Eric, 212–213, 218, 219
Architecture School, 179, 194–197, 200
Asbury, Herbert, 50
Aural objects, 69
Axe in the Attic, The, 157–158

Bacon, Kevin, 200
Bad Lieutenant: Port of Call New Orleans, 8
Benjamin, Walter, 203, 206
Berlosconi, Silvio, 145
Big Easy, The, 2
Big Oil, 51
Biopolitics, 90
"Blame the victim" discourse, 51
Bohemian Town, 152, 155, 160
Bones, 7, 25, 26, 30, 31, 33–38, 40
Bourbon Street Beat, 24, 39
Brakhage, Stan, 156, 167, 168
Bringing Down the House, 134
Brown, Michael, 18
Bush, Barbara, 136
Bush, George W., 51, 74, 76–77, 86, 114, 116, 132, 199, 221, 225
Butler, Judith, 61

California wildfires, 113, 115
Canemaker, John, 163
Cape, Frances, 46
Center for Home Movies, 162, 163, 170

Central Business District, 11
Chan, Paul, 43, 207–208, 218
Charm School, 190
Childress, Cindy, 133
Cleveland Street Gap, 157
Cloverfield, 10
Concert for Katrina Relief, A, 5
Cooper, Anderson, 7, 144
Cops, 24, 29, 30
Corporation for Public Broadcasting, 69
"Creative Economy," 11
　see also Florida, Richard
Crier, Rondell, 57
Criminal Minds, 25, 29
Crocodile Hunter, The, 118, 121
　see also Irwin, Steve
CSI, 31
Culinary Tourism, 146–147
Curb Your Enthusiasm, 145
Curious Case of Benjamin Button, The, 15–16

"Da Mayor in Your Pocket," 78–79
　see also Aural objects
Dante's Peak, 8
Day After Tomorrow, The, 8
Decasia, 160
Deep Impact, 8
Déjà Vu, 8
Derrida, Jacques, 203, 205, 227
Dimock, Wai Chee, 1
Dion, Celine, 144
Discovery Channel, 7, 73, 114–117, 120–128, 129, 190
Disney Princesses, 146
Dog Whisperer, 190

Domino, Fats, 110
Douglas, Mary, 45
Duggan, Lisa, 93, 109
Dunlap, Blaine, 169
Dyson, Michael Eric, 204, 217

e2, 179, 180, 183, 187–191, 194, 197, 200
East Coast Blackout, 1
Edwards, John, 220–222
Egan, Courtney, 156, 157, 159, 167, 169, 170, 171, 173
Ehrenreich, Barbara, 12
Emergency: This Book Will Save Your Life, 19, 117
"Empathy Deficit," 12
ER, 38
Extreme Makeover: Home Edition, 114, 176, 178, 184

FEMA, 18, 25, 35, 116
Ferrari, Matthew, 123, 129
Film for Rosie, 153
Fish, Adam, 119
5 Spells, 155
Fleetwood, Nicole R., 17, 38, 39, 90, 137, 145
Floodwall, 42, 44–49, 53–62
  see also Napoli, Jana
Florestine Collection, The, 163, 166, 167
Florida, Richard, 11, 139–140
Food Not Bombs, 152, 155, 166
Forensic Culture, 31–32
48 Hours Mystery, 160
Fox News, 5
Francis Pop's Hallowe'en Parade, 157

Gailiunas, Paul, 151
Gilroy, Paul, 134
Giroux, Henry, 19–20, 36
Godard, Jean-Luc, 158
Gothtober Baby, 156
Gray, Herman, 193–194
Great Flood of 1927, 12
Grylls, Bear, 120–127

Haggins, Bambi, 216
Hall, Stuart, 55
Halloween in New Orleans, 156
Ham Radio, 77
Harvard Film Archive, 163
Hatchet, 7
Hawaii Five-O, 24
Healthism, 138
Hill, Helen, 9, 44, 149–174
Hogan, Patrick Colm, 210
Holmes in New Orleans, 179, 193, 197
Holmes on Homes, 179, 184, 191–194
"Home," 45–48
Homicide: Life on the Street, 40
hooks, bell, 45
Horisaki, Takashi, 42
House M.D., 14, 38, 90–91, 98, 99–105, 108, 110
House of Sweet Magic, 151, 164, 168
Houston Astrodome, 136
How Do I Look?, 176, 177, 197
Hurricane Andrew, 6, 30
Hurricane Digital Memory Bank (HDMB), 158, 169
Hurricane Gustav, 17, 76, 82
Hurricane Katrina
  "anniversarizing of," 10, 68, 76–77, 82–86
  and crime television, 23–38
  and horror genres, 7–8
  and material culture, 9, 51
  online presence of, 9, 80–82, 203–229
  in relation to makeover culture, 7, 175–198
  relationship to 9/11, 3–4, 12, 16, 17, 21, 31–32, 38, 42, 52–53, 81, 83, 84
  and tattooing, 133–134
Hurricane on the Bayou, 8, 19
Hurricane Rita, 17
Hurricane Season, 21

I Love Nola, 153
I Shouldn't Be Alive, 114–117, 120–123, 126–128

Imus, Don, 67
Inconvenient Truth, An, 8, 114
Independence Day, 10
Indian Ocean Tsunami, 8, 113, 116
International Flag Burning Day, 159, 164
Interview with the Vampire, 2
Irwin, Steve, 118–119

Judge Judy, 29, 30

Kardashian, Kim, 133, 144
Keeping Up with the Kardashians, 18
Kinchen, Florestine, 156, 167, 173
Klein, Naomi, 3, 92, 109
K-Ville, 8, 24, 25, 114

Lagasse, Emeril, 135, 145
Laissez les bon temps rouler, 14
Last Holiday, 7, 13, 131–143
Law and Order, 32, 34, 38
Law & Order SVU, 7, 23, 24, 30
LeBlanc, Phyllis Montana, 105–106
Lee, Spike, 89, 90, 114, 160
Lee, Susanna, 32, 37
Left Behind series, 13
Left behindness, 11, 13
Left 4 Dead 2, 13
Lessin, Tia and Carl Deal, 90–95
Life or Something Like It, 135
Like Water for Chocolate, 135
Limbaugh, Rush, 67, 71
Lipstz, George, 51, 131, 134, 208
Littler, Jo, 199
"Livestrong," 3
Looting vs. supply gathering, 75, 203–205
Lopez, Jennifer, 133, 144
Louisiana Purchase, The, 50
Lyons, James, 10

Madame Winger Makes a Film, 152, 153, 155, 163, 164, 165, 166, 167
Maddow, Rachel, 67

Make It Right Foundation, 183, 187, 188, 192
 see also Pitt, Brad
Man vs. Wild, 114–117, 120–128
Mardi Gras, 21
Marsalis, Wynton, 107
Martin, Randy, 18
Massey, Doreen, 49
Matta-Clark, Gordon, 46, 61, 62
Mayer, Aric, 5, 6, 139
McCain, John, 223, 225
McCarthy, Anna, 117, 191, 200
McMurria, John, 184, 215
McPherson, Tara, 20–21
Melamud, Jodi, 107
Mr. Pregnant, 203, 215–221, 222, 226, 227
Mizejewski, Linda, 134
Mobility (in American culture), 136
Monahan, Torin, 13
Monster in New Orleans, A, 157
Morley, David, 45–46
Mouseholes, 152, 153, 163, 166

Nagin, Ray, 9, 51, 78–80, 84
Nakamura, Lisa, 215
Napoli, Jana, 42
National Geographic Channel, 7
National Public Radio, 7, 10, 67–77, 80–86
Necropolitics, 13–14, 34, 39, 137
Neoliberalism, 14, 90–92, 95–109, 175, 178–198
"New Economy," 1, 132, 140, 143
New Orleans
 as Caribbean City, 2
 relation to New York, 41
 ties to Europe, 2, 25, 136
New Orleans Center for the Creative Arts (NOCCA), 155, 156, 160, 167, 170
New Orleans Film Collective, 155, 163, 166
New Orleans International Human Rights Film Festival, 169

Newitz, Annalee, 31, 32
No Reservations, 135
NOPD: After Katrina, 24

Obama, Barack, 198, 221, 222, 223, 229
Obsession, 2
Oklahoma City Bombing, 31, 54
"Old South," 2, 20–21
Orphan Film Symposium, 159, 162, 163, 167
"Orphanistas," 161–164
Ouellette, Laurie, 29, 86, 188, 199

Penn, Sean, 144, 190
Pitt, Brad, 144, 175, 183, 187, 188, 190, 192, 197
Polidari, Robert, 43
Poster, Mark, 81
Princess and the Frog, The, 15, 141–143, 146

Queen Latifah, 132, 133–134, 135, 137–138, 140, 142, 144, 146

Rain Dance, 151
Reaping, The, 7
Recipes for Disaster: A Handcrafted Film Cookbooklet, 153, 154, 159, 160, 164, 165
"Reckoning Texts," 61
Roberts, Kimberly, 91–99, 109
Robinette, Garland, 78
Rojecki, Andrew, 11, 12
Rose, Nikolas, 90, 199
Rosie Wonders What to Wear, 156
Ross, Andrew, 18
Rozario, Kevin, 12–13

Sconce, Jeffrey, 114–115, 128
Scratch and Crow, 150, 152, 168
Seelig, Mike, 105
Shavers, Dinerral, 160–161, 172
Simplify Your Life, 186
Smith, Shepard, 5

Social Dress New Orleans – 730 Days After, 42, 44–48, 49–50, 58–62
see also Horisaki, Takashi
Spigel, Lynn, 51, 180
Springer, Kimberly, 109, 132, 143
Stabile, Carol A., 4
Streetcar Named Desire, A, 159
Stroud, Les, 120–128
Sturken, Marita, 3, 53, 54
Suh, Do-Ho, 46
Survivor, 119, 122
Survivorman, 19, 114, 120–128
"Swine Flu," 211

Tabloid culture, 26, 31
Terror Dream: Fear and Fantasy in Post-9/11 America, The, 21, 63
"Them not us," 12
Think of Me First as a Person, 161–162
thirtysomething, 70, 72
Tomorrow Begins Today, 220–222
"Tourist Romances," 135, 145
Treme, 14
True Blood, 14–15, 20
Truth about Hurricane Katrina, The, 9, 212–213
Trouble the Water, 7, 77, 90–99, 108–109
Tuana, Nancy, 2
Tunnel of Love, 152
2012, 8

"Urban Tornado," 1–2

Van Malssen, Kara, 162, 163, 172
Vessel, 151
Voodoo, 32, 35

Waiting for Godot in New Orleans, 43, 64, 207–208, 218–219
see also Chan, Paul
Walker, Janet, 110, 172, 228
Walsh, John, 6, 19, 25–30, 38
Wanzo, Rebecca, 143

War of the Worlds, 8
Wassup 2008, 222–225
Weather Channel, The, 7, 18, 53
West, Kanye, 5, 116
When the Levees Broke, 7, 89–91, 98, 99, 105–114, 160, 172
Where is Santa Clause, 217–220, 221, 222
White, Hayden, 211, 216, 220
Whiteread, Rachel, 45

Wikipedia, 208–212, 213, 214, 219, 221, 225
Wild at Heart, 2
Without a Trace, 25, 30
World's Smallest Fair, The, 151
"Wound culture," 23, 35, 38

YouTube, 9, 116, 168, 212–228
Your New Pig is Down the Road, 153